ECONOMICS, POLITICS AND SOCIAL STUDIES
IN OXFORD, 1900–85

By the same author

PUBLIC CONTROL OF
ROAD PASSENGER TRANSPORT

LESSONS OF THE BRITISH WAR ECONOMY (*editor*)

CENTRAL AND LOCAL GOVERNMENT

ORGANISATION OF BRITISH CENTRAL
GOVERNMENT, 1914–56 (*editor*)

QUESTIONS IN PARLIAMENT (*with N. Bowring*)

NATIONALISATION OF BRITISH INDUSTRY, 1945–51

ENGLISH ADMINISTRATIVE SYSTEM, 1780–1870

ECONOMICS, POLITICS AND SOCIAL STUDIES IN OXFORD, 1900–85

Norman Chester

MACMILLAN

© Norman Chester 1986

All rights reserved. No reproduction, copy or transmission of this publication may be made without written permission.

No paragraph of this publication may be reproduced, copied or transmitted save with written permission or in accordance with the provisions of the Copyright Act 1956 (as amended).

Any person who does any unauthorised act in relation to this publication may be liable to criminal prosecution and civil claims for damages.

First published 1986

Published by
THE MACMILLAN PRESS LTD
Houndmills, Basingstoke, Hampshire RG21 2XS
and London
Companies and representatives
throughout the world

Printed in Hong Kong

British Library Cataloguing in Publication Data
Chester, *Sir* Norman
Economics, politics and social studies in
Oxford, 1900–85.
1. University of Oxford—History 2. Social
sciences—Study and teaching (Higher—
England—Oxford (Oxfordshire)—History
I. Title
300.7'1142574   H62.5.G7
ISBN 0-333-40837-3

Contents

Acknowledgements		vi
Introduction		vii
1	Establishment of the Diploma 1903	1
2	Developments 1903–18	17
3	Modern Greats 1920–39	30
4	Creation of a Faculty of Social Studies	46
5	Development of University Facilities	52
6	Lord Nuffield's Benefaction	63
7	Social Reconstruction Survey	83
8	Emergence of Nuffield College	114
9	Training for Social Work	130
10	The Institute of Economics and Statistics	144
11	General Developments after 1945	161
Glossary		185
Notes and References		188
Name Index		196
Subject Index		200

Acknowledgements

The book would not have been possible without the help of many colleagues and friends. The whole typescript was commented upon by Michael Brock, David Butler, Rod Martin and Chelly Halsey and particular chapters were read by Lord Franks, Sir Henry Phelps-Brown, Frank Pickstock, Kenneth Robinson, Robert Skidelsky, David Worswick and John Wright. I also benefited from being able to discuss some aspects with Lord Fulton, Lord Roberthall, Eric Hargreaves, A. F. Madden and Lord Morris of Grasmere. I am grateful to the Vice-Chancellor and to other University authorities for permission to draw upon the University Archives, and to the staff of the Registry and of the Archives for their ever-ready help. I also owe a good deal to the help and encouragement of my very good friend, Janet Fenwick. Mrs K. Rogers did most of the typing in her usual efficient way. Finally, I have been sustained and helped in many ways by the Warden and Fellows of Nuffield College. To all these I owe my warmest and most sincere thanks. I absolve them from any blemishes in the finished work.

NORMAN CHESTER

Introduction

Social Studies or the Social Sciences can be variously defined. At their widest they include economics, political science, social, economic and political history, international relations, public and international law, social psychology, anthropology, geography, demography and so on. That would be a vast canvas to cover. Instead this book contents itself with those subjects and aspects which fall within the jurisdiction of the Faculty of Social Studies. Oxford has separate Faculties for Law, Psychological Studies, Anthropology and Geography. The book, therefore, is primarily concerned with Economics, Politics, Recent History, Philosophy and cognate subjects.

The expansion of Social Studies, so defined, has been a major feature of Oxford University in the present century. Though there had been a general interest in political economy and political studies in the last years of the nineteenth century it was not until 1903 that the creation of a Diploma gave the subjects a distinctive place in the University curriculum. It was not an auspicious start and the Diploma always bore the marks of the hesitant and conflicting views of its originators. Yet from such an uncertain beginning there grew a Faculty with the largest number of undergraduate and graduate students in the University. The first purpose of this study, therefore, is to show the steps by which this growth was achieved.

Three features of this growth deserve attention. First, there was the period when aspirations were by no means matched by the teaching resources available. This was clearly the situation until the late 1920s. Those who urged the provision of training in economics and in business management in the first part of the century had to recognise that not only were first-class teachers scarce, but that the subjects themselves were not yet clearly defined, at least as subjects to be taught to young men and women straight from school. That this was not the only obstacle can be seen by the progress made in these subjects at certain other Universities and by the successful launching of Modern Greats in the early 1920s.

Modern Greats or PPE or the Final Honour School of Philosophy, Politics and Economics was established when Oxford teaching resources were little different from what they had been in say 1910. But the desire to enter this field of study was now overwhelmingly greater than in the tentative earlier years. Moreover the burden of teaching fell at first on the philosophers and modern historians, two well established faculties. The appointment of economists did not begin to catch up on needs until some years after the establishment of the School, indeed not until the School began to produce its seed corn.

The growth in the teaching resources available in Social Studies provided the basis of the more specialised developments after 1950. The B.Phil./M.Phil. was a major landmark followed by the growth of the new combined Honour Schools and the high level of the University's contribution to training for Social Work.

The second feature is the attitude towards specialisation. In 1903 Cambridge decided that three years studying just economics was a perfectly suitable University education. Oxford took a different view. True the different view may have reflected the vested interests of the philosophers and historians in Oxford but the opposition to a purely economics degree was much wider than that. The combination of philosophy, politics and history with economics that eventuated in 1920 was generally felt to provide a more liberal education. Even the option of a bipartite School made available in 1970 still provided scope for a wider ranging degree than the Economics Tripos. By then, however, the emphasis had shifted to postgraduate work. Specialisation was considered appropriate for second Degrees such as the B.Phil./M.Phil. and the M.Sc. in Applied Social Studies.

Thirdly, it is interesting to see how the University responded to outside pressures and events. What the Universities of Cambridge and Manchester or the London School of Economics were doing in the social sciences; the fear that rich businessmen might give their benefactions to the newer Universities rather than to Oxford or Cambridge; the recognition that Oxford was not providing the training and qualifications that would attract the able graduates from Commonwealth and American Universities – all these were arguments used at various times to secure the expansion and improvement of what the University had to offer in the field of social studies.

During the course of the expansion of this field there arose in two different ways an issue central to the development and character of the University - the extent to which teaching and research should be College- or University-based. The first occasion was the proposal for an Institute of Statistics. In the early 1930s the dozen or so newly-appointed Economics tutors found that the facilities available to them for research and advanced study were inadequate. The textbooks required for undergraduate reading were usually available in their College library, the Barnett Library or the Bodleian. But statistical abstracts and other specialist publications were seldom to be found in any of those places. This is not an unusual situation with a rapidly growing new subject, for library provision is geared to long established demands. Had the Economists been concerned only with greater availability of published material their needs would have been met by increased acquisition of library holdings in their field. But for their research into the working of the economic system they needed expert assistance and equipment for their statistical analyses. Hence the demand for an Institute of Statistics.

This would not be an unusual demand in the great majority of British Universities. In Oxford it represented a break with tradition. In the Sciences it had become customary for the University to erect and finance the laboratories. In the Humanities it had so far been thought sufficient if the University provided the Bodleian. All the teachers of economics had rooms and facilities in the Colleges of which they were Fellows. In addition they wanted the University to provide them with accommodation and facilities for their research activities.

The point was recognized in the letter which the University sent to the Rockefeller Foundation in 1934 asking for a grant of £5000 a year for Social Studies. The letter emphasised that the work of the University was inextricably interwoven with the College system. It would be undesirable to develop social studies in Oxford on lines inconsistent with that tradition. Hebdomadal Council considered that the development of Social Studies ought to continue along the lines which had proved so fruitful for other humane studies, thus securing not only the easy and informal co-operation of scholars in every subject able to contribute to the solution of social problems but also the financial support of the Colleges.

The fact that the Institute became established with its own building does not contradict what was written in 1934. Its main service to the mass of economics teachers has been its provision of a first-class library of books and statistical sources. Owing in part to the accident of War it became a research institute with its own staff and programmes. A few Economics tutors benefited from its research facilities but by and large it developed as a self-contained institute.

The issue arose again on the occasion of Lord Nuffield's Benefaction of October 1937, the primary purpose of which was to establish a College for postgraduate studies. However A. D. Lindsay, the Vice-Chancellor, talked in terms of the College being the University's instrument for social research. To this end the affairs of the College were vested in the hands of Hebdomadal Council. At the same time, true to Oxford traditions, the College was to have its Warden and Fellows, students and chaplain, and on the surface appeared little different from other Colleges. Council proved an unsuitable body to direct the affairs, including a major research programme, of this new institution and indeed had little or no wish to do so. Gradually the Warden and Fellows became more and more the governing body of the traditional College until in 1958 the original Trust Deed was superseded by a Royal Charter and Nuffield was admitted to collegiate status by the University.

The story is complicated by Lindsay's attempts to secure an integrated structure for all the bodies engaged in social studies. But those concerned with the Institute of Statistics and Barnett House were not prepared to give up their independence and become part of a College and yet money from the Benefaction had to be spent on College purposes and could not legally be used to develop quite independent institutes. The gap created by the War years and the very changed financial circumstances facing the College meant the end of Lindsay's earlier plans. It is, however, a most interesting aspect of the development of social studies and is a major reason why Nuffield College has such a prominent place in the story.

1 Establishment of the Diploma 1903

An analysis of the subjects examined in the various Schools in late nineteenth century Oxford would not reveal any great concern on the part of the University with contemporary society. Yet at the time there was considerable interest among both senior and junior members in current social, economic and political problems. It was in the nature of the Oxford system that teaching and learning were not confined to the demands of the Examination Statutes: Tutors, Professors and the more able undergraduates were ready to take a wider view. The problems of contemporary Britain were debated in the numerous societies, for example, the Political Economy Club. Three other features of the Oxford academic scene at this time need mention.

First, there was the major contribution and pervading influence of the Honour School of *Literae Humaniores*. It is not necessary to go as far as Alfred North Whitehead and claim 'as a training in political imagination, the Harvard School of Politics and of Government cannot hold a candle to the old-fashioned English classical education'.[1] Lit. Hum., or Greats, to give it its popular title, did however give the undergraduate an insight into the political systems of Rome and Athens and the ideas of Plato and Aristotle. The philosophy content of the School went beyond the period of history studied to cover, for example, Kant, Mill and Bentham, and was greatly influenced by Hegel. Tutors, such as T. H. Green, were intimately concerned with the philosophical and moral basis of the State and with current political and social problems. To be an undergraduate at Balliol in the 1890s was to have the opportunity to learn most of what was important in political science at the time.

Second, the Honour School of Modern History as it had developed late in the century offered much of what could be regarded as social studies: political and economic history and, as an optional subject, political economy.

Finally, it is important to appreciate that the high degree of specialisation in the social sciences now currently the fashion had hardly begun. Scholars in the humanities found it possible to cover a range of subjects well beyond the means, or the aims, of their present-day successors. The number of important books on any subject was much more limited and there were few specialised periodicals. Academics were not readily labelled as they now are as philosophers or economists or political scientists, let alone political theorists or econometricians. It seemed perfectly natural therefore that John Stuart Mill should produce important works on Logic, Political Economy, Representative Government and Liberty, and equally natural that these should be read by Greats or History tutors.

The great interest in social and economic problems which was a feature of Oxford in the last twenty years or so of the century stimulated a great interest in political economy, a subject very different from economics as taught today. Dealing with unemployment and poverty, tariffs and taxation, it became a favourite subject for the lectures to working-class audiences provided by the Oxford Extension Lectures Committee in different towns. Thus, though the subject did not have a significant place in the curricula of the University it was thought important enough to be taught by Oxford men in other places.[2]

CAMBRIDGE TRIPOS - OXFORD DIPLOMA

In 1902 there was a good deal of discussion in both Oxford and Cambridge about the need to make greater provision for Political Economy or Economics and associated subjects. On 26 April 1902 a Memorial was presented to the Council of the Senate in Cambridge signed by 130 members of Senate, respectfully requesting the Council 'to nominate a Syndicate to enquire into and report upon the best means of enlarging the opportunities for the study in Cambridge of Economics and associated branches of Political Science'. On 12 May, 88 members of Convocation of Oxford University presented a Memorial to Hebdomadal Council respectfully suggesting consideration of the desirability of affording greater encouragement to the systematic study of Economics and cognate subjects.

It was no coincidence that the moves took place at the same time. There were, for example, personal links between the two Professors, Alfred Marshall in Cambridge and Francis Edgeworth in Oxford. Marshall, the driving force, had many friends and acquaintances in Oxford dating from 1883, the year he spent as a Fellow and Lecturer in Political Economy at Balliol. One of his Balliol pupils, L. L. Price, who was Treasurer and Fellow of Oriel, anticipated the Memorial by sending a printed open letter to the Vice-Chancellor in January 1902, i.e. before the date of the Cambridge Memorial.

The arguments used in support of the two Memorials were very similar. In Cambridge, Marshall published an 18-page booklet: *A Plea for the Creation of a Curriculum in Economics and associated branches of Political Science* dated 7 April 1902. He circulated this to all members of the Senate. There was no similar cogently argued Plea in support of the Oxford Memorial, though there was a little in Price's letter. But, before considering what action to take, Hebdomadal Council asked to see a copy of the Cambridge Memorial and almost certainly had the opportunity to read Marshall's arguments.

Marshall had three main considerations in mind when pleading for a more thorough study of economics. First, economic issues were growing in urgency and in intricacy and economic causes were exerting an increasing control on the quality of human life. Second, such studies offered abundant scope for the training and the exercise of those mental facilities and energies which it was the special province of a university to develop. Third, those looking forward to a business career, or to public life, were likely to be preferentially attracted to a residential university which offered a good intellectual training and opportunities for distinction in subjects that would bear on their thoughts and actions in after-life. The Oxford Memorial mentioned the value of the study of economics to those taking up business careers, administrative or similar posts.

Point had been added to this last consideration by the development of new universities which had shown a special interest in political economy. In 1895, the London School of Economics and Political Science had been founded, helped by a grant from the Technical Education Board of the London County Council and the goodwill of the London Chamber of Commerce. The School became a recognized institution in the reconstituted University of London, in 1900. At the same time the University established a Faculty of Economics, of whose ten original members eight were recognized teachers at the London School. The first Director, W.A.S. Hewins, had been a Fellow of Pembroke College, Oxford, where he taught economic history. At Birmingham William Ashley became Professor of Commerce in 1901. He had obtained a First in Modern History at Balliol in 1881 and after a Fellowship at Lincoln College had held Chairs at Toronto and Harvard. He was a candidate for the Oxford Chair in 1891. At Manchester, Sydney Chapman became Professor of Political Economy in 1901 after two years as Lecturer in Economics and Political Science at Cardiff. He had obtained a First in both Parts of the Moral Sciences Tripos.

Both Marshall and Price were worried that their Universities would fall behind other universities. In his letter, Price claimed that merchants and businessmen would increasingly send their sons to the younger universities rising in the great centres of commerce, who were experimenting with curricula suitable for students preparing for business.

Marshall sent his Plea to a number of industralists, businessmen and civil servants for their observations. He received replies, *inter alia*, from the General Manager of the North Eastern Railway, an Ironmaster, a Shipowner, the Secretary to the Board of Agriculture, and from A. J. Balfour, James Bryce, and John Morley. All were favourable and copies of the salient passages were circulated in Cambridge.

In the Senate Debate on the Syndicate's Report on 7 May 1903, Marshall wound up his speech thus:

> The providing a good education for businessmen was indeed not the main object of the movement: the main object was to render possible a thorough scientific and therefore realistic study of economics. But as a secondary aim it was important, for its own sake; and possibly also in relation to the poverty of the University . . . For if this University should refuse to do what business required: if in return they should, as it was said they were already doing, tend more and more to send their sons to new Universities (even though thereby the glorious training of Oxford or Cambridge corporate life were lost); and if, in consequence, the rising generation of wealthy businessmen became the loyal sons of the newer and not the older Universities, then he thought this University might regret too late

Establishment of the Diploma 1903

that it had seemed somewhat indifferent to the opinion of businessmen.[3]

There was, however, a major difference in the approach of the two sets of memorialists. Though the Cambridge Memorial asked only for an enquiry into the best means for enlarging the study of Economics, Marshall's lengthy and well-argued supporting Plea talked in terms of a new Honours Degree. In marked contrast the Oxford memorialists, though talking of the desirability of constituting 'a new School of Economics and Political Science', suggested that it should be confined to persons who had taken the degree of BA, B.Sc., or B.Litt. It was referred to as being postgraduate. The Oxford Magazine explained that the petitioners had most wisely disarmed opposition by explicitly not asking for a new Honours School.[4]

In both Universities there were seen to be four main ways in which greater emphasis could be given to Economics and cognate subjects: (i) by introducing new papers in the existing Honour Schools; (ii) by creating a new Honour School; (iii) by providing a suitable examination at the 'post-graduate level'; and (iv) by providing more teaching. In Cambridge each of these possibilities had support. Marshall had for some years been successful in increasing the amount of Economics in Part II of the Moral Sciences Tripos. In the Senate Debate, Dr W. Cunningham argued that a one year's postgraduate course was not to be altogether despised since it would give a large number of able men an opportunity of knowing and doing something at Economics.[5] Marshall, however, decided to go all out for a new Honour School. For one thing he wanted Economics to be studied over three years. At one time he had hoped that one year's reading for the second part of the Moral Sciences Tripos might set Mathematicians and other trained students fairly on their way to becoming economists. But, since taking the Chair, experience had shown him that one year's study was insufficient. In his eighteen years only two men in their third year had shown a knowledge of the realities and a grasp of the machinery of their science such as a tolerably able student of Physics had in his third year. This was a major reason why he did not think a one year postgraduate course would meet the needs.[6] In any case neither Marshall nor his main supporters believed that having spent at least three years on acquiring a degree, many would have the wherewithal or the inclination to do a further year devoted to

economics. Similar doubts must have occurred in Oxford, for writing at the time Edgeworth said that evidence had been laid before the Committee considering the Oxford Memorial that a Diploma 'was not likely to prove a dead letter'.[7]
Marshall was concerned with Economics rather than Political Economy. Maynard Keynes described him as

> the first great economist *pur sang* that there ever was; the first who devoted his life to building up the subject as a separate science, standing on its own foundations, with as high standards of scientific accuracy as the physical or the biological sciences . . . after his time Economics could never be again one of a number of subjects which a Moral Philosopher would take in his stride, one Moral Science out of several, as Mill, Jevons, and Sidgwick took it.[8]

There was no support in Oxford for a new Honour School devoted to this conception of Economics. Nor was there much if any room for new compulsory papers in Lit. Hum. or Modern History. The choices canvassed, therefore, were the provision of more teaching unrelated to any examination or an award of a status lower than a Degree.

The different approach and course of events in the two Universities were mainly due to three factors:
(i)   the greater extent to which Economics already had a place in the degree structure of Cambridge;
(ii) the absence in Cambridge of any Honour School, affected by the extension of the subject, with the prestige and dominance of Literae Humaniores;
(iii) the widely differing outlook and character of Professor Marshall and Professor Edgeworth.

In his letter of January 1902 L. L. Price made it quite clear how small a place proficiency in Economics occupied in the Oxford examination system. In the Final Pass School only part of one of the four Groups of subjects was devoted to Political Economy. In the Final Honour School of Literae Humaniores the 'leading principles of Political Economy' were, as a division of Political Philosophy, recommended for study and one or two questions were set on them. But, Price commented, 'it is a matter of common opinion that a candidate does not gain, but lose, by addressing himself to such questions at the risk of omitting others to which more importance is assigned'. Political Economy was also one of a list of 40 Special Subjects which candidates might elect to take, but, according to Price, was seldom chosen. In the Final Honour School of Modern History there was a compulsory paper entitled 'Political Science and Political Economy with Economic History'. But candidates not aiming at either a First or a Second Class could omit either Political Science or Political Economy with Economic History. According to Price 'neither the standard of attainment in economic knowledge which is generally reached by the candidates, nor that which is expected by the examiners, is very considerable'. Since 1900, Political Economy[9] had been included among eight Special Subjects which a candidate aiming at a First or Second Class could offer. Summing up the position Price said: 'the place given to Economics in our Honour Examinations was never large, and has hardly tended to become more considerable during recent years'. In contrast Price claimed that in Cambridge Economics occupied a very prominent position in the Moral Sciences Tripos and a larger place in the Historical Tripos than in the Oxford School of Modern History. As a result Cambridge was 'continually producing young economists of capacity and attainment'.

At Cambridge [10] each Tripos (or Honour School) was divided into two parts. In the case of most of them it was possible to obtain a BA by spending three years on Part I and passing the examination. It was also possible to spend one or two years on Part I and take Part II in the third or fourth year of residence. Under certain circumstances it was possible to combine one part of one Tripos with part of another. The Cambridge arrangements made for flexibility and choice.

The examination for Part I of the Historical Tripos (success in which did not qualify for a degree) was usually taken at the end of the second year of residence. There was the choice of a paper in either Comparative Politics or General European History (Ancient) and a paper in either English Economic History or Political Economy. In Part II, in addition to an Essay paper and two prescribed periods of history, candidates could offer not less than two, nor more than four of the eight subjects. The list included Comparative Politics, Analytical and Deductive Politics, International Law and two papers in Political Economy. The Economics papers were much more theoretical and less historical than the Oxford treatment.

It was, however, the Moral Sciences Tripos as it had recently developed, largely under Marshall's influence, which offered the greatest opportunity for those who wished to specialise in Economics. Part I, which could be taken at the end of the second or third year of residence, contained two papers each in Psychology, Logic and Methodology, and Political Economy; one in Ethics and an Essay. In Part II, candidates could specialise either in (A) Philosophy and Psychology or (B) Political Philosophy and Advanced Political Economy. Group B contained a paper in Political Philosophy and three in Advanced Economics (including English Economic History and History of Economic Science). Candidates were warned that the papers would consist largely of questions involving considerable scientific difficulty. In particular students would be required to have made a careful and exact study of the mutual inter-actions of economic phenomena, and to have grappled with the difficulties of disentangling the effects of different causes, and of assigning to each as nearly as may be its relative magnitude and importance. Some scope would be given for the diagrammatic expression of problems in pure theory, with the general principles of the mathematical treatment applicable.

Marshall was appreciative of what Part II of the Moral Science Tripos offered to the economics specialist. But he disliked Part I, claiming that a boy coming straight from school was bewildered by its large and heterogeneous mass of difficult notions. Consequently, hardly any who obtained a First Class in Part I came to it straight from school, but usually by way of another university. The situation had been eased recently by changes in the Historical Tripos, thus making Part I of that Tripos a better preparation for Part II of the Moral Sciences. Even so, Marshall disliked the arrangement because Part I was primarily concerned with Mediaeval, not recent, history.[11]

The task of those who wished to provide a more important place for Economics in the Examination structure was thus very different in the two Universities. At Cambridge the subject already had a significant place in Part II of a Tripos. In practical terms it was largely a matter of establishing a more suitable Part I. At Oxford, on the other hand, little or no progress had been made in obtaining a place for the subject in either of the two main Honour Schools in Arts – Lit. Hum., and Modern History. The weight given to the subject in either School could be

Establishment of the Diploma 1903

increased only by the Historians' (Ancient and Modern) and the Philosophers' accepting that less weight need be given to their subjects, which they were not prepared to do.

It might be thought that this would be a situation favourable to the acceptance of a new Honour School. Indeed it was the development of a subject beyond the capacity of the Honour School of which it formed part that had led to the creation of new Schools in the past half-century. There was no overwhelming opposition to the establishment of new Honour Schools; that in English Language and Literature was agreed in 1894 and one in Mediaeval and Modern Languages and Literature was being agreed at the same time as the Diploma. The fact was, however, that Oxford in general, including most of those who signed the Memorial, believed that Economics was best studied, not in isolation, but along with such other disciplines as Philosophy and History. Only thus could it be regarded as a liberal education. If it had to be studied in isolation then a Diploma following upon the education provided by an Honours Degree was probably the most suitable arrangement.

There was, therefore, no support for an Honours Degree so overwhelmingly devoted to Economics as was the new Cambridge Tripos. It would have had to contain a substantial amount of history and philosophy and as such might be seen as a potential competitor by Literae Humaniores and Modern History. The former was the pride of the University. It covered Greek and Latin, the histories of ancient Greece and Rome (studied as far as possible in the original authors), Logic and the outlines of Moral and Political Philosophy. Candidates had to offer at least two philosophical treatises by ancient authors. The writings of modern philosophers were admitted, but not required. The School was widely claimed to present the ideal liberal education and training for the mind. It was Greats, requiring four years residence, which provided the bulk of Oxford's successful candidates for the Home and the Indian Civil Services. In recent years the numbers taking Modern History had increased and the School had gained in prestige. Those who taught in these two Schools were hardly likely to believe that a new School devoted in large part to Economics would have anything like the same prestige. And if, in the process, the content and fabric of their Schools were to be upset, even damaged, there could be a serious loss.

Two of the main advocates of more economics teaching in

Oxford – F. Y. Edgeworth, holder of the Drummond Chair of Political Economy established in 1825, and L. L. Price, later Reader in Economic History – were both products of Greats. In an Obituary notice, Price said that Edgeworth's attitude towards the changes advocated in 1920 had been greatly influenced by 'a loyalty, with which I sympathised, towards the ancient school of Literae Humaniores, ... and unwillingness to depreciate or impair so admirable an education as that, in our joint belief, had proved'.[12]

At the time probably the most prestigious School in Cambridge was the Mathematical Tripos, of which Marshall was a product. But this was not directly affected by the development of an Economics Tripos. The Cambridge Historical Tripos also had grown in prestige and the Board responsible for it might have proved a serious obstacle. But Marshall got G. Lowes Dickinson on his side by giving his scheme a Political Science content and Dickinson used his persuasiveness to win over the History Faculty. In any case, having conceded the general principle, as even Cunningham did, of the need for a larger place for Economics, there was little or no room for more of it in the Historical Tripos. Some, including Neville Keynes, tried to keep Economics within the Moral Sciences Tripos but the Philosophers and Psychologists who dominated it were not unhappy to be allowed greater scope for their disciplines.

With the establishment of an Economics Tripos, the Board for Moral Science decided it was no longer desirable to retain Political Economy in either Part. The two Political Economy papers in Part I were replaced by an additional paper in Ethics and a new paper entitled Elements of Philosophy. The removal of Economics from Part II enabled candidates to devote themselves exclusively to advanced study in one of three groups: (1) Metaphysical and Ethical Philosophy; (2) Logic; or (3) Psychology. Speaking in Senate on the changes J. Ellis McTaggart said it was not a question of looking for a substitute to fill the gap left by the removal of Economics: it was an opportunity for making better provision for Philosophy which was very much needed.[13]

It is improbable that even had Marshall been Professor of Political Economy in Oxford in 1902–3[14] he would have been able to persuade the University to establish an Honour School of Economics. Circumstances and attitudes would have been against him. Of course, in Cambridge he had been campaigning for ten or so years during which time he had won over or worn down many of his main opponents. There was, however, nothing in Oxford comparable to the Moral Sciences Tripos to offer fertile ground for expansion. What is even more improbable is that had Edgeworth held the Chair in Cambridge he would have fought for and achieved the Economics Tripos.

Marshall and Edgeworth differed about Economics as a subject. Marshall believed that it took three years to make a good economist, Edgeworth appeared to believe that economics was a subject one could master fairly readily with the training of a good first degree, preferably Greats. Marshall was interested in the market place and the actual processes of production and exchange. According to Maynard Keynes, Edgeworth wished to establish theorems of intellectual and aesthetic interest, whereas Marshall wished to establish maxims of practical and moral importance.[15]

The difference between the two men comes out strongly in their Inaugural Lectures. Edgeworth started his by calling attention to a certain congruity between the theory of political economy and

> the studies which are particularly characteristic of . . . the great Oxford School of *Literae Humaniores*. . . . It is in economics only, when we have excepted the mathematical physics, that there is realised with some perfection the type of science to which Greek thought aspired, . . . The logical methods, which are studied in the School of *Literae Humaniores* may be exemplified in political economy without going beyond the range of subjects co-terminus to that school.

A little later on he dwelt on 'a certain affinity between the mathematical physics and the one social science which is largely occupied with measurable quantities . . . The differential calculus, the master-key of the physical sciences, unlocks the treasure chamber of the pure theory of economics.'[16]

One short passage from Marshall's Inaugural of 1885 is sufficient to bring out the contrast.

> The only resources we have for dealing with social problems as a whole lie in the judgement of common sense. For the present and for a long time to come, that must be the final arbiter. Economic theory does not claim to displace it from its

supreme authority, nor to intefere with the manner nor even the order of its work, but only to assist it in one part of its work.[17]

L. L. Price, who probably knew Edgeworth better than most people, described him as hesitating and tentative, always seeking shelter behind deference to multiplied authority yet ready to show up minute discrepancies in the numerous texts consulted. Price and others who longed to raise Economics 'from the ignoble level, at Oxford, of a tolerating, grudged, subordination to other studies to the prominent status of recognised autonomy, won at Cambridge through Marshall's influence and effort, sighed sometimes at the absence of pugnacity and the dread of assertiveness, which Edgeworth courted'.[18]

So the Oxford memorialists did not ask for, nor were they given, a new Honour School, but got a Diploma in Economics first examined in 1905, and a Committee to provide for teaching in the subject. In Cambridge, on the other hand, Marshall and his friends asked for and were successful in establishing a new School, with the usual type of Faculty Board to manage it. Part I of the Economic Tripos was first examined in 1905 and Part II in 1906.

POLITICAL SCIENCE AND ECONOMIC HISTORY

Though in both Universities the stress was on economics initially, both talked in terms of associating the development with related subjects. But whereas the new Tripos carried the title of 'Economics and associated branches of Political Science', the new Diploma was confined to economics and economic history.

The full title of the Tripos exaggerated its political science content.[19] Of the seven papers in Part I there was one on the existing British Constitution and two on Recent Economic and General History. But some of the candidates for Part II would have taken Part I of another Tripos, for example, the Mathematical Tripos. In Part II the paper on Modern Political Theories, the two papers on International Law and the two on Principles of Law as applied to economic questions were optional whereas the Essay paper and the three papers on General Economics were compulsory. Candidates could, therefore, concentrate on three

General and two Advanced Economics papers. After being remodelled in 1911 the Tripos contained only one law paper (International Law) and 'Modern Political Theories' became 'Political Science': both were optional. A new compulsory paper 'Economic Functions of Government' was, however, introduced.

The same point might be made of the place given to Economic History in the new Tripos. Two papers in Recent Economic and General History had to be taken in Part I, but there was no specific reference to the subject in Part II. Marshall stated that if time sufficed an economist should know all history; but in a three years course, in which some room had to be found for political science and perhaps for law, the economist could not afford to give the equivalent of more than one year to the subject and could not acquire more than a very superficial knowledge if it were spread over many centuries. The aim of the two papers in Part I was to lead the student to develop the study of general history he had made at school, 'by tracing the action of modern influences, and especially of those which enable anything important said anywhere to be heard within twenty four hours over the whole civilised world'. In Part II, while mainly occupied with a realistic study of those economic conditions in which he was specially interested, the student would be expected to trace their roots as deep into the soil of the past as might be necessary. Those who wanted to give a greater part of their three years to economic history could do so by combining a Part of the History Tripos with a Part of the Economics Tripos.[20]

The Oxford Diploma had two compulsory papers in Economic Theory and one in Economic History. Candidates also had to offer two special subjects, chosen from economic theory; economic history; and applied economics. The Memorial had talked in terms of 'a new School of Economics and Political Science' and earlier had referred to 'Economics and cognate subjects'. But the Statute made no mention of political science nor of cognate subjects. Possibly this was because, unlike Cambridge, it was not necessary to placate the History Faculty. It may also have owed something to Edgeworth's views.

In his letter to the Vice-Chancellor dated 26 June 1902,[21] Edgeworth said there appeared to be two divisions of the general field of political economy. There was Economics proper and a wide outlying ill-defined region of miscellaneous knowledge compressed in what might be called Political Science. He thought it might plausibly be asserted that the latter was more useful, but 'the former has that kind of utility on which value depends, the utility which is attended with rarity or difficulty of attainment'. Men trained in the School of Literae Humaniores would not derive much benefit from lectures on Political Science, but had something to learn from the Economic specialist.

In February 1909, however, the words 'and associated branches of Political Science' were added and the Diploma henceforth had the title of Economics and Political Science. As such it was first examined in June 1910, the old Diploma being examined for the last time in that year. It is interesting that the additional words were exactly the same as those used in the Cambridge Tripos. The change was recommended by the joint Committee on Oxford and Working Class Education of 1908.

The expanded coverage inevitably reduced the place accorded to Economics. The three compulsory papers were henceforth to be in Economic Theory, in Applied Economics and Political Science and in Economic and Constitutional History. To the existing list of groups of special subjects was added two new choices – History of Political Ideas and the Development and Working of Political Institutions.

PROVISION OF TEACHING

In the light of its subsequent history, probably the most significant element in the establishment of the Diploma was the statutory Committee with 'power to make arrangements for lectures and courses of instruction to be given within the University on Economics'.

The Committee for the Diploma, which was set up in November 1903, was composed of 13 members: four elected by the Board of Literae Humaniores, four by the Board of Modern History, two nominated by the Vice-Chancellor (who nominated in the first instance Edwin Cannan and L. L. Price), the Vice-Chancellor, the Proctors and the Drummond Professor of Political Economy. L. L. Price was appointed Secretary and held office continuously until 1921.

The provision of more teaching was seen by some to be the major part of any plan to afford 'greater encouragement to the systematic study of Economics'. In a letter to the Vice-Chancellor in June 1902 Edgeworth gave as the first of four 'conspicuous ways' of affording fresh incentive to the study of Economics 'Course of teaching open to persons who are not members of the University; on the analogy of the School of Geography'. A similar view was presented by W. Cunningham, and J. Ellis McTaggart in Cambridge. In opposing the creation of the Economics Tripos they stated: 'What is required in our opinion is not more examining but more teaching.'[22]

It must be remembered that, at this time, Faculty Boards played very little part in the arrangement of lectures. These were mainly provided by the inter-collegiate lectures offered by the Tutors of the various Colleges. Only a minority of the teachers were under an obligation to lecture by virtue of holding a Chair or other University appointment. Colleges were unlikely to feel any obligation to provide lectures and classes for the new Diploma, hence the need for a University Committee specially charged with the duty. And so from Michaelmas 1904 there appeared each Term in the Gazette a lengthening list of lectures and courses of instruction in Economics and Politics.

In 1904 only the lectures which the Professor of Political Economy was required to give were readily available. As the University had not provided the Diploma Committee with money to make appointments, teachers at first were left to charge, within a prescribed maximum, such fees for attendance as they thought desirable, retaining these as their remuneration. Thus during 1904 H. B. Lees-Smith charged a fee of £1 a term to those who attended his twice-weekly 'Outlines of Economic Theory' and Sidney Ball and Edwin Cannan each charged £5 a term for informal instruction. The work of the Committee was assisted financially by several Colleges, among them All Souls, Oriel and St John's, and by the Oxford Political Economy Club. At Cambridge, Marshall privately paid out of his own pocket stipends of £100 a year to two, sometimes three, young lecturers for which the University made no provision.[23]

A Lecturership in Economic History was created and L. L. Price was appointed for 3 years from June 1907. Two years later this was raised to the status of a Readership by a grant from All Souls, L. L. Price continuing in the post and remaining a Fellow of Oriel College.

As might be expected All Souls were particularly interested in furthering the new subjects. In 1910 they elected N. B. Dearle to a Fellowship by Examination in Political Economy. Dearle, after a First in Modern History, had obtained a Distinction in the Diploma in its first year. Following the enlargement of the Diploma to include Political Science, a Lecturership in Political Theory and Institutions was established in 1909 by the Chancellor's Fund for the further endowment of the University. W. G. S. Adams was appointed and All Souls thereupon provided the extra money to convert the post into a Readership tenable with a Fellowship in the College. In 1912 the Committee for the National Memorial to Mr Gladstone offered about £6000 for the endowment of a Chair of Political Theory and Institutions to be called the Gladstone Professorship, with the result that the Readership and its holder were raised to this new status.

Thus by 1914 the teaching resources provided by the University had been markedly strengthened. No longer was the Professor of Political Economy in isolation: he was flanked by a Professor of Political Theory and Institutions and a Reader in Economic History. There was also an All Souls Fellowship devoted to Economics. However the numbers needing instruction had greatly increased.

2 Developments 1903–18

THE STATUS OF THE DIPLOMA

Looked at dispassionately in 1903 it was not altogether obvious that Cambridge was taking a much bigger step forward than was Oxford in the place it would be giving to Economics. Admittedly a Tripos or Honour School would at the time be regarded as a level above that of a Diploma. A Diploma was a new idea in Oxford, having only just been introduced for Geography and for Education. In the next five years other Diplomas were established in Scientific Engineering and Mining Subjects (1904); Anthropology (1905); Classical Archaeology (1907). There was, however, a suggestion that the new Diploma was to be postgraduate. This was how it was understood in Cambridge during the debates on the Tripos proposal.[1] Today the term post-graduate implies a course or examination confined to candidates who already possess a degree and at a level higher than that expected from first degree candidates. If that were to be the case the new Diploma might be expected to produce economics specialists of a level not less than that achieved by those who had reached Part II of the Economics Tripos by way of Part I of another Tripos.

The three candidates for the first examination in June 1905 were all graduates. One had recently obtained a First and another a Second in the Oxford Modern History School and the third was a graduate of the University of Paris. All obtained a Distinction. Two years later another History First (Miss C. V. Butler) was awarded a Distinction. But these were above the quality of candidates implied by the Statute of 1903 which established the Diploma. Candidates had either to have been matriculated by one of the regular Colleges or by the Non-Collegiate Society, i.e. be a member of the University; or if not, had to show that they had received 'a good general education'.

In 1907 the words 'and are qualified to pursue the study of Economics' were added.

The booklet explaining the Diploma, put out in 1904 by the Diploma Committee, stated that because the Statute had been drawn up on lines similar to those followed in the case of the Diplomas in Geography and in Education it had been possible to secure considerable elasticity in the regulations for admission both to the Examination and to the preliminary instruction. As a result some students might be enabled to combine their reading for a University degree with simultaneous study for the Diploma. But some, unable or unwilling to seek the ordinary degree, or to spend the full time required for it might become candidates.

In their Report for 1905–6 the Diploma Committee commented on its advantage to Rhodes Scholars, who had first arrived in force in Oxford in October 1904. Two of the five candidates in 1906 were Rhodes Scholars, one Canadian and one German. The Diploma offered to such candidates 'who can generally spend no more than two years at Oxford, and cannot take a regular degree, an opportunity of carrying back to their native country documentary testimony bearing the *imprimatur* of the University, of the success with which they have pursued their studies'.[2] In their next annual Report the Committee mentioned the advantage of the Diploma to Rhodes Scholars from Germany. An explanatory pamphlet about the Diploma had been translated into German by 'official authority at Berlin for the use of intending students'.[3]

Nowadays those holding a good degree from a university in another country would normally be granted Senior Status and so be entitled to proceed to the Final Public Examination after two, not three, years' residence. There was, however, no general provision of this kind in 1904 and each university was granted the concession, as the case arose, by a decree of Congregation. The Diploma was thus a useful safety net for candidates from universities not yet so treated. But no doubt this meant that some who took it did so *faute de mieux*, not out of an enthusiasm for economics.

The academic level of the Diploma was reflected in a university decision of 1908 that successful Diploma men were exempted from a Group (two if they obtained Distinction) from the Final Pass School.[4] Thus success in the Diploma could enable a man to obtain a Pass degree. The Diploma Committee expected the change 'to bring an accession of students of a new description, consisting of the better type of passmen'.

WORKING-CLASS EDUCATION

During 1908–10 the purpose and character of the Diploma became involved in the public discussions of what Lord Curzon, the Chancellor of the University, called 'The Admission of Poor Men' and 'A Curriculum for a Business Career'.

The formation of the Labour Party after its success in securing 30 Members of Parliament at the 1906 Election, the growing strength of the Trade Union movement and other happenings focussed attention on the status and education of working men. Aware that they were regarded as providing for the education of the rich and the privileged, some in the University felt the need to consider ways in which Oxford could be brought more closely in touch with, and further working class education. The Extension class movement of the 1880s had aimed at doing this outside Oxford, but there still remained the question of what could be done intramurally.

An important landmark was the appointment of a Committee composed of seven from the University and seven from the Workers' Educational Association. The University side included Sidney Ball, J. A. R. Marriott and H. B. Lees-Smith with experience of teaching for the Diploma. The Dean of Christ Church (T. B. Strong) was Chairman and the Labour and Trade Union leader, D. J. Shackleton was Vice-Chairman. The joint report was published in 1908 and entitled 'Oxford and Working Class Education'.

It was a very thorough report dealing *inter alia* with the Purpose, History and Endowments of the University and Colleges; the Extension Movement and the Functions of a University in a Democratic Community. Extramural teaching they thought, however excellent, must not be regarded as a substitute but as a preparation for study in the University. Assuming money could be found for scholarships for working men these could come up as members of the normal College or as Non-Collegiate or as members of Ruskin College. They were of the opinion that the majority of working-class students would desire to study some of the various branches of Political Science. They would naturally tend to read for a Diploma for they would rarely be in a position to pass Responsions, with its compulsory requirements of Greek and Latin.

Of the present Diploma courses the most desirable for such students was the Diploma of Economics. The course of reading for this could be adjusted to give special attention to the industrial problems in which working people were particularly interested. Facilities should also be offered for studying questions which were not strictly economic but a grasp of which was essential to the understanding of modern society, e.g. local government and political geography. On this they waxed eloquent. 'We hold strongly, moreover, that not only in the interests of workmen students, but in the interests of the scientific study of political problems, political science in the broadest sense of the term, or Sociology, should be given a much more prominent place in the curricula of Oxford.' After mentioning the work of Sidney and Beatrice Webb, the endowment of two Chairs of Sociology at London University, and the research work at the London School of Economics and Political Science the Report went on: 'We think it most desirable that the theoretical and analytical study of politics and economics, which has hitherto predominated at Oxford should be supplemented by inductive investigation of political and economic problems'.

However their only recommendation under this heading, was that a Diploma in Political Science should be established either as part of or in parallel to the Diploma in Economics. In the body of the Report, but not as a recommendation, the Committee expressed the hope that 'ultimately the University will organize a School of Politics and Economics and that one or more Chairs of Sociology will be endowed.' They thought that the Labour Organizations might be willing to contribute to their endowment.[5]

The Committee contained several prominent members of the Executive Committee of Ruskin College. But apart from that it was obvious that that institution would have a role to play in the development of University education for working men. Founded with the support of the Trade Unions in February 1899 the College was housed in Oxford but without any formal links with the University. It provided teaching and facilities for some fifty working men mainly from the North of England and Wales.

The Joint Committee made two recommendations which were to link Ruskin with the Diploma. They were:

(i) that residence for one year at the College, together with a Certificate from the College, agreed by two University representatives appointed for the purpose by the Diploma Committee, stating that the student has reached a satisfactory standard in the course of study pursued at the College, should be accepted as satisfying the requirements of the University that he had received a good general education and was qualified to pursue the study of Economics; and
(ii) that under any scheme of Scholarships or Exhibitions for working men a certain number should be placed at the disposal of Ruskin College for second-year students who had qualified for the Diploma Course.

The proposals for opening the doors of the University to Ruskin students was disliked by those who envisaged a Marxist College or who feared that the working-class viewpoint would be submerged in the traditional Oxford teaching. There was a sharp conflict involving the resignation of the Principal (Mr Dennis Hird) and a strike of the 54 students in March 1909. This led to a major change in the Governing Council of which at the time only a minority were representatives of working-class organizations. Henceforth the Council was to consist of two representatives each of the Trades Union Congress, the General Federation of Trade Unions, the Cooperative Union and the Working-Men's Club and Institute Union, with one representative of every working-class organization that contributed to the College. There were also to be three academic advisory members without votes. The new Principal was Dr Gilbert Slater, the economic historian.[6]

The University agreed to widen the Diploma to cover Political Science and to admit Ruskin students to it. The first two Ruskin candidates were examined in 1910 and both gained a distinction. In 1911 Ruskin students took 8 of the 13 distinctions and 4 of the 12 passes. In the following year they took 6 of the 12 distinctions and 6 of the 13 passes and in 1913, 6 of the 13 distinctions and 7 of the 15 passes. In those years they almost doubled the numbers taking the Diploma.

BUSINESS EDUCATION

In his Memorandum of 1909 the Chancellor (Lord Curzon of Kedleston), said he would like to see the University interest itself in the creation of special facilities for the education of businessmen. He had been disturbed by the view expressed by commercial men that Oxford gave the wrong sort of training. A symptom of this attitude was to be found in 'the large financial contributions which the merchant princes are in the habit of making to the younger universities as compared with Oxford and Cambridge'. He suggested a two-year Diploma to include History, Political Economy, Accounting and Commercial Geography.[7]

The proposal was referred to a Committee appointed by Hebdomadal Council. Reporting in May 1909 the Committee said: 'it would raise the University in the estimation of public men if a suitable curriculum could be arranged . . . the University itself would benefit if it could be shown that those destined for commerce could profitably spend two or three years of their lives at Oxford'.

The Committee, helped by a memorandum from L. L. Price, looked at what Birmingham, Cambridge, Liverpool and Manchester were doing in this field. At Cambridge there was an Economics Tripos, the course of study for which was 'to a large extent a course in Commerce'. The aim of the Faculty of Commerce and Administration of Manchester University, according to its prospectus, was 'to afford a systematic training in higher commercial subjects, in the study of government and administration, and in the work of economic and social investigation'. At Birmingham the Regulations stated that in planning courses of instruction in the Faculty of Commerce 'two objects have been kept in view – (1) the combination of liberal culture with utility, and (2) due regard to the different requirements of different branches of commercial life'. The curricula of both Birmingham and Manchester contained much that was found in the Oxford Diploma, the inclusion of Accountancy and a Modern Language being the most important differences.

The Committee thought a Lecturer in Accountancy would be required and that the Diploma would need to include modern foreign languages.[8]

The Agenda of Hebdomadal Council was overloaded with the consideration of other aspects of the Chancellor's Memorandum. The Committee's Report was not, therefore, formally discussed until 17 March 1910. At that meeting a motion to defer consideration until a detailed curriculum was available was narrowly defeated by 8 votes to 10. A motion in favour of a scheme was carried by 11 votes to 4.

Even so no progress was made. On 12 October 1910, however, the Chancellor attended a meeting of Council and pointed out that a decision in respect of a Curriculum for Business Education was one of several items still pending. Council thereupon agreed to resume the discussion.[9] The ad hoc committee presented a scheme to Council on 27 January 1912.[10] The scheme was considered, amended, referred back, drafted and redrafted over the next year until in February 1913 it emerged as a draft Statute and was submitted to Congregation in April 1913.[11]

Candidates had to be members of the University and have kept two years' residence. The compulsory papers were the three then required for the Diploma in Economics and Political Science plus Principles of Banking and Foreign Exchange, Principles of Accounting, English Law of Contracts and either French or German, (or Spanish with the approval of the Committee). The papers in Law and Languages were those as set for the Final Pass School. It was to be a Diploma in Commerce and Economics and was to be under the jurisdiction of the Committee for Economics and Political Science.

The Preamble, stating the purpose of the Statute, was approved on 13 May 1913, but only by 35 votes to 26.[12] When, however, Congregation tackled the Statute itself a number of amendments were moved on 3 June 1913. The crucial one was the addition of the words 'who have passed all examinations necessary for the Degree of Bachelor of Arts' after 'members of the University'. Moved by A. J. Carlyle and seconded by Professor J. A. Smith the amendment was carried by 50 to 26. The purpose of this and the four other successful amendments was to tighten up the qualifications required of candidates to the new Diploma.[13] The Diploma was to be postgraduate, it being claimed that the University ought to be very careful not to give an education and a certificate which meant nothing really adequate and liberal: 'the old firm ought to deliver the old goods'. Speaking for Council Mr P. E. Matheson argued that the amendments 'would go far to render the scheme a dead letter'.[14]

The amended draft was put to Congregation on 28 October 1913 and was carried by 24 votes to 5. However it then had to go before Convocation where on 11 November 1913 it was rejected by 2 votes to 16.[15] From an early stage there had been a lack of enthusiasm for the general idea. Though the amendments made in Congregation should have ensured that its academic standard and status would be higher than that of the Diploma in Economics and Political Science many believed that they would kill off any potential demand. In the end only two voted in its favour. Four years had passed since the idea had been first suggested by the Chancellor.

Undoubtedly there was a prejudice against the general idea which was not put into rational argument. Where the opposition was articulate it ranged itself chiefly around two distinct points of view. On the one hand, there were many who doubted whether a satisfactory course of business training could be given in the University. The President of Corpus protested against a diploma being awarded for 'subjects of which the University is so profoundly ignorant as banking, accountancy and foreign exchanges'. On the other, there were those who feared that the training would be too effective and too attractive. The Warden of New College thought 'it would indeed be a pity if too much of the brains and vigour of the country were attracted into a business career, and the more important and more ennobling careers of the clergyman, the student, the man of science, the lawyer, the doctor, and even the public servant, should be neglected'. In the latter group there were some who believed that the 'wealth-amassing career of commerce or business had an ignoble and sordid taint and the University would be degraded if it undertook to direct young men into such a career'.[16]

THE MASTER OF CIVIL SCIENCE(S)[17]

The lengthy, inconclusive discussion about a possible Diploma in Commerce and Economics must have left some people rather unsatisfied. Anyhow in May 1915 Hebdomadal Council accepted a motion proposed by Professor W. G. S. Adams to appoint a Committee 'to report on the advisability of instituting a course of study and examination in Political Economy, Political Science and Public Law leading to a Degree, and, if thought desirable to prepare a scheme for the consideration of Council'. The members included Professors W. G. S. Adams and W. M. Geldart, E. Barker, and the Warden of All Souls (F. W. Pember) with the Vice-Chancellor in the Chair.[18]

The Committee reported a month later.[19] They thought that three main groups of possible students should be borne in mind:

(i)   those seeking to enter on political or administrative work;
(ii) those seeking higher positions in commerce and business; and
(iii) those wishing to teach or do research in political, social and economic subjects.

They then considered three possible degrees:

(a) An Honours BA for students who had satisfied the preliminary qualifications for entrance to the Final Honour School of Literae Humaniores.
(b) An Honours BA restricted to students who had passed a Final Honour School at Oxford or who had graduated at other Universities.
(c) A course leading to a new degree analogous to the Bachelor of Civil Law (BCL) open to graduates of Oxford and other Universities.

The Committee rejected the creation of a new Honour School. They were of the opinion that students would be much better prepared for the study of the proposed subjects after completing one of the courses leading to an Oxford B.A. or some similar course at another university. Such students would however find the new course much more attractive if it led to a new degree. For reasons which they did not fully explain they came down in favour of the third possibility. This 'would enable a higher course in the proposed subjects to be established at Oxford which would be distinctive in character and attractive to an important group of graduates both of this and other universities'.

They therefore recommended the institution of a new Degree in Political Economy, Political Science and Public Law. The course would normally take two years but candidates who had already graduated at Oxford might take the examination at the end of one year from the date they obtained their BA. This concession was analogous to the provisions for the BCL. They reported that they had considered various suggestions for the title of the Degree. As it would be 'of a post-graduate character' they recommended that it should carry the title of Master and be known as Master of Civil Science.

Hebdomadal Council quickly adopted the general proposal and asked the Committee to draft the statute which would need to be passed.[20] The draft Statute submitted by the Committee in November did not go into any detail about the subjects and papers. The examination was to include Political Economy, Political Science and Public Law (which was deemed to include Jurisprudence, Constitutional Law and International Law). It was to be under the jurisdiction of a board of Studies composed of six ex-officio members and two appointed by each of the Faculty Boards of Literae Humaniores, Modern History and Law. Again, the Committee's efforts had a favourable reception and with one or two amendments the draft was referred by Council to the three Faculty Boards concerned and to the Committee for Economics and Political Science for their observations.[21]

In the meantime, however, the Board of the Faculty of Natural Science began to take an interest. They asked to be consulted and when this request was supported by the General Board of Faculties it was agreed to by Hebdomadal Council, albeit with some reluctance.[22]

The replies from the various bodies received in May 1916 were generally favourable in principle. Natural Science, however, thought that if the aims of the course were as stated by the Committee then, before admission to it, candidates should produce evidence that they had a sufficient knowledge of Natural Science, a view supported by the General Board. They also asked for representation on the Board of Studies. The Lit. Hum. Board preferred the title of Bachelor to that of Master of Civil Science. The Law Board thought the degree should be a Baccalaureate not a Mastership.[23] The replies were referred to the Committee which reported at the end of June 1916. They were against both the proposals of the Natural Science Board. As for the title they pointed out that the Preamble to the draft Statute did not state whether the degree should be Bachelor or Master. The question could therefore be left for further consideration when the Statute came before Congregation.[24]

Again Council supported the views expressed by the Committee but the rejection of the representation for the Natural Science Board on the Board of Studies was carried only by 11 votes to 8. The draft Statute was referred back to the Committee for further consideration[25] and there it rested apparently without further action. The Committee on Civil Science remained in being until 1919 when it was asked to consider a somewhat different scheme.

The proposals for the new degree showed substantial changes in thinking about the best way of developing the study of economics and related subjects in the University. There was now no longer any thought of making do with a Diploma: the new courses would lead to a Degree. No doubt this reflected disappointment in the way the Diploma in Economics and Political Science had developed. In terms of numbers it was a success: there were 42 candidates in June 1914, more than were attracted by several of the Final Honour Schools. But it had developed outside the mainstream of College and University interests and activities. It did not attract the brightest students nor their tutors. Its aim was not to produce professional economists as had been Marshall's at Cambridge. Though in its early years the Diploma produced three who subsequently taught economics in Oxford (Violet Butler, N. B. Dearle and T. H. Penson) by 1910–14 it does not appear to have been attracting candidates of that quality. In contrast Part II of the Economics Tripos was producing W. Layton (1907); G. F. Shove (1911); H. D. Henderson and D. H. Robertson (1912) and C. W. Guillebaud (1913) – all placed in the First Class.

Nevertheless the existence of the Diploma had proved something of a godsend to the University authorities. It had provided a ready-made vehicle for encouraging working class education and in particular Ruskin College. It had provided at least a reasonable talking point in the discussion about the education of men destined for careers in business and commerce. And it had provided a safety net for those who could not satisfy the requirements for the BA, particularly the compulsory Greek and Latin. In doing these things the Diploma enabled Lit. Hum. and the Modern History School to remain unaffected by external forces and events.

Though the Annual Report of the Diploma Committee usually quoted the rising number of candidates as a measure of its success, their honest appraisal was probably that given in their Report for 1919–20.[26] This was at the time the proposals for an Honour School in Economics and Politics were under consideration. Contrasted with a Final Honour School, they declared, the Diploma had been obviously handicapped:

(a) as it did not qualify for a degree, except as a substitute for the Final Pass School, it could not appeal to the great mass of students, and it was not inaccurate to describe many of those who had taken it as perforce 'waifs and strays', unable for various accidents or reasons to follow a normal University course;

(b) it could not give, in time of preparation or in width or intensity of study, the scope desired by ability of the highest honour type, and those of such calibre had been the few post-graduate candidates able to spend one additional year after the completion of a regular course for some established Honour School;
(c) the teaching had been provided largely by the help of tutors and lecturers mainly occupied in their preparation of pupils for the recognized Schools.

A new factor had emerged to underline the need for a degree. Thanks largely but by no means wholly to the creation of the Rhodes Scholarships, Oxford now attracted a substantial number of graduates from Commonwealth and American universities. Few of these were interested in Greek and Latin and the glories of Greats. They preferred more modern subjects. Oxford had little or nothing to offer in the fields of Economics and Politics. The increasing number of overseas graduates had led to the introduction of senior status. The University were driven to acknowledge that students with three years' study, with Honours degrees from Sydney, Harvard, Princeton, Melbourne and other Universities could not be treated as though they were fresh from school. Such students were granted senior status, which exempted them from Responsions and the First Public Examination and enabled them to take an Oxford Honours Degree after two years' residence. But there was no such degree in Economics and the social sciences.

Even so, there does not appear to have been any enthusiasm for following Cambridge's successful Economics Tripos. In some part this must have been due to a desire to avoid competing with the existing Honour Schools, particularly the powerful Lit. Hum. and Modern History Faculties. There were, however, two genuine academic considerations which influenced the views even of many of those who wanted to see Economics have a more prominent role in the University curricula.

On the one hand there were doubts whether the study of Economics, Government and similarly contemporary subjects could properly constitute a liberal education. Such doubts had been expressed at the beginning of the century when the Diploma and the Economics Tripos had been under discussion. They had still not been resolved. On the other hand, there were many who believed that Economics required a certain maturity in those who studied the subject and was more likely to be better understood and appreciated by students who had spent time studying other subjects than by those fresh from school. Both these lines of thought were present during the discussions on the Diploma in Commerce and Economics. The amendment requiring candidates to possess a first degree was partly to ensure a higher standard but also to ensure that they had a liberal education and were mature enough to tackle 'commerce'.

The Bachelor of Civil Law (BCL) was a possible model. This was a long standing degree which had recently risen in academic standard and prestige. It could be taken only by candidates who had already obtained the Oxford BA or who held a similar qualification from a recognized university. It could be granted with Honours. That being so, it is somewhat puzzling that the Committee did not recommend the title of Bachelor of Civil Sciences. In the Oxford of the time the degree of Master was not awarded for academic prowess shown either by examination or thesis. Any person having taken his BA and having kept his name on the books of his College for 5 years by paying the proper fees could apply for the status of Master. Doubts were raised about the title and one suspects that the Committee's proposal would not have received much support in Congregation.

Finally it is noticeable that Law was to be the partner of Economics and Politics. When after the war a tripartite school was established it was Philosophy that became the partner, indeed the senior partner. The Committee thought that Political Science and Public Law were so closely related that it was desirable to group them together, e.g. Jurisprudence and the Theory of the State and English Constitutional Law and Administration. The History of Political and Economic Theory was to be a compulsory subject.[27]

Probably the proposals on the law side owed much to Professor W. M. Geldart. Not only was he the Vinerian Professor of English Law and a Classical Scholar of note, he was a member of Hebdomadal Council from 1905 to 1921. There is, of course, much to be said for linking the study of political institutions and government with the study of constitutional and administrative law. Anyhow in 1916 at least the Lit. Hum. Board approved of the general idea without committing itself to the details. Three years later they were to propose a different scheme.

3 Modern Greats 1920–39

During the war of 1914–18 the number of teachers and undergraduates declined markedly. The University limped along. By 1919 with the return of peace the numbers increased and there was a strong urge to get back to pre-war activities and aspirations. So far as Economics and cognate subjects were concerned their future seemed to be with the Diploma in Economics and Political Science and the draft Statute for a degree in Civil Science awaiting action by Hebdomadal Council. Yet neither of these blossomed and by the end of 1920 an entirely new Honour School had been established in Philosophy, Politics and Economics.

The creation of this School was the major step in the development of Social Studies in Oxford. For its establishment led to a Board of Studies, later to a Faculty, and as the School grew in popularity, College and University appointments in Economics and Politics were made to provide the teachers.

The original impetus came from the philosophers, an important element in the Honour School of Literae Humaniores. Though the School is predominantly concerned with the history and languages of ancient Greece and Rome and though much of the philosophy teaching, e.g. of Plato and Aristotle, is closely linked with those civilisations, the ideas with which the philosophers deal are not so confined. This was recognised in the Special Subjects which at that time included Descartes, Spinoza, Locke, Hume and Kant. Many philosophy teachers took more than a passing interest in Political Economy, reading John Stuart Mill's *Principles of Political Economy* as well as his *System of Logic*, and *Representative Government*. A. D. Lindsay and many of his philosophy colleagues were, therefore, interested in any proposal that would enable philosophy to be taught and examined in its own right, not tied to ancient history, but in association with 'modern' subjects.

As early as 1912[1] the Lit. Hum. Board had agreed in principle to a School which combined Philosophy and Natural Science. They submitted a detailed scheme to Hebdomadal Council in December 1914. In explaining the reasons for the proposal the Board referred to students of such subjects as mathematics, natural science, history, psychology or anthropology being interested in philosophy. There was no mention of Economics or Politics. The new Honour School of Modern Philosophy would be confined to modern philosophy since the study of Greek philosophy was already provided for in Lit. Hum. In detail the proposals were very similar to those put forward and rejected in 1923.[2]

War prevented the matter being discussed but early in 1919 the Boards of the Faculties of Lit. Hum. and of Natural Science raised the issue afresh. In May 1919 the former Board resolved that the time has now come to consider the general question of a philosophical course connected with subjects other than Ancient History.[3] They followed this up in November by submitting a scheme for an Honour School of Modern Humanities and asking Council to introduce a Statute embodying the proposals.

The scheme had been prepared by a committee of the Board, the report being signed by H. H. Joachim, A. D. Lindsay, J. L. Myres, C. C. J. Webb and H. H. Williams. They had consulted the Boards of Modern History and of Mediaeval and Modern Languages. At the outset of their report they said they were convinced that the Honour School they proposed would meet the need 'not only of those students who approach philosophy from other sides than classical literature and history, but also of those numerous students who desire to study politics and economics on a broad and systematic basis'.[4] If the new School were not to overlap with Lit. Hum. or Modern History it had to be regarded as concerned with the study of the foundations of the nineteenth-century and present day civilisation in its three branches: philosophy; science; and political, economic and social development. The School should include such study of the earlier history of these subjects as was necessary for an understanding of them and should admit the study, as a special subject, of the philosophy, science, or political, economic and social development of any period. But, except as studied as a special subject, the philosophy should be modern, from Descartes, and the history should not go further back than say 1776.

The Committee envisaged an Honour School of Modern Humanities covering Science and Economics and Politics with Philosophy providing the common element, that is, candidates could take either Philosophy and Science or Philosophy and Politics and Economics. The School would be under a Board of Studies appointed by the Faculty Boards of Lit. Hum., Natural Science and Modern History.

The idea of a 'Science Greats' did not arouse sufficient enthusiasm either among the philosophers or the scientists to give it any real hope of success. It was quite different in purpose and scope from the proposal which became known as 'Modern Greats'. There were already Honour Schools covering science whereas economics and modern politics were not catered for at that level. It was therefore likely to attract only the few candidates who wished to learn something about the principles of science along with modern philosophy. In contrast, the other part of the scheme had attractions to both philosophers and historians who wished to concentrate on recent times as well as providing for the study of economics and political science at the Honour School level.

The Lit. Hum. Board proposed that candidates could specialise in philosophy, politics or economics but would be required to take papers from each. They suggested nine papers.

(1) An Essay with choice of subjects: philosophical, psychological, and economic and political.
(2) Moral and Political Philosophy.
(3) Social, Economic, and Political History from say 1776.
(4) Set books on any two of the following three subjects:
    (i) Logic and Metaphysics; (ii) Moral and Political Philosophy, and (iii) Economics.
(5) Unseen translation from any two of the following languages: Latin, French, German and Italian.
(6) A special subject of either a philosophical, political or economic character. The report listed *inter alia*: The Theory of Law, History of the House of Commons; Federalism; the Relations between Capital and Labour; and Finance, Currency and Banking.
(7)–(9) Three papers out of the following list:
    (i) Logic and Metaphysics
    (ii) History of Modern Philosophy from Descartes
    (iii) Theory and Organisation of Modern Political Institutions

(iv) Economics, including the History of Economic Thought.

The attractions of this scheme to the philosophers was obvious: a candidate could take six papers (1, 2, 4, 6, 7 and 8) in modern philosophy. It offered less to the economists: even so there were four papers central to their subject (1, 4, 6 and 9) as well as the paper in Social, Economic and Political History. Politics had a reasonable coverage if Moral and Political Philosophy and the History paper were regarded as central.

Council referred the report and its proposals to a small committee of its members which met in February 1920, with H. A. Prichard and A. D. Lindsay in attendance. After consultation with the Sub-Faculty of Philosophy and with members of the Board of the Faculty of Natural Science, Council's Committee recommended: (1) that the proposal for a School of Modern Philosophy in relation to Science should be postponed for further consideration by the two Faculty Boards,[5] and (2) that the Committee should be authorised to proceed with the drafting of a Statute for a School of Modern Humanities, 'i.e. Philosophy in combination with modern political, economic and social development'.[6]

The recommendations coincided with a letter from the Committee for Economics and Political Science requesting Council to establish a Final Honour School in Economics and Politics.[7] Accompanying it was a draft syllabus which, however, had not yet received formal approval of the Committee.[8] The letter together with the Draft Statute for the Degree in Civil Science were referred by Council to a Joint Committee composed of the Committees on Modern Humanities and for Civil Science, to which representatives of the Committee for Economics and Political Science were invited to attend.

This Joint Committee were clear that the Lit. Hum. proposal would not satisfy the wishes of the Committee for Economics and Political Science who were, therefore, asked to draft a Statute embodying their ideas. This they did in May 1920.[9] Their School of Economics and Politics was to consist of the following ten papers:

1/2 Economic Theory, including its history.
3 Modern Economic History from 1700.
4 Political Philosophy.

5   History of Political Thought.
6   British Constitutional History, including that of the Dominions, from 1688.
7   The Economic Organisation of Modern Society.
8   The Political Organisation of Modern Society.
9/10 Special Subjects.

The draft stated that 'Candidates will be expected to show such knowledge of Economic and Political Geography and Jurisprudence and Statistical Method as is necessary for the proper study of the subjects of this Examination'. The Board of Studies proposed for the Examination was the Committee for Economics and Political Science.

The Joint Committee had in the meantime drafted a Statute which modified a little the original proposals of the Lit. Hum. Board. They thought that the Examination should consist of eight, not nine, papers. This was notwithstanding the History paper being divided into two: British Political and Constitutional and British Social and Economic History both from 1760. But candidates would have to offer only one further subject, not three. Two other changes were made in the main papers: (a) Logic and Metaphysics became Metaphysics and Moral Philosophy, and (b) Latin was dropped from the list of languages for the Unprepared Translation paper.[10]

There were thus now two possible schemes. On 22 May 1920 the Joint Committee recommended that if Council did not feel able to submit simultaneously both draft Statutes to Congregation it should submit first that for Modern Humanities, because (1) it fitted most naturally into the scheme for the degree of Master of Civil Science already adopted by Council, and (2) while it made provision for almost as great an amount of Economics as the other scheme it also made provision, as the other did not, for the inclusion of Philosophy and thus afforded a broader range of choice for candidates. They recommended that the Diploma Committee's scheme should be submitted subsequently.[11]

On 3 June, Council agreed to send the draft Statute for a School of Economics and Politics to the General Board of Faculties where consideration was deferred *sine die*.[12] On 14 June a motion in Hebdomadal Council that the Modern Humanities Statute should be referred back was lost on a division by 5 votes to 15 and so was sent to Congregation.[13] On 16 June 1920 therefore, the Statute appeared in the Gazette,[14] the Preamble reading 'Whereas it is expedient to promote the study of the structure, and philosophical, political and economic principles, of Modern Society, and for this purpose to provide an Examination in Philosophy, Politics and Economics as an Honour School of the Second Public Examination, the University Enacts'. It first came before Congregation on 19 October 1920.

The proposal aroused criticism and opposition mainly from those who wanted an Honour School devoted to Economics and Political Science. They disliked the important, indeed dominating, place afforded to Philosophy. The proposal for a degree in Civil Science had broadly met their views for though a significant place was given to Law it was felt that public law had greater relevance to the study of contemporary society than general philosophy. In some quarters there was annoyance at what was seen as the arrogance of the philosophers. The proposals of the Philosophy Sub-Faculty were in effect for an Honour School in their subject with Economics and Politics hitched on. The new degree was even to be entitled 'Philosophy, Politics and Economics'.

In his Autobiography Professor Lionel (Lord) Robbins recalling his experience as a Lecturer in Economics at New College in the mid 1920s says that discussion of Modern Greats

> tended to be swamped by the then ruling school of philosophers, a race of men who were all too apt to assume that their own discipline gave them spiritual jurisdiction over all, or nearly all, others, regardless of their degree or relevant technical qualification – to hear, for instance, J. A. Smith, Waynflete Professor of Moral Philosophy pontificating on the methodology of economics, with which his acquaintance was zero, was to gain new conceptions of the possibility of human absurdity.[15]

Edwin Cannan who, though a Professor of Economics at the London School of Economics and Political Science until 1926, did his best in various ways to stimulate the development of Economics in Oxford, organised regular meetings of Oxford economists in the inter-war years. He called his group 'Some Oxford Economists' and refused to allow any philosopher to be a member.

Those who wanted an Honour School devoted to Economics and Politics put forward their claims vigorously in public. Sir

Henry Penson (a Lecturer in Economics at Worcester) produced a pamphlet. The Committee on Economics and Political Science submitted a memorandum to the recently appointed Royal Commission on Oxford and Cambridge Universities. It claimed that, in spite of no more than limited encouragement, Economics and Politics had had a strong and growing attraction. The two subjects could be joined together with advantage. The Diploma was handicapped because it did not qualify for a Degree, except as a substitute for part of the Final Pass School and many of those who took it were 'waifs and strays', unable to follow a normal University course. The Royal Commission invited Edwin Cannan and L. L. Price to give oral evidence but their report, published in 1922, did not deal with curricula or examinations.[16]

The Professor of Political Economy, Edgeworth, by now aged 75, was not an active supporter of those who wished to exclude philosophy. He still retained a loyalty to Greats. When asked for his opinion about the merits of the two schemes at a conference called for the purpose of enabling Council to make a choice 'he gave the halting, albeit honest answer that there seemed much to be said on either side'. He took no part in the debates.[17] No doubt this was a major reason why Edwin Cannan, though a Professor in London University, was asked to express the case for the Committee.

In the circumstances of the Oxford of the time the Economists were most unlikely to win the day. There were far too few teachers of economics, even including economic history, for them to be trusted with a completely new Honour School. Their almost complete rejection of philosophy meant that they forfeited support from that important body of teachers. It might have been better tactics to argue for more economics and less philosophy in the proposals of the Lit. Hum. Board which the Joint Committee claimed provided almost as much Economics as did the Diploma Committee's proposal. But the philosophers would have been unlikely to accept that. To their mind Economics and Politics were being treated as on a par with Philosophy, for all candidates would be able to take five papers on the side of the School on which they wished to specialise.[18] As a contributor to the Oxford Magazine wrote at the time 'one suspects that a School of political and economic study with a definite philosophical background might be of great value to these subjects'.[19] Instead Price moaned that the new School marked the continuation of the old policy of regarding Economics as the 'Cinderella' of the subjects taught in Oxford,[20] and spoke against it in Congregation.

The second main line of criticism was that the promoters of the proposed new School had two aims 'admirable in themselves but fundamentally inconsistent with one another': to create a Modern Humanities School analogous to Greats and to give scope for the teaching of Economics. H. J. Paton (then Junior Proctor, Fellow of Queens and Lecturer in Philosophy) claimed that neither of these was properly secured and indeed could not possibly be so in any single School. He then made a detailed comparison between Greats and what was coming to be referred to as Modern Greats. Greats, he claimed, gave a training in Philosophy, in History and, to a lesser degree, in Language 'three most fundamental departments of human thinking on its so-called humane as opposed to its so-called scientific side'. The new School was inferior to Greats in each of these disciplines. Instead of Logic and Metaphysics there was the History of Philosophy since Descartes, chosen because it was a soft option to the weaker man. British history since 1760 was not an adequate parallel to the close acquaintance required by Greats with one period of Greek and one of Roman history. As for languages the new School demanded merely unprepared translation from two modern languages 'and we know how little that is worth'.

Paton summed up his views by saying 'A school . . . . which is content to neglect modern languages, to ignore Continental History, and to truncate modern philosophy . . . cannot be accepted for a moment as a satisfactory school of Modern Humanities and it cannot profess even to compare with Greats in any of these three fundamental departments of human thought'. At the same time the proposed School was grossly inadequate to meet the demands for teaching in Political Economy. There were far too many subjects in the School 'and each has been ruined by the necessity of providing room for the others'. He pleaded for a School of Political Economy and History.[21]

It is probable that the term 'Modern Greats' which quickly came to be applied to the new School misled many people. It was not intended, as Paton suggested, to provide exactly the same training for the modern world as was provided for the Greek and Roman civilisations. Instead it was designed to liberate Philosophy in Oxford from its hitherto close links with Ancient History and to provide something at the Honour School level for economics, recent history and politics. In any case Greats took four years and there does not appear to have been any serious proposal that Modern Greats should take longer than three. All in all Modern Humanities was probably a more appropriate description: in terms of the Statute and in practice it was the Final Honour School of Philosophy, Politics and Economics.

The Preamble to the Statute came up for discussion in Congregation on 19 October 1920. It followed a long debate on quite a different topic and the House was said to be weary, many having left on the impression that the debate would be adjourned. However a division was unexpectedly taken at 4 p.m. and by 46 votes to 29 the Preamble was carried.[22] On 19 November 1920 the Statute was agreed by 95 votes to 58, no notice of any amendments having been given. It was agreed by Convocation *nem. con.* on 30 November 1920.[23]

The Statute which established the Final Honour School of Philosophy, Politics and Economics laid it down that the Examination should always include the following subjects:

(1) Moral and Political Philosophy
(2) British Political and Constitutional History from 1760
(3) British Social and Economic History from 1760
(4) History of Philosophy from Descartes
(5) Political Economy
(6) Prescribed Books in two of the following:
    (a) Metaphysics and Moral Philosophy
    (b) Political Philosophy
    (c) Political Economy
(7) A further subject in Philosophy, Politics or Political Economy
(8) Unprepared translation from French, German and Italian authorities – at least two of the three.

The Board's Regulations modified the list slightly by putting a terminal date of 1914 on the Constitutional History paper. The Board also indicated the contemplated scheme of papers. There were to be ten papers, the Prescribed books being the subject of two papers and a paper entitled Political and Economic Organization being added. All were three-hour papers except the language paper which was two hours.

The Regulations made by the Board of Studies amplified the statutory requirements. Candidates for Political Economy would be expected to show a knowledge of economic theory, of its history, and of its application to the most important aspects of modern economic conditions. The Prescribed books were Adam Smith's *Wealth of Nations*; Ricardo's works (the McCulloch edition); Vol. 1 of Marx's *Capital*; Jevons's *Theory of Political Economy* and List's *The National System of Political Economy*. The further subjects in Political Economy were Currency and Banking; Capital and Labour; and Labour Movements 1815–75. The further subjects in Politics were Public Administration; the Development of International Relations since 1815; and the Reform Movements in British Colonial Policy (1830–50) and the Development of the new Colonial System. Candidates in the two history papers were expected to show such knowledge of the contemporary history of Europe and America as was necessary for their proper study.

The Statute provided that the Examination was to be 'so arranged that Candidates may give special attention either to Philosophy or to Politics or to Political Economy by the choice they make of prescribed books and of a further subject'.

It should be explained for the benefit of those not familiar with Oxford University that undergraduates spend six terms (two years) or seven terms working for their Final School. The first two, possibly three, terms of residence are spent on preparing for their First Public Examination. If by virtue of possessing a suitable Degree from another university they have been granted Senior Status they are exempt from the First Public Examination which means they need to spend only six terms residence to qualify as candidates for the Second Public Examination.

There was a choice of several First Public Examinations but most candidates for Modern Greats took Pass Moderations. This required a knowledge of Latin or Greek, French or German and in the early twenties a choice of Mathematics, Logic or the Elements of Political Economy. By the time of the changes of 1933 the list of non-language papers, now eight, included English Constitutional Law and History and European History. The Books recommended for the Political Economy paper were Gide's *Principles* followed by Nicholson's *Elements* in the early years. Then for a time they were: Henderson, *Supply and Demand*; Lehfeldt, *Money*; and Dalton, *Public Finance*. From October 1936 candidates were told that they would be given an opportunity of showing knowledge of the elements of economics theory and organisation as comprised, for example, in Taussig's *Principles of Economics*, Books I and II; Book III except chapters 20–21 and 27–31; Book IV except chapter 35; and Book V. The Board's Committee which had recommended the change disliked the current list of books but thought no other list would be generally acceptable. The Regulation was worded to avoid any implication that Taussig's text book was recommended for textual study. English Constitutional Law and History could be studied in Dicey's *The Law of the Constitution* and Maitland's *Constitutional History*.

The experience of the working of the new School gained by Tutors and Examiners and the emergence of a strong group of Economists led to changes.

In their report on the Examination of 1925 the Examiners said they were 'impressed by the difficulties presented to the candidates by the extent, variety, and heterogeneousness of the matter required to be studied ... difficulties obviously felt by their teachers and advisers in organising their preparation'. They believed that 'the danger is very considerable in the case of Philosophy' and the Philosophy Examiners therefore suggested 'that the philosophical requirements and instruction should be more brought into touch with the subject matter of the other branches'.

In March 1926 the Modern History Tutors submitted a memorandum criticising the Politics side of the School. There were, they claimed, too many half papers, which made for scrappiness rather than thoroughness. The requirements arose from:

> the early fear, that was widely felt, that it would prove a soft option. To prevent this it [had been] loaded with a large number of subjects, many of them disconnected, and with a requirement that a candidate must stand in three separate lines, which is too many. The attempt to prevent the School being made a soft option has defeated itself. It overweights the School with information, hampers the good man, but makes it easier to get a low class merely because the questions... have to be very often too general, and capable of being answered from small text book knowledge.

The Regulations were slightly revised for the 1928 Examination and onwards. The terminal date on the Constitutional History paper was removed and the word Modern was placed in front of Political and Economic Organization. All the papers were now listed in the Regulations. The Labour Movements paper remained but Currency and Banking became Currency and Credit and

Capital and Labour was replaced by Advanced Economic Theory. This last paper was spelt out in a way which revealed the growing professional character of the teaching of Economics in the University. Candidates for this new paper were told that they must show acquaintance with the works of such authors as Marshall, Cassel, Böhm-Bowerk, J. B. Clark, Edgeworth and Pareto in formal theory, and of special writers on such problems as money, prices and wages, interest, trade fluctuations and foreign trade. Candidates were expected to be 'generally acquainted with modern statistical methods and concepts as applied to measurement of economic data; and with the methods of quantitative analysis now generally in use'.

Late in 1929 the Board of Studies appointed its Chairman (A. D. Lindsay), Professors Adams, Coupland and Macgregor, and T. D. Weldon to consider the Statute governing the School. Their report was circulated to the Faculty in June 1930 and considered by the Board in the following two Terms. The Committee reported that there was considerable dissatisfaction with the present Examination, both in general and in detail. It involved, they said, 'an excessive quantity of diffuse study but left little scope for adequate specialisation in the candidate's main subject'. They then considered three possible kinds of improvement.

The first was to reduce the School from three to two sides either by omitting one or by allowing candidates to select two out of three. They rejected this unaminously because, in their opinion 'any such alteration would destroy the claim of the School to be the "study of the structure and principles of modern society" '.

The second possibility was to create a distinction, analogous to that in the Modern History School, between strong and weak candidates and allow the latter to omit a paper or papers. The Committee thought the differentiation would be invidious and unsatisfactory. Therefore, they inclined to favour a third possibility which was to reduce the number of papers required from all candidates.

They then looked at the requirements in the light of detailed criticism. This led them to recommend that the two Philosophy papers should remain virtually unchanged but Political Theory was to become a compulsory subject in Politics. Questions about economic organisation were to be included in the compulsory Political Economy paper. The Committee claimed that their proposals would reduce the amount of work required from weaker candidates and would allow all candidates to concentrate more thoroughly on their main subject.

Their views were not shared by the Tutors to whom the report was circulated. Comments submitted by such Philosophers as Ryle, Hardie, Franks, Wolfenden and Price, and by several Politics dons (Costin, Fulton, Keir, McCallum, Maud, Sumner and Sutherland) mainly concentrated on points of detail. The Economists, however, were up in arms in a major way, for Lindsay's Committee had proposed that the two compulsory Economics papers should be Economic Theory and Organisation and Economic History since 1815.

The Economists (Bretherton, Phelps Brown, Fraser, Hall, Hargreaves, Hugh-Jones, Rodger, Sutherland and Miss Wilson) said 'it will be little short of disastrous if the School does not provide one full paper in Economic Theory'. Harrod had made a similar point in a separate note. The Philosophers criticised the combination of theory and organisation in one paper, since abstract theory being more difficult than the accumulation of information, candidates would concentrate on organisation. The Economists proposed a compulsory paper confined to theory, with economic organisation becoming a special paper. They also criticised (i) the starting date for Economic History: 1815 might be significant for politics but had less meaning for economic history; and (ii) the special paper headed Finance covering both Currency and Credit and Public Finance: the former was indispensable whereas the latter was not.

The Economists thought that the effect of the changes in the constitution of the School would be to widen the distinction between those who were and those who were not doing advanced work in Economics. It would be difficult to set an Economic Theory paper for both classes and, therefore, they suggested two distinct papers in Economic Theory: one containing reasonably advanced questions in Theory in the narrow sense, to be taken by candidates offering Economics as their first subject and another, of a more general character, to be taken by candidates concentrating on Philosophy or Politics.

The criticisms and their lengthy discussion led to the proposals being revised as can be seen from the Statute agreed by Congregation in June 1931.[24] The new arrangements, which came into operation from the June 1933 Examination, differed from the old in several significant ways.

First, the Board were given a wide discretion to determine and change the content of the Examination without being tied to a detailed Statute. The new Statute did not therefore specify even the papers, but stated the principles. There was to be a general part of the Examination in which candidates had to take six subjects or any larger number which the Board should determine, but these had always to include two in Philosophy, two in Politics, and two in Economics. A list of Further Subjects had to be offered from which candidates had to select two, the list having to include at least two subjects in Philosophy, two in Politics and two in Economics. Finally there had to be a paper of unprepared translation from French, German and such other modern European languages as might be prescribed. This treatment made the Statute much shorter and much less informative about the contents of the School than had the original Statute of 1920. All the detail was now to be found in the Regulations made by the Board.

Second, there was a significant change in the wording of the Preamble which states the purpose of a Statute. The old Statute, dating back to 1920 had stated that the subject of the School 'shall be the study of the structure, and the philosophical, political and economic principles, of Modern Society'. The new Statute stated that the subject 'shall be the study of modern philosophy, and of the political and economic principles and structure of modern society'. There is nothing in the scanty recorded proceedings of the Board which indicates the purpose of the changed wording. The implication would, however, appear to be clear: this was a School for those who wanted to study modern philosophy in its own right not just as a means of understanding the principles and structure of modern society.

Third, the three groups of prescribed books, from which candidates had to choose two, were replaced by a list of Further Papers divided under the headings Philosophy, Politics and Economics. Candidates still had to choose two but now the two could come from one side of the School. The Philosophy list was Kant, and Logic; the Politics list was Public Administration, International Relations, the Political Structure of the British Empire or Political Theory since 1760; and for Economics the choice offered was Currency and Credit, Public Finance, Statistical Method and the use of statistics in economics, and either the economic works of Adam Smith and Ricardo or Labour Movements since 1815 (the Advanced Economic Theory paper was dropped).

Fourth, a similar recognition of the specialised needs of the three sides of the School had changed the compulsory papers. Philosophy retained General Philosophy since Descartes and Moral and Political Philosophy but there were now two clearly Economics papers – Economic Theory and Economic Organization – and Politics had papers in Political Institutions and in British Political and Constitutional History since 1760. The Committee's proposal for a compulsory paper in Political Theory was dropped no doubt because of the Moral and Political Philosophy paper. There was a seventh compulsory paper: either British Social and Economic History since 1760 or Political History from 1871 to 1914. Candidates who chose both their further papers from the Economics list were required to take the Economic History option.

Fifth, there still remained the paper of unprepared translation but the languages had been widened by the addition of Spanish, and candidates had to offer either French or German.

As a result of the changes the School offered a more coherent and satisfactory vehicle for those who wished to specialise in economics. The criticisms and demands of the growing band of economics teachers had been substantially met, whilst retaining the tripartite character of the School. There were now compulsory papers in Economic Theory and in Economic Organisation and a choice of two further subjects from a list of four. Economics specialists had also to take British Social and Economic History since 1760, and so had five papers of direct relevance to their specialism.

The Politics side also gained in clarity for it now had a paper in Political Institutions with Moral and Political Philosophy not being too far removed from a Political Theory paper. The Philosophy side was hardly changed, with four essentially philosophical papers.

From the beginning of the School the Regulations of the Board had made it clear that highest Honours could be attained by excellence either in Philosophy or in Politics or in Political Economy (changed to Economics in 1932) provided that the candidate showed an adequate knowledge in the other subjects of the Examination. The changes clarified the three sides and offered the specialist a group of papers which linked with each other. Nevertheless the wide, tripartite character of the School was retained.

How this worked can be seen from the Report of the Examiners in 1934. There were 146 candidates of whom 21 specialised (i.e. took the two further papers) in Philosophy, 35 in Politics and 44 in Economics. Of the remainder, 6 combined Philosophy and Politics, 7 combined Philosophy and Economics with the majority (33) combining Politics and Economics. Of the twelve candidates who obtained a First Class: 5 took Philosophy, 1 took Politics and 5 took Economics as their first choice.

The School so restructured remained unaltered in any significant way until the unprepared translation was dropped after June 1938. According to B. H. Sumner of Balliol, who moved the amending Statute: 'The standard had sunk to a pass standard, and it was impossible to raise it without adding to the labour of a School already overburdened.' The Faculty were unanimously in favour of the abolition.[25]

By 1939 the Economists had made a few later changes. For the 1937 Examination a limit of 1914 was put on the Labour Movements' Paper: Agricultural Policy and Organization became an alternative paper but only until 1939 when it was replaced by Economic Theory, the compulsory paper of that title being changed to Principles of Economics. The rubric for the new subject shows the increasing specialisation in Economics. Candidates were expected to show 'knowledge of the development of economic theory since 1890, including the main problems that have been discussed in recent periodical literature'. The scope of the paper was to include 'the theory of international trade and such parts of monetary theory and of the theory of fluctuations as relate to the general problem of equilibrium in the economic system'. An opportunity would be given to show a knowledge of mathematical methods in economic theory, but such knowledge was not essential for the attainment of the highest honours.

Viewed in terms of tutorial time over the whole period of preparation, having spent the first two terms of residence preparing for the First Public Examination, candidates then usually spent their next two terms on General Philosophy and Economic Theory and, by covering two subjects each term, were able to complete their tutorial work for the compulsory papers by the end of their second year. By then they were certain as to which side of the School they wished to concentrate on, and had two terms available for this purpose.

4 Creation of a Faculty of Social Studies

Normally the management of an Honour School is the responsibility of the Board of a specific Faculty. The scope of Modern Greats, however, was wider than the responsibilities of any existing Faculty and, therefore, the Statute creating it provided for a Board of Studies. This was composed of twelve members: four elected by the Lit. Hum. Board and two each by the Modern History Board and the Committee for Economics and Political Science, all from among their own members. These eight could co-opt four other members.

It is not surprising that the task was not entrusted to the Committee for Economic and Political Science. Their opposition to the philosophy content of the new School reduced what support they might possibly have mustered for being given this important new role. In any case the Committee were closely associated with running a Diploma regarded by many as low level and for a limited, specialised clientele. The Committee remained in existence until 1946 when its functions were taken over by the Board of the Faculty of Social Studies.

Thus for some 25 years there existed side by side two University bodies concerned with Economics and Politics. True they had different functions – one to run a Diploma, the other an Honour School. But the success of Modern Greats steadily reduced the role and importance of the Diploma Committee. In 1923–24 there were 178 undergraduates reading for this new Degree, and the numbers rose to 350 in 1928–9 and 495 in 1938–9. In contrast the Diploma Committee became increasingly concerned with social training. In 1919 they were empowered to issue Certificates of Training for Social Work. Though only two or three awards needed to be made each year the function pushed the Committee further into a specialised field not regarded by most as central to the interests of the University and the Colleges. Their concern with social training was further emphasised in 1936 with the creation of a Diploma in Public and Social Administration. The rise in importance of Barnett House in the 1930s reduced the scope of the Committee's work and their function of organising lectures for Diploma candidates was taken over by the Lecture List organised by the Faculty Board.

In the absence of a suitable Faculty Board the Diploma Committee acquired two functions which are still a feature of the social studies scene. The more significant was the George Webb Medley Scholarships. In her will Mrs Maria Louise Medley, who died in 1919, left money to the University for the promotion of the study of the science of Political Economy. The Scholarships, of a value of not less than £80 nor more than £300 a year, were tenable by undergraduate and graduate members of the University under such conditions of eligibility and tenure as the Committee for Economics and Political Science thought fit. The first Senior Scholarship was awarded in 1923 and the first Junior in 1924. The former came to be made on the results of the Final Honour School: the latter as the result of a special examination.

The other was the annual Sidney Ball Lecture. In 1919 the Council of Barnett House offered £500 of 5 per cent War Loan Stock to the University to provide an annual lecture on modern social, economic and political problems in memory of Sidney Ball. He had been concerned for a lifetime in promoting social studies and the discussion of current problems in a variety of ways in Oxford.

Satisfying the teaching requirements of Modern Greats posed little or no problem on the side of Philosophy. There were several University posts and all Colleges had one or two Fellows well qualified to teach the subject. That was one reason why Philosophy played such a major role in the formation of the School. For their Politics teaching Colleges turned partly to their Philosophy Tutors but mainly to their Historians. There were two compulsory History papers and a choice of two others in the Further Subjects. When most Colleges had only a handful of candidates they could manage but sometimes at the expense of stretching the resources of their Modern History Tutor. So, for some years there was little pressure to create new Fellowships in Politics. J. P. R. Maud was probably the first: with a First in Greats, he became a Junior Research Fellow and Lecturer in Political Institutions at University College in 1930 followed by Patrick Gordon-Walker at Christ Church and R. B. McCallum at Pembroke. W. J. M. Mackenzie became the Tutor in Politics at Magdalen in 1934. They were followed by such well known names as Kenneth Wheare and Robert Blake. There is little wonder then that, writing in January 1932 on the study of Politics in Oxford,[1] R. B. McCallum had this to say: 'The subject is taught by a very few specialists and a large number of philosophers and historians who approach it with varying degrees of enthusiasm or disgust.' He asked whether the instruction given in political theory by a Greats tutor primarily interested in logic to a Modern Greats man interested only in currency was to be regarded as 'Politics' and thought it to be 'a moot point'.

In contrast there were hardly any Fellows available to teach Economics so Colleges, having admitted candidates to read for the new School, had to appoint teachers. Henry Clay had a Fellowship at New College, 1919–21, and F. W. Ogilvie at Trinity, 1920–6, but both left to take Chairs in Economics at Manchester and Edinburgh respectively. A First in Greats in 1921 and a First in Modern History in the following year by Roy Harrod led Christ Church in 1922 to think this was a good qualification to teach economics and he went to Cambridge for six months to improve his knowledge of, if not actually to learn, the subject.[2] Greats provided several other Economics tutors. Eric Hargreaves was appointed a Fellow of Oriel in 1925 to teach economics: he had obtained a First in Greats in 1921, a distinction in the Diploma in Economics and Political Science and a Ph.D. of London University. Lindley Fraser elected by Queens in 1929 had obtained a First in Greats. Several Colleges went outside Oxford to recruit economists. New College recruited Lionel Robbins from the London School of Economics as Fellow and Lecturer in Economics in 1927 but he left to take up a Chair at the School in 1929. Balliol went outside Oxford for Maurice Allen, and Magdalen for Redvers Opie, both elected in 1931. Soon, however, Modern Greats was beginning to produce its own teachers. H. K. Salvesen took a First in 1923, the first year the School was examined, and was elected to a Fellowship by New College in 1924. Robert Hall who obtained a First in 1926 was elected by Trinity in 1927; R. F. Bretherton, a First in 1928, by Wadham in 1928; Henry Phelps Brown took Firsts in both Modern History (1927) and Modern Greats (1929) and was elected a Fellow of New College in 1930; J. E. Meade, a First in 1930, by Hertford in that year. The women's Colleges had Violet Butler (Society of Home Students) with a First in Modern History and a Distinction in the early years of the Diploma, and Evelyn G. Wilson (Lady Margaret Hall) with a First in Modern Greats in 1925 and a Senior Webb Medley Scholarship in the same year. In 1925 a legacy enabled University College to establish the Mynors Readership and Fellowship in Economics with G. D. H. Cole as the first holder. By 1932 the majority of Colleges had a Fellow or a Lecturer in Economics.

It is the Oxford practice for all teachers in a particular area of studies to have the right to vote in the election of the members of the Board charged with the conduct of those studies. In the case of the Board of Studies set up for Modern Greats the election was indirect: members of the Lit. Hum. and Modern History Facilities electing their respective Faculty Boards, who in turn appointed those responsible for the conduct of the new degree. But several of those who taught in the new School, principally economists, were not members of either Faculty and did not even have an indirect say.

In June 1926, therefore, A. J. Carlyle moved a resolution in the Board of Studies asking for the establishment of a Faculty of Philosophy, Politics and Economics which would also take over the functions of the Committee on Economics and Political Science. This not being successful, he moved in 1927 that the Board should be directly elected by members of the Faculty of Modern History, of the Philosophy Sub-Faculty of the Lit. Hum. Faculty and by teachers of Economics, in certain proportions. The substance of the demand was met by a Statute approved by Congregation in February 1928.[3] The Board was in future to consist of six Official and six Ordinary members and not more than three co-opted members. There was the usual list of those qualified to be Official members – twelve in all – to which two Readerships were added shortly afterwards. The Ordinary members were elected by and from those on the list of Faculty Lecturers kept by the Board. The functions and powers of the Board were widened to become little different from those possessed by the Board of a Faculty.

The change improved the status of the Board, for its members now drew their mandate direct from the teachers in their subjects as was the normal practice with Boards of Faculties.

Late in 1931 the Secretary of Faculties was asked by the Board to circulate a memorandum about becoming a Faculty. He pointed out that the Board of Studies already possessed most of the functions of the normal Faculty Board, e.g. power to appoint University Lecturers. It differed, however, in that few of those who lectured for the School were entitled to vote in the election of Ordinary members.[4]

A more particular defect was stressed in a note which D. H. Macgregor, G. D. H. Cole and L. M. Fraser prepared for the General Board of Faculties. They pointed out that Economics Tutors *per se* were not members of any Faculty. They were thus unable to elect representatives to the General Board of Faculties and this might seriously prejudice the interests of their subject at a time when the University was reviewing its needs, financial and otherwise. More significantly, not being part of a Faculty they could not form a sub-faculty; they therefore had no formal means of organising their schedule of lectures except by informal gatherings and conclaves.[5] Most met informally at Edwin Cannan's home.

The Board agreed to ask to be raised to the status of a Faculty. But what should be its title? Philosophy, being under the Lit. Hum. Board, could not be incorporated in the name of another Faculty. The Secretary of Faculties suggested Social Sciences on the analogy of the Faculties of the Physical and Biological Sciences. The Board, however, preferred Social Studies, influenced by the doubts usually expressed that Economics and Politics could not claim to be sciences. That change was agreed by Congregation in May 1932.[6] Social Studies thus becoming the eleventh Faculty. The first meeting of the Board of the Faculty of Social Studies took place on 10 June 1932.

One of the first decisions of the Faculty Board was to constitute a Sub-Faculty of Economics. A Sub-Faculty of Politics was not set up until 26 October 1934.

The merging of the Committee for Economics and Political Science was mooted at various times. In 1930 for example the General Board asked the Board of Studies whether the time had not come to take over the functions of the Committee. But a joint committee of the two bodies took the view that there was no advantage to be gained by their amalgamation. The Board thought that co-operation could be improved if it could nominate some members of the Committee.

When the new Diploma was established in 1936 the constitution of the Committee was changed. The four members appointed by the Lit. Hum. Board were replaced by two appointed by the Law Board and two by the Social Studies Board. In May 1937 the Committee agreed unanimously that their functions should be transferred to the Faculty Board, providing the management of the two Diplomas and the Certificate were entrusted by it to a Standing Committee with power to co-opt members. This was achieved in 1938, not by abolishing the Committee but by making it in effect a committee of the Social Studies Board. It was to be composed of five members of the Board, all appointed by the Board, with the power to co-opt not more than three other members.[7]

The Committee finally came to an end in 1946 when a Delegacy of Social Training was established and took over the training functions performed by Barnett House. The other work of the Committee, e.g. in respect of the George Webb Medley Scholarships and the annual Sidney Ball Lecture passed to the Board.

5 Development of University Facilities

Until the early 1930s the development of teaching in social studies had been a College response to the rising number of candidates for the new Honour School. The University was involved in the legislation which established the School and first a Board of Studies and then a Faculty. But the University had provided only the Montague Burton Chair of International Relations in 1930 and converted the Readership in Economic History into a Chair in 1931. Nor had it increased the facilities available for the increasing number of College teachers. Then came two general initiatives on the part of the University which gave the Faculty, and in particular the teachers of Economics a real opportunity to secure more and better facilities.

The first arose out of an increasing awareness of the inadequacy of the Bodleian Library to meet the ever-growing claims upon it. Already by 1928 there was talk of a major extension in Broad Street. In November of that year a Committee of Council recommended that Faculty Boards and the Board of Studies of Philosophy, Politics and Economics should be asked to report 'on the adequacy or inadequacy of the existing facilities for research and higher study in the subjects of the Faculty, with particular regard to the facilities offered by the Bodleian Library, by Departmental or special Libraries and by College Libraries'.[1]

The Board of Studies asked W. G. S. Adams, G. D. H. Cole and D. H. Macgregor to draft a reply. They considered the availability of (a) official publications of this and other countries; (b) records of unofficial organisations; (c) files of the more important periodicals; and (d) books now out of print, or not easily obtainable. As regards (a) and (c) there were some important resources outside Bodley, especially the libraries of All Souls and of Barnett House. But Oxford was very defective in

Development of University Facilities 53

such foreign materials as census reports and statistical year books (almost entirely lacking). Even the British material was imperfect and scattered: for example, no complete file of the Economist was available. The records under (b) were fragmentary and inconsiderable. As for (d) the library of All Souls contained a valuable collection but was not open to women. They asked for a central record to be prepared covering all sources, but thought that the problem would be solved as a whole only by the creation within Bodley of a sectional library, with a reading room in which the most important periodicals and records were on open shelves.[2] The Board replied in that sense to Council.

Late in 1933, however, in response to an enquiry from Bodley's Librarian the Social Studies Board decided not to apply for any accommodation in the Special Library Building.[3] The Board had by then decided to press for an Institute of Economic Statistics, which would contain a specialised collection, and for a section of the new Bodley providing open access to books and periodicals central to Politics and Economics.

The second initiative started in February 1931 when Hebdomadal Council decided that a general review should be made of the probable financial needs of the University during the next few years and asked its Committee on Financial Questions to report. Faculty Boards were asked to submit a statement of the developments, arranged in order of importance, necessary for the progress of the studies for which they were responsible. The Social Studies Board appointed a committee to examine the needs of the School.

After mentioning the library needs and supporting two proposals which affected it in common with other Boards, viz. the need for a Department of Experimental (including Social and Industrial) Psychology and for a Chair of Geography, the Committee's report went on to point out that Oxford was well adapted for political and economic research. There was the 'close association of Oxford through its alumni with the government of this country and of the Empire'. Rhodes House, Barnett House and the Agricultural Economic Research Institute were mentioned as was the growth of PPE, a School now exceeded in size only by Lit. Hum., Natural Science, Jurisprudence and Modern History. 'With all these favourable conditions it will be very regrettable if the University does not take the steps which are needed for the further development of these studies.' The specific proposals were for Chairs of Political Philosophy, Public Administration, Finance, Currency and Economic Organisation and a Readership in Statistics.

Revised in the light of the discussion on the Board, the report which went forward to Council listed three posts as necessary immediately: (1) Readership in Statistics; (2) Chair of Public Administration, and (3) Chair of Finance and Currency, with a further two Chairs needed in the near future: in Economic Organisation and in Political Philosophy. More significant a new paragraph was added which read: 'The proper development of economic and political studies requires also the establishment of a Department or Institute of Economics furnished with equipment and apparatus for statistical research, and of a Department or Institute of Political Science.'

The proposals by the various Faculty Boards, for all considered they had needs, were quickly considered by the Committee on Financial Questions. Reporting on 20 June 1931[4] the Committee regarded five proposals as most urgent, in the following order:

(1) Extension of the Taylor Institute
(2) An Institute for post-graduate Clinical Research
(3) Readership in Biochemistry
(4) Readership in Statistics
(5) Department of Experimental Psychology (for which the existence of a strong philosophical school provided the best kind of atmosphere).

Council and the General Board agreed the recommendations and they were circulated as a statement along with the Gazette. In the public version, as edited by the General Board, only three new posts were listed for Social Studies: Readership in Statistics, Chair of Finance and Currency and a Chair (or Readership with a substantial stipend) in Public Administration. Economic Organization and Political Philosophy were mentioned as other subjects in which further provision was desirable.[5]

Two points are worth noticing. First, the University was thinking in terms of appealing to Foundations and outside benefactors for funds to make these developments possible. It was already accepted that the large sum required for the extension of the Bodleian would need such help. Strangely enough these discussions were taking place about the time of the Government's Economy campaign when Colleges had agreed to defer until 1933

Summer Balls that would normally have been held in 1932 and the Warden of New College had had to explain to Council that his College were not in breach of that arrangement: they were holding only a Dance.[6]

The second point was that a Readership in Statistics had emerged as number four in the University's list of priorities. Moreover the idea of an Institute had been aired to a wider audience than the Faculty. True the version circulated to Congregation did not mention an Institute or Department either of Economics or Political Science, but it did mention that facilities for research in economics could be obtained by making use of vacant rooms in the new buildings of the Agricultural Economics Research Institute.[7]

In a letter of 23 May 1934 All Souls generously offered 'to contribute to a satisfactory scheme for an Institute of Economic Statistics by the establishment of a Readership in Statistics at a stipend of £600 per annum'. Council's Committee on Financial Questions considered that this afforded a reasonable basis for approach to the Rockefeller Foundation which, it was understood, was 'anxious to contribute on a considerable scale to the advancement of the study of social sciences in the University'. It was also understood that the Foundation would be more attracted by a comprehensive scheme, including Anthropology, Psychology and Statistics, than by the proposed Institute of Statistics by itself and would no doubt require the University to make a substantial contribution to the total cost of any scheme. Having explored this last point the Committee concluded that the University could meet the recurrent expenditure involved with the aid of the All Souls' contribution. The Committee also recommended that the University Grants Committee should be informed of what was under consideration and their attention drawn to the need for a special contribution from the University if benefactors were to be attracted.[8]

On 28 May 1934 Council appointed a Committee which included A. D. Lindsay and Roy Harrod[9] to advise 'how best to secure the orderly development of Social Studies in the University', it being understood that an application to the Rockefeller Foundation might be involved. They asked the Faculty Board for information and suggestions. The Board appointed their Chairman (Professor G. N. Clark), D. H. Macgregor and the Warden of All Souls (W. G. S. Adams) to meet Council's

Committee. In addition to having the advice of the Faculty Board's representatives, that Committee also received a memorandum from 'a Group of Economists'. The Committee submitted to Council the draft of a letter to the Rockefeller Foundation in January 1935.[10]

The draft started by explaining how the work of the University was 'inextricably interwoven with the College system'. It would be 'undesirable to attempt to develop social studies in Oxford on lines inconsistent with that tradition'. It was true that the study of the physical and biological sciences was carried on somewhat apart from the College system but that arrangement was forced on the University by the necessity for numerous large-scale laboratories. Council considered the development of social studies ought to continue along the lines which had proved so fruitful for other humane studies, thus securing not only the easy and informal co-operation of scholars in every subject able to contribute to the solution of social problems but also the financial support of the Colleges. Because teaching of undergraduates was so important the resources of the Colleges almost entirely and of the University very largely, were devoted to securing its adequacy. One result was that insufficient support could be given to those subjects which were not suitable for or had not yet fully developed for study by undergraduates. Therefore money was needed to support additional senior research workers and to attract promising research students in such departments. The University was not ready with proposals for particular posts. In the meantime they asked the Foundation to make a grant of £5000 a year for five years. The provisional budget included £1600 per annum for strengthening departments in which there was little undergraduate teaching and £750 a year for capital expenditure for a Statistical Institute.

The draft letter was approved with a few amendments by Council on 12 November 1934 and sent to the Foundation. On 21 January 1935 Council were told that the Foundation had agreed to make a grant of £5000 a year for 5 years from 1 July 1935.[11] The Social Studies Board were asked to advise or make recommendations on certain points. With this further information representatives of Council and of the Board were to meet representatives of the Rockefeller Foundation for a discussion of 'the type of research project which would be particularly welcomed by the Foundation'. The Board were asked to consult such other bodies as seemed desirable in making their recommendations on the scheme as a whole.[12]

The Board's report reached Council on 2 March 1935. It started by expressing the hope that attention would be paid to two main principles: (a) that, under the scheme, research should, in the first instance, be related as far as possible to the current problems of modern society, and (b) that, in assigning preferences to one claim over another, regard should be paid to the balanced development of the various branches of social study carried on in the University. They could not specify in detail what accommodation and equipment should be provided at once for the Institute; that would have to wait until a Director had been appointed. But the Board felt that in considering the claims of the Institute 'the fact of its utility to other branches of Social Studies besides Economics should be borne in mind'. It also ventured to hope that the needs of Geography and Anthropology would be given due regard. There were two long paragraphs stressing the claims of Politics, particularly the study of Administration. As regards new appointments the Board proposed two Research Lecturerships – one in Colonial Administration and one in Public Administration – at £300 a year for 5 years, and a grant of £300 a year for the same period to Barnett House for the maintenance of training for social work.[13]

The Committee of Council supported the two proposed appointments and the £300 a year for Social Training, but went further, adding a Research Lecturership either in Public Finance or in the Economics of Development. They also suggested that posts in African Social Anthropology, in Geography and in the social aspects of experimental psychology should be provided out of the £1600. Council agreed with the bulk of their Committee's recommendations as a basis for discussion.[14]

The Master of Balliol (A. D. Lindsay), Roy Harrod, and the Registrar, met Mr Kittredge of the Foundation immediately after this meeting. Kittredge thought that the scheme now drawn up went as far in defining the objects of the work to be undertaken as was reasonable to go at present. He approved the appointment of a research Board which would gradually give definite shape to the scheme of studies in the light of experience. He also said that, if in the course of the five years, any particular piece of work emerged which could not be met out of the £5000 the Foundation would be prepared to consider an application for an *ad hoc* grant.[15]

The General Board of Faculties gave its approval and put forward a draft Decree for the establishment of a Social Sciences Research Committee. This was approved by Council on 27 May 1935, the word 'Sciences' being altered to 'Studies'[16] And so, on 1 July 1935, there came into existence a Social Studies Research Committee, for five years, charged with the duty of administering the £5000 a year from the Rockefeller Foundation. It was composed of the Vice-Chancellor and Proctors; seven other ex-officio members; four persons elected by Council; and two by the Social Studies Board. Power was given to co-opt not more than two additional members who need not be members of Congregation. At a meeting in October 1935 the President of Corpus (Richard Livingstone) and H. D. Henderson were co-opted.

The specific duties of the Committee were:

(a) to administer such part of the Benefaction, not exceeding in any year one third of the £5000, as was not specially allocated by Decree;
(b) to make recommendations for further allocations by Decree having special regard to provision for an Institute of Statistics and for research in the following or in allied subjects; (i) Colonial Administration; (ii) Public Adminstration; (iii) Public Finance; (iv) Economics of Development; (v) Social aspects of Experimental Psychology; (vi) Social Anthropology; and (vii) Geography;
(c) to frame reports to the Foundation, Council, the Social Studies Board, etc.;
(d) in general to co-ordinate the work carried on as a result of the Benefaction.[17]

The new Committee was given a significant status by having the Vice-Chancellor and Proctors as members: the Senior Proctor usually attended. Moreover its terms of reference were much wider than the distribution of the special research fund of £1600 a year as originally envisaged. It was given a general responsibility for the allocation of all the £5000 and for the co-ordination of all the work carried out in the spending of the grant. This was a substantial sum at a time when junior Lecturers could be obtained for a salary of £300 a year.

It was, however, too large a body to deal with a wide range of applications for grants and other day to day matters. At their fourth meeting (22 October 1935) therefore, the Committee appointed the President of Corpus (Richard Livingstone), Sir Arthur Salter, and H. D. Henderson, to act as a Co-ordinating Committee. After that, all the business first went through this Committee before being discussed, accepted or rejected by the Research Committee. The 'Full Committee' was often poorly attended but even when well attended the minutes of the proceedings quite often merely recorded that the report of the Co-ordinating Committee was adopted. It is seldom that any reference is made to the Board of the Faculty of Social Studies, the Scheme financed by the Rockefeller Grant clearly being regarded as going beyond normal Faculty business.

The Research Committee were principally concerned with appointments and grants. At a meeting on 8 October 1935 five Research Lecturerships were filled:

(a) Human Geography by E. W. Gilbert (then in charge of the Department of Human Geography at Reading University).
(b) African Sociology by E. E. Evans-Pritchard, then engaged in research in Africa.
(c) Colonial Administration by Miss M. Perham, Research Fellow of St Hugh's College.
(d) Public Finance by R. F. Bretherton, Fellow of Wadham.
(e) Public Administration by Mr. G. Montagu Harris, Head of the Foreign Branch of the Intelligence Division of the Ministry of Health 1919–33, and Secretary of the County Councils Association 1902–19. This appointment was originally only for one year: for the remaining four years it was to be held by J. P. R. Maud, Fellow of University College but, when he left Oxford for Birkbeck, Montagu Harris's appointment was extended yearly until 1940.

The Committee rejected a proposal to establish a Research Lecturership in Psychology. They thought it would necessitate an excessive expenditure on Lecturerships in relation to the whole sum available. Instead they suggested help should be given to a research project in Social Psychology. Subsequently a lump sum of £500 for capital expenditure and an annual grant of £150 was made for experimental psychology.

No further appointments to Research Lecturerships were made out of the grant. But the Committee continued to be generally concerned with the work of these five appointments, e.g. granting leave of absence and approving programmes of research.

Applications for grants came from individuals (Professors or graduate students) or from institutions. They were a significant element in the policy of the Research Committee. In June 1936, for example, a grant of £250 a year for four years was made to both a Politics and an Economics Group, each for a programme of research agreed and put forward by a group of Tutors in that discipline. During the financial year 1936-37 small grants were made towards the cost of the Colonial Services Summer School; to the School of Geography for a social survey of Kenya and for the expenses of an Air Transport Inquiry, in addition to objects already mentioned. The Committee allocated £1500 to Barnett House to be spent over three years for a social survey of Oxford and district. The financing of an Institute of Statistics is dealt with later.

Towards the end of 1935 Mr Kittredge met the three members and told them that the Foundation had a Project Fund from which grants could be made to assist specific pieces of research. The Foundation would welcome applications for such grants but it would be desirable for all those connected with Social Studies should reach it through one channel. Following this, a successful application was made to the Foundation for a supplementary grant. In March 1937 a further £1700 a year for two years was granted of which £580 a year was for a study by the Institute of Statistics of trade fluctuations; £600 a year for an investigation into the trade cycle in Great Britain under the general direction of H. D. Henderson and £460 a year for H. Phelps Brown's research into the Trade Cycle. A small sum was included for the cost of publication.

THE APPEAL

On 24 May 1932 Congregation had accepted unanimously an offer of the Rockefeller Foundation to contribute up to three fifths of the toal cost of building the Bodley Extension up to a limit of $2.3 million. The offer was conditional upon the University finding the remaining two-fifths (£337 720) by 31 December 1936. The time was very unfavourable for launching a public appeal. But privately and in various ways the University had within a year raised almost £250 000 in cash or promises to pay. The balance required to make up their share was obtained by the University Chest guaranteeing an annual contribution of £7000 a year pending the provision of equivalent funds from other sources. The Foundation thereupon expressed their willingness to make their contribution.[18]

Late in 1935 Council agreed that the time was now ripe for launching a public appeal. They thought, however, the Appeal would be likely to be more successful if it were not confined to the Bodley Library and were also to be for the advancement of research generally. This meant that the document launching the Appeal had to make both a general case and state some of the urgent needs. After dealing with the Extension of the Bodleian, said to require about £250 000, the Appeal pointed out that modern research was increasingly expensive. The number of students reading the Honour Schools had increased as had the number of research students. On the Science side there was a pressing need for a new Physics Laboratory, a new building for Geology and an extension of the Botany buildings. Sooner or later Physical Chemistry, the study of which was flourishing, would need to be concentrated in a single laboratory.

The Appeal then singled out Social Studies as 'but one conspicuous example of the increasing attention now paid to research in all the humane faculties', research 'for which for many reasons the University is peculiarly fitted'. The development had been made possible by a grant of £5000 a year for five years by the Rockefeller Foundation. But at the end of the five years the University would be able to get money from the Foundation for specific schemes of research only 'if it is able to support from its own resources the necessary teachers for advanced work and to provide the equipment they require. It must maintain from its own funds its new Institutes of Statistics and of Experimental Psychology'.

A minimum of £250 000 was required to cover the pressing needs of research in science and the humanities.

The Appeal was launched publicly in February 1937. Contributors could either leave the spending of their donation to the general discretion of the Trustees and the University or they could earmark it for a particular purpose. Lord Nuffield, for example, contributed £100 000 for the general purposes of the Appeals Fund, thus keeping a promise he had made at the time of his large Medical Benefaction in 1936. On the other hand, the Rhodes Trustees specified that their £100 000 should be used for research 'into problems of modern Government, particularly in the British Commonwealth and American Republic, and such institutions as the League of Nations'. The general fund was entitled the Higher Studies Fund, and was under the control of seven Trustees.

The response to the Appeal, even apart from these two substantial contributions, was very good. Then in October 1937, the University and the public learnt of Lord Nuffield's new benefaction of £1 million for the establishment of a new College and the building of a new Physical Chemistry Laboratory. As a result, nine months after the Appeal had been launched the University found that the capital sum required for the new Bodley Extension was assured, Lord Nuffield and the Rhodes Trustees had 'between them supplied what is needed to make Oxford a great centre of research in Social Studies' and the money was available for a new Laboratory. It was, therefore, decided not to proceed further actively with the Appeal but to encourage people to go on contributing to bring the total of the Fund up to £500 000, from the £421 000 it had reached by the end of October.[19]

6 Lord Nuffield's Benefaction

THE OFFER

Lord Nuffield went to see Lord Halifax, the Chancellor of Oxford University, in London on the morning of 8 July 1937. Halifax was then Lord President of the Council, becoming Foreign Secretary in February 1938. That same day Halifax telephoned the Registrar (D. Veale) about the conversation and wrote a confirmatory letter. Nuffield had told Halifax that 'he had it in mind to offer to build on the waste ground that he has recently bought below St Peter's Hall a College of Engineering'. Nuffield 'had been much impressed with what seemed to him the gap in the equipment of Oxford on those lines, and felt that Oxford compared in this respect very unfavourably with Cambridge with the result that she lost many good men'. To build such a college would cost £250 000 and Nuffield said 'he would be prepared to put up something in the nature of three-quarters of a million for endowment'.[1] Though he mentioned only Engineering in his letter Halifax told Veale and the Vice-Chancellor that Lord Nuffield had talked in terms of a College of Engineering and Accountancy.

The offer was totally unexpected. But the work put into the Survey of Needs undertaken in 1932 and the subsequent thought which had gone into the preparation of the Higher Studies Fund Appeal meant that the Vice-Chancellor, Registrar and leading members of Hebdomadal Council were well informed about currrent needs and aspirations. Neither Engineering nor Accountancy had been part of the University's thinking, so that money donated specifically for these purposes would not in effect be a response to the Appeal. Any Vice-Chancellor would have been bound to try and steer Lord Nuffield's money into one or more of the major objectives of agreed University policy.

It so happened that the Vice-Chancellor of the time was A. D. Lindsay, Master of Balliol, who had played a prominent role in the development of Social Studies in Oxford. He had been active in the founding of the Honour School of Philosophy, Politics and Economics; had been a member of the original Board of Studies and then of the Faculty Board and had taken his turn as their Chairman; had been active in formulating the needs of Social Studies, including the idea of an Institute of Statistics, and was, as Vice-Chancellor, currently the Chairman of the Social Studies Research Committee. In the Special Number of 'Oxford' published by the Oxford Society in February 1937, it was Lindsay, not the Chairman of the Social Studies Board nor one of its Professors, who wrote the chapter on Social Studies in Oxford. Social Studies, singled out for special mention in the Appeal, were an aspect of University development very dear to Lindsay's heart. He was also aware that most of the recent University appointments in the subject were financed out of a grant which came to an end in July 1940, a point stressed in the Appeal.

There was, however, a new factor which kindled Lindsay's enthusiasm and imagination. Lord Nuffield was very interested in bringing academic learning and research into closer contact with the outside world. This had been a major reason for the very large Medical Benefaction he had given a year earlier and with which Lindsay was very familiar. The possibility of linking academics and men of practical affairs in the study of current economic and social problems had a special attraction. It was not difficult to show that an approach of this kind was likely to be particularly fruitful in Social Studies and so give Lord Nuffield what he really wanted.

Nevertheless Nuffield had mentioned Engineering which might have interested the Science Faculties who so far had obtained little or no earmarked contributions to the Appeal. A new Physical Chemistry Laboratory had been listed as necessary, the subject being then studied in two laboratories provided by three Colleges, some of the research being carried out in the cellars of Balliol. If Lord Nuffield could be persuaded to earmark £100 000 of his new benefaction to build such a laboratory one of the University's pressing needs would be satisfied.

Nuffield saw the Registrar on 9 July. The course of the conversation (on pp. 65–6) was reported by Veale to Halifax.[2]

Thanks to your timely warning I was able to have a little private conversation with Hobbs [Lord Nuffield's Private Secretary] yesterday afternoon and with the Vice-Chancellor this morning. I was therefore prepared to put to Lord Nuffield a scheme which carries out the esssential parts of his idea in a way which is far more acceptable to us than a residential Engineering College...
In Applied Engineering Cambridge is pre-eminent, and Cambridge and the Provincial Universities supply the entire demand for Commercial Engineering. For us to set up a rival School would not only be contrary to the arrangement to which we have come with Cambridge that we should not unnecessarily duplicate services but would, by sterilizing capital sunk in the Cambridge School, be thoroughly bad policy from the public point of view... There is, however, one branch of Physical Science, namely Physical Chemistry, which is an Oxford product and in which Oxford has an undisputed pre-eminence. It is of essential importance to engineering and most other branches of Commercial Science. If, therefore, Lord Nuffield wants to do something for Oxford which will enable it to talk with Cambridge at the gate, Physical Chemistry is the thing to go for and what Physical Chemistry needs is a new £100 000 Laboratory in the Parks.
That building, however, will not restore, as he wishes to do, the beauty of his site. For that he wants a residential College. What we want is a Post-Graduate College, rather on the lines of Mansfield or Manchester, where people who have already graduated at other Colleges, or more mature scholars than the undergraduate, can go for higher study. The Overseas student of 25 or 26 who comes here to do a research degree does not fit in very well with the boys at the undergraduate Colleges. If this Post-Graduate College, though open to post-graduate students of all kinds, were also made the centre of our Modern Studies, it could be run as a centre to which the practical man is brought to give the benefit of his practical experience to the dons. This is in line with two things which are already being done in Oxford:

(1) the approach to the theory of Local Government through instruction in its practical working
(2) the approach to Political Economy through the way that its problems strike the business man. This is the foundation of the work on trade cycles which, under H. D.

> Henderson's inspiration is being done by the Economists here, with the help of money from the Rockefeller Foundation.
>
> This, you will see, gives effect to what Lord Nuffield meant by 'Accountancy' when he was talking to you.
>
> I think I can safely say that he accepted this scheme as fulfilling exactly what he really had in mind, when talking to you, in all essentials, much as it differs from it in details.
>
> I may add that I mentioned the growing needs of the Nuffield Medical School, as something already associated with his name, as a possible alternative if I was wrong in thinking that the first part of what I had said was congenial to his ideas. He said, as to that, that he would rather fill what he thought to be a serious gap in Oxford education before developing the Medical School further, but that when we wanted more money for Medicine, we could go back to him.
>
> The way it was left was that I was to tell the Vice-Chancellor exactly what I had said to him and let him know whether the Vice-Chancellor is prepared to support it. Lord Nuffield will then probably see the Vice-Chancellor, make up his mind finally, and then we are to work out the details in September ready for an announcement in October on the lines of last year's startler.

This last referred to Lord Nuffield's gift of a £2 million for Medical research. Veale scribbled at the end of his letter 'Excuse a rather incoherent letter. I am in rather a flutter of excitement...' Later that day Veale wrote to Hobbs:

> Will you tell Lord Nuffield that after I left him today I saw the Vice-Chancellor as he had requested. I had felt very little doubt that the Vice-Chancellor would approve of what I said, because I thought I knew his mind pretty well on this sort of subject. He is satisfied that the method of disposing of Lord Nuffield's benefaction which is at the same time most in accordance with Lord Nuffield's desires and with the interests of the University is
> (1) the erection at a cost of £100 000 of a Laboratory for Physical Chemistry on the site proposed for it in the Parks;
> (2) the establishment on the new site of a Post-Graduate

College which would also serve as a centre of Modern Studies developed on the present lines, viz. of bringing in people of practical experience in the world to cooperate with the academic people. This plan was started by the Vice-Chancellor and possible developments have been in his mind for a very long time. This College would require of course substantial endowments for Fellowships and so on, but the Vice-Chancellor thinks that the whole scheme can be carried out well within the limit of the funds suggested by Lord Nuffield to the Chancellor.

At the end of the letter Veale wrote 'The effect of this, of course, is that the Vice-Chancellor approved what I said to Lord Nuffield'.

Ten or so years later Lord Nuffield was very inclined to say that the University had cheated him when they claimed that engineering was a subject best left to Cambridge. It was, however, true that discussions had quite recently taken place between Oxford and Cambridge, in which Veale had participated, about the need to avoid unnecessary duplication of their academic activities. A Committee advised Council in June 1935 that 'while it is clearly inevitable and right that there should be a good deal of duplication of work in the two Universities, it would seem likely that with good will on both sides much unnecessary duplication could be avoided, and the expenditure thus saved would become available to meet the constantly increasing claims for new expenditure'. Council agreed to have informal talks with Cambridge and these took place towards the end of the year.[3]

In any case the Cambridge argument was one used by the Registrar. Lindsay had a more positive argument for he fully believed, probably rightly, that he was interpreting what Nuffield really wanted and in such a way as to meet a pressing need of the University. Speaking in Congregation on 16 November 1937, he said that what had first moved Lord Nuffield to purchase the site was 'to give beauty and dignity to the western approach to the City'. He went on:

> The function of the new College has a certain likeness to the function of the medical benefaction.... It was designed to bridge the gap beween the scientific research in the laboratory and the clinical practice in the wards of the hospitals, not by

confounding the functions of laboratory and ward but by bringing the two into close co-operation. This College is concerned to bridge what is I think an even more disastrous gap in our modern life, the gap between the theoretical student of society and those responsible for carrying it on.

There can be little doubt that this interpretation of his intention appealed to Lord Nuffield at the time and in the long run. Had it not done so he had already shown himself very capable of getting his own way even with the University. His threat to withdraw his offer of the Medical Benefaction unless the University agreed to his proposal that one of the new Medical Chairs should be in Anaesthetics had been quite successful.[4] Moreover he was still a very rich man and could easily have afforded to give a large sum elsewhere to foster engineering. Instead he gave little or nothing for that kind of academic activity. Indeed when early in 1943 he gave £10 million to establish the Nuffield Foundation its terms of reference included such phrases as 'the advancement of health and the prevention and relief of sickness', 'the advancement of social well being' and 'the comfort and care of the aged poor'.

Lord Nuffield was not much of a correspondent. Communication was usually by word of mouth or by way of a short letter from Hobbs the legal aspects being handled direct by Andrew Walsh, Lord Nuffield's Solicitor. It would appear, however, that towards the end of July Lindsay showed Nuffield a Note headed 'Scheme for a Postgraduate College especially devoted to the study of the facts and problems of contemporary society'. The first part of the Note stressed the separation between the theoretical students of contemporary civilisation and the men responsible for carrying it on; between the economist, the political theorist and the student of government on the one hand and, on the other, the businessman, the politician, the civil servant and the local government official. This separation was probably more disastrous than that between the scientific researcher in the laboratory and the clinical practitioner in the wards, a separation which Lord Nuffield's Benefaction for Medicine was intended to end. The coping stone of the new Benefaction would be a College of Postgraduate Studies. Lindsay then sketched out his ideas about the College: the five possible kinds of Fellows, the character and number of postgraduate students and added something about the building and the needs it would satisfy: 'particular attention would have to be paid to opportunities for discussion.... The beauty and quiet of the garden would be of importance'.

Lindsay sent a copy of his draft scheme to the Chancellor, Registrar, the President of Corpus (R. Livingstone) (presumably as Chairman of the Co-ordinating Committee), Dr F. A. Aydelotte (President of Swarthmore and American Secretary to the Rhodes Trustees) and to Lynda Grier, Principal of Lady Margaret Hall. In a letter dated 29 July 1937 he told Miss Grier of Lord Nuffield's offer of the site in New Road with money to build on it 'his original proposal of a College for Engineering and Accountancy'. But Nuffield 'has agreed that in place of Engineering he will give us £100 000 for a Physical Chemistry Laboratory in the Park; and in the case of Accountancy he is ready to give the money... for a postgraduate College of what he called Modern Studies but is prepared to mean what we call Social Studies'. Lindsay said he had showed Lord Nuffield the draft and had agreed to 'try and work out the thing more elaborately and see what it would cost' and asked her, and the others to whom he showed the draft in confidence, to think about it and let him have anything that occurred to them sometime during August. One of Lord Halifax's comments was that he did not feel 'that All Souls ought to have any serious misgiving because... some of its most valuable features are deemed worthy of imitation!' Several saw the parallel with All Souls College.

It had been agreed with the Chancellor that the matter should be kept confidential. The Long Vacation had already started and Hebdomadal Council, and most University bodies, had ceased to meet. Council did not receive papers about the new benefaction until 9 October 1937, shortly before the beginning of the Michaelmas Term, and discussed them on 11 October.

The offer became public on 12 October 1937 when Lord Nuffield, with Veale present, gave a press interview. According to the *Oxford Mail* for October 13, 'Three times his enthusiasm overcame his diffidence and he broke out with "This is the thing which may go down the ages... it was too early yet to predict its outcome".' *The Times* of the same date printed his letter of offer in full along with a long leader headed Learning and Life.

The Benefaction was made the occasion for an inspired act on the part of the University. Appreciating that a 'thank you letter', however warmly and felicitously worded would not express adequately their feelings, Council decided to offer Lord Nuffield the status of MA which would entitle him to take part in the government of the University as a member of Convocation. He was already an honorary DCL, but that degree did not confer membership. Nuffield was clearly pleased by this imaginative gesture and on 2 November 1937 he was made an MA and so became in the Vice-Chancellor's words 'an ordinary member of the University'.

LINDSAY'S VIEWS

Lindsay's Note of late July 1937[5] is so important for an understanding of the early development of the College, of Social Studies generally, and the way in which Lindsay approached the issues, that parts are worth quoting *in extenso*. Referring to the raison d'être and basic purpose of the benefaction, Lindsay wrote:

> We are living in a world of extraordinary complexity, where expert and unbiased knowledge is a vital necessity if civilization is to survive, where yet expert and unbiased knowledge in social affairs is at a discount. The theorist complains that the practical man is so short-sighted that he cannot see what is beneath his nose; while the practical man, with equal excuse, retorts that the theorist is so long-sighted that he cannot see what is beneath his nose. There is no need to labour the disadvantages of this divorce between theory and practice in our study of contemporary society. What is important to realize is that, like the separation between the laboratory scientist and the clinician, it cannot be fundamentally cured by changing the theoretical training of either the theorist or the practical man. The right training will help each to understand and cooperate with the other, if they get the chance; but the opportunity for co-operation has to be created. No theoretical training will teach a man horse-sense, and the experience in the world which most easily teaches a man horse-sense debars him from becoming an expert in theory and tends to blind him to the need of theory. Just so the expert clinician becomes such from clinical experience, and his absorption in clinical work debars him from the intense scientific research in which the pure scientist spends all his time. The two sets of men *ought* to

be different and have different qualities; and the most fruitful research can only come from collaboration between men of these different qualities. That is the principle behind the Nuffield research scheme; and the same principle must be applied to research into the problems of contemporary society.

The University Committee for Research in Social Studies, which has been in existence now for two years, has been trying to work on those lines. Barnett House is making a survey of the social services in Oxford and the neighbourhood, and in that survey University scholars are enlisting the help of local government officers and of men and women in the district actually engaged in the social services. In the Colonial field, a group of scholars is going out to Kenya to conduct a piece of planned research there; and the University is bringing here colonial civil servants to a summer school in Oxford. There are plans afoot to elaborate this idea of collaboration between the colonial administrator and the Oxford students of colonial administration. The Economics tutors who are studying the factors governing fluctuations in British business activity are inviting leaders of industry and commerce to meet the group for discussion. The group of students of politics which is studying the use of advisory bodies in relation to central government is inviting students of public affairs who are working outside the University to join it, and is asking men of affairs, civil servants and others, to come to the periodical meetings of the group.

The defect of these schemes as they exist today is that the co-operation between the theorist and the practical man is too sporadic and too formal. Men have to know each other before the co-operation between men of different training becomes really fruitful. In the study of contemporary society, there is nothing quite like the hospital where clinician and scientist can work together over a long period.

Much might be done by using the opportunities for intimate talk, discussion, and common understanding, which an Oxford college can give. The coping-stone of the scheme which we have been trying to work out would be a College of Post-graduate Studies especially devoted to the study of the facts and problems of contemporary society.

The early drafts of the various formal documents which put Lord

Nuffield's ideas into words, showed how much Lindsay and Veale strove to emphasise collaboration between academic and non-academic persons. This is understandable in that this was the feature which attracted Lord Nuffield, but it was also something that both believed in strongly. The Committee of Council[6] which examined the drafts at the end of October thought they gave too much emphasis to this feature. They amended, for example, the wording of the draft Decree 'to make the College a centre of co-operation and research between academic and non-academic persons' to read '... a centre of research especially by co-operation between...'

Lindsay's Note then turned to the form, character and status of the College. Lord Nuffield's gift of £100 000 for a Physical Chemistry Laboratory was straightforward business. The purpose was clear and only a Decree of Acceptance needed to be drafted and passed by Congregation. But the part of the benefaction to be devoted to 'Nuffield College' was both vague and unfamiliar. When making the offer Lord Nuffield had not stated his ideas in any detail. The only readily recognisable element of his offer was the piece of land in New Road on which he wished a College to be built.

Nuffield did not know much about Oxford Colleges. He was 'town' not 'gown' and to him Colleges were buildings rather than independent centres for teaching and learning. His academic contribution was to stress the need for the University to undertake its studies in closer association with the outside world. But however enthusiastic one might be for that aim in general, it was by no means clear what it meant in practice. In the case of his medical Benefaction the money had been given to the University for what were well recognised University purposes, e.g. Chairs and Departments of Medicine and Surgery. Had Nuffield talked in terms of putting a University department or institute on the site, that would have been just as straightforward an operation as erecting a Physical Chemistry Laboratory. Or had he enquired about how to found a College similar to the great names with which he was familiar, All Souls, Balliol, Magdalen and so on, he might have been handled in the way that Besse was in 1948 when founding St Antony's. He would have learnt that the University did not run Colleges, which were independent foundations.

Lord Nuffield's Benefaction

The Vice-Chancellor and the Registrar do not appear to have presented Lord Nuffield with either of these alternatives. Veale may have had the problem in mind when in a very early draft he used the term 'Hall' not College for, as in the phrase of 'hall of residence', the word did not carry the implications in Oxford that the word College did. Distinctions of this kind would probably have been completely lost on Lord Nuffield. He wanted to erect a College and Lindsay was ready to provide him with one. There was never any suggestion that the building should be called a Department. Moreover, it is clear that Lindsay set great store on a residential building, with dining facilities and common rooms where academic and non-academic persons could mingle and exchange ideas. This pointed to the collegiate rather than the institute form.

Nevertheless Lindsay was equally clear that the money and the College should be in the hands of and under the control of the University. He wanted to use some of the money to meet all or part of the expenditure being financed for the time being out of the Rockefeller Grant. In part he saw the new Benefaction as a means of furthering the work of the Social Studies Research Committee.

There is no evidence that Lindsay would have preferred the establishment of an ordinary University department though others were inclined that way. Beveridge, who had recently resigned from the Directorship of the London School of Economics and Political Science upon being elected Master of University College, and with whom he talked on 14 July, was of the opinion: 'It would be a thousand pities if the benefits of the new institution were concentrated predominantly on a very limited number of students – say 100 or so – for whom residence could be provided to the exclusion of men in other colleges.' His practical conclusion was that the new institution was likely to gain in value 'the more it approximates, not to an ordinary residential College, but ... a post-graduate School of Social Studies ... This does not mean that the institution could not be called a "College" if that is felt to be important'. The Warden of All Souls (W. G. S. Adams) was quite clear in his letter of September 3 that he wanted:

> a school rather than a College. Like the Brookings Institute at Washington it should draw to it graduates from other

Colleges ... also it should be the centre with which particularly the Oxford Colleges cooperate in considering their individual contributions in the fields of social and economic studies. In that sense it should be more like a University Department ... with a Director at the head of it. It is very desirable that the funds should not be tied up in any great measure in Fellowships but should be free to be applied in whatever ways can best advance teaching and research ... I have put this all dogmatically – not least for brevity.

But University departments did not provide common rooms, residence and eating facilities – only Colleges did that. Yet to Lindsay such facilities were essential to the basic idea of bringing the academic and the man of practical affairs into close contact. It was also apparent to Lord Nuffield that residence for Students was the true mark of a College. It is not without significance that from an early stage Lindsay was thinking in terms of a Chapel and Chaplain: in the 1930s it would have been unthinkable for a College not to have a chapel. To Lindsay concern about current social and economic problems was an essential element in his Christianity. In his letter to Miss Grier quoted earlier he wrote: 'I think the framework within which the plan must be made is (a) it has to be something which can be called a College (though it need not technically be so) and which would involve some residence; and (b) the idea [of the collaboration of the theorist and the practitioner] is essential to it.' He used a very similarly worded phrase in his letter to Dr F. A. Aydelotte dated 31 July 1937: 'it must be a College in the sense that there must be some residence'.

Having stated that the new College would be the coping-stone of the scheme Lindsay had to admit that it 'would be unlike anything at present existing in the University'.

(a) It would be unlike the ordinary college because

(1) It would be the University's instrument of research into the facts and problems of contemporary society, and would therefore have to be under the control of the University in a way which the ordinary college is not: its endowments, etc. would have to be the property of the University, and its Head and salaried researchers would have to be appointed by the University.

(2) University and college teachers concerned with the above special studies would therefore have to be in some sense members of this 'college' as they can now be members of or associated with the Social Studies Research Committee (without of course giving up their special attachment to their existing college).

(3) Women as well as men graduates ought to be eligible for its posts.

(4) It should be possible to attach to it or connect with it such University institutions as the Institute of Statistics or the Extramural Delegacy, and such an institution as Barnett House.

(5) It should also be the centre for postgraduate advanced studies throughout the University.

(b) On the other hand, if the best use is to be made of the possibilities of bringing together University men and men outside the University, the College would have to be to some extent residential, and that side of it would have to have considerable autonomy. There are clearly analogies with Rhodes House.

The College would, however, be like an 'ordinary' College in that it would have a Head and a body of Fellows. In his view: 'The Head of the "College" should be a University man who has had plenty of practical experience and knowledge of affairs, who would be in touch with all sorts of people in the world of affairs, and had the gift of making people work together'.

He had in mind five kinds of Fellows:

(1) Two or three Directors of Studies, such as were already being found to be valuable in the Social Studies Research scheme.

(2) Six to twelve Senior Research Fellows and Lecturers, who would cover those branches of the study of modern society not covered by the ordinary university teacher.

(3) About twenty non-university men of affairs, businessmen, civil servants, local government officials, etc. They would have equal rights with others in the government of the College, and would have rights to rooms, dining, etc. But their service to the College would mostly be fulfilled by

coming there as often as possible (probably mostly at weekends) and joining in discussions. Their practical advice would be invaluable to the theorists, and common membership of the College would produce the understanding necessary for co-operation. They would all be non-university in the sense that they would not be resident university teachers. Some of them would not have been at the University at all; some of them might be Extramural teachers. All Souls had fellowships of this kind by which the College kept in touch with its old members who were distinguished in the world of practical affairs. (The value of these Fellowships could be the same as that of the corresponding ones at All Souls, £50.) It would also be desirable, if it could be managed, obviously to bring such men to reside for a term, like the Rhodes Lecturers.

(4) Ten to twenty Junior Research Fellowships for young men who had taken their degrees and were doing definite pieces of research. It would be essential that they should not remain in Oxford all the three years of their Fellowship, but should conduct some of their investigations on the spot.

(5) Associate Fellows, not members of the Governing Body: University and College teachers who are members of other Colleges but would be associated with this College for research and would have dining rights, etc.

Besides the Fellows there would be (in place of undergraduates in the strict sense of the term) men reading for research degrees, postgraduate students in addition to those holding Junior Fellowships. They would be either men from other colleges who had just taken their Schools, or men from other universities rather older than the men who go to other colleges to do research. Their number should be limited, not more than fifty perhaps. It would not be desirable to withdraw any considerable number of postgraduate students from other colleges. They might be men researching in any field, not only in that which is the especial concern of the College. They would not be paid anything by the College, but would be to some extent a source of income.

In the planning of the building of the College, Lindsay believed that particular attention would have to be paid to opportunities for discussion. There would have to be plenty of common rooms and rooms for discussion, besides a conference hall. The beauty and quiet of the garden would be of importance. The College ought to be a place where men could talk at leisure together as well as work together, if the best kind of co-operation between the theorist and the practical was to come into being. The College would of course have to have a library.

Towards the end of his Note he saw the problem posed by the unlike and the like features. He wrote:

> Since the College would be the centre of the University's research into the facts and problems of contemporary society, the government would have to be so arranged that this should be a reality, and yet the College be left with a certain autonomy. Those within the University and those from without would clearly join in the direction of the College's work. How constitutionally that should be arranged need not now be considered.

So it was not considered. It was left to be worked out during the next twenty or so years.

In fairness to Lindsay it must be stated that nobody seems to have openly questioned the desirability or practicability of a College being under the control of Hebdomadal Council. That may be because the scheme and the resulting Statute had all the outward signs of the normal College, e.g. with a Warden and Fellows. Miss Grier saw the proposal 'as far as I understand it, more like a modern All Souls than Rhodes House'. Richard Livingstone thought it better for the Warden to be appointed by the University but for the Fellows to be elected by the Governing Body. He finished his comments on Lindsay's Scheme:

> One problem I suppose we ought to consider later is the College's control over its funds; I mean over endowments and gifts which it might get at a later date; and whether you will let it become (like the other Colleges) an independent star, or retain it as a controlled member of your University solar system.

For some years at least the College was to be very much a part of Lindsay's solar system.

Veale's early drafts placed the emphasis on the University. The draft Statute he sent to Lindsay on September 6th stated that the money was to enable the University to establish University Fellowships to be held by members of the University and to be associated with a Hall of residence for [post-] graduate students which shall also be used as an Institute of political and social studies, or such other studies as may hereafter in the opinion of the Hebdomadal Council more urgently require such provision.

Though there is little or no evidence on the files to show how the change came about, there was clearly a switch in the drafting to the money being for a College and not for the general use of the University. Thus the draft Statute circulated to Hebdomadal Council on 4 October 1937 made no mention of an Institute, the money was for 'a College for post-graduate studies especially but not exclusively in the field of social studies'.

The Trust Deed, which was the legally binding document, stated quite clearly that the purposes of the Trust so created were:

(A) the erection of a Physical Chemistry Laboratory and its equipment
(B) (1) the erection on the site of a College (hereinafter called 'the College') for post-graduate work especially in connection with the study by co-operation between academic and non-academic persons of social (including economic and political) problems and also for any other post-graduate research or work
(2) the laying out of the rest of the site as the garden or grounds of the College, and
(3) the equipment of the College
(C) the maintenance and carrying on of the College.

But a letter of 8 October conveying the offer, drafted by Veale and signed by Lord Nuffield stated that: 'In order that there may be power to vary the use of its resources from time to time in such ways as will best promote the general policy of the University, the College and its endowments are to be under the direct control of the Hebdomadal Council.' That kind of wording could be interpreted to mean that the money was given to the University to achieve certain general purposes with the College as an instrument of University policy.

It must have been difficult for Veale, and indeed for Lindsay, to find words which conveyed both the dominance of the University and the traditional concept of a College. The

Fellowships tenable in the College were originally described as University Fellowships even though the word Fellowship was used in Oxford only in the case of Colleges, the University titles being Professor, Reader and Lecturer. The word University was deleted by the Committee of Council which examined the drafts submitted by Veale.

In passing it is interesting that Lindsay did not see anything contradictory between his first and last reasons why Nuffield would be unlike an ordinary college. For the College to be 'the centre for postgraduate advanced studies throughout the University' would surely have taken it quite outside 'research into the facts and problems of contemporary society'. Yet, he envisaged, that its students could be 'researching into any field, not only in that which is the especial concern of the College'. The Draft Statute circulated to Council referred simply to 'a College for post-graduate studies' and it was the Committee of Council which added the words 'especially but not exclusively in the field of social studies'. The Committee for Advanced Studies told Council that it did not wish to see ruled out the possibility that the official centre for research students should be in the College. The Committee of Council replied that this was not ruled out by the Statute and thought it 'a valuable suggestion which should be explored at a later stage'.

The Committee also received a suggestion that Common Rooms should be provided for all students working for research degrees in the faculties of Theology, Law, Modern History, English and Social Studies. They thought this 'would need to be considered at a later stage when the financial position is more clear'.

Suggestions of the last kind reflected partly uncertainty about the purposes of the new Benefaction, partly a concern about the growing number of students working for research degrees and the inadequacy of the University's facilities for them, and partly an exaggerated notion of what could be achieved with the money. It was perhaps not appreciated that the money would be paid in thirteen half-yearly instalments of almost £77 000. As the Physical Chemistry Laboratory might take £100 000 and the College buildings about £300 000, their immediate building would absorb the whole of the capital contributions of the first two and a half years.

It is also probable that there was a certain amount of concern, even a certain jealousy, at such a large sum going to a limited area of academic activity. The Appeal had asked for about £500 000 for research and development in the whole of the sciences and humanities. Yet on top of £100 000 from the Rhodes Trustees, Social Studies were also to get another £900 000. Professor Powicke, Lindsay's brother-in-law and a distinguished Mediaeval Historian, expressed his worries in an early note to Lindsay.

> My own reaction is rather that, while it is doubtless right to bridge the 'separation' between the students and responsible agents of contemporary civilisation, it would be unwise to incur the great risk of throwing the weight of the University and deflecting its future history in this direction *alone*. I should much prefer to see a graduate mainly non-residential college of a less specialised kind which could gather together the graduate work in the older faculties and in English literature (excluding Medicine as well as Science as subjects of study, though not necessarily excluding their graduate students from the social opportunities provided by such a centre). In other words a Graduate College of Arts. I have not touched on the strong feeling which would be aroused – I think with some justification – if, so soon after the Rockefeller endowment of social studies, another enormous endowment were altogether devoted to the same purpose. This is not a matter of jealousy between 'departments'. It affects the whole 'idea of a University'.

There was in any case a reluctance on the part of Lindsay to reject out of hand any of the suggestions and claims. He appreciated that some of the features of the Benefaction would not be popular and there was a fear that criticisms would be voiced in Congregation. However unrepresentative such criticism might be, Lord Nuffield might feel that his money and ideas were not appreciated. This would be misleading, for Council and the University generally were overwhelmed by his generosity. It might also cause him to turn elsewhere for his next major benefaction.

The concern to avoid major controversy in Congregation can be illustrated by the treatment of the issue of whether the College should be open to both men and women. When Lindsay put the

question specifically to Miss Grier she replied 'I see no reason why everything should not be open to both. The College is postgraduate and therefore does not present the problem of children straight from schools in which they have never set eyes on members of the opposite sex.'
Livingstone, however, told Lindsay:

> Women will be a great difficulty . . . You can hardly have both sexes living together; and if you appropriate a wing to women, you will tie yourself down to having as many women Fellows as will fill it, i.e. to allotting a definite number of fellowships to women, which seems undesirable. Yet one sees of course the difficulty, and in a sense undesirability of excluding women. I should have thought however it would be best from the start to assume that you will have no women *residents*, but (without saying anything about it) to keep a spot free where a women's wing could be erected later.

In their comments on the draft Statute the Social Studies Research Committee resolved on 20 October 1937 that the Statute 'should be so drafted as not to exclude women from the College'. Right from the beginning Lindsay believed that 'Women as well as men graduates ought to be eligible for . . . posts' in the College. The early drafts of the Statutes left the issue open by referring to persons and by not mentioning men or women. When the draft was considered by the Committee of Council they reported that the position of women in relation to the College might be a controversial subject. It would be ungracious to Lord Nuffield and unfortunate in itself, if the Statute which, under the provisions of the Deed of Trust, must be passed before his gift becomes effective, was made to include controversial topics and was delayed in consequence. They assumed that it was 'the question of the residence of women in the College which might arouse controversy, and that no one would dispute that it is desirable for women to be as closely associated as possible with research in social studies'. They, therefore, suggested an additional clause which 'provides a *mezzo termine* and postpones any controversy until it has been ascertained what provision for women it is practicable to make'. This read: 'Women shall be eligible for Faculty Fellowships, Visiting Fellowships (exclusive of the right of rooms in College . . .)' The clause was replaced by Council with the clearer statement 'Women shall be eligible for Fellowships and Studentships but shall not be permitted to reside in the College.'

THE TRUSTEES

The Deed of Trust and Covenant contained one other important provision. It established a permanent body of Trustees, composed of a Chairman appointed by Lord Nuffield, the Vice-Chancellor, three other members appointed by Lord Nuffield and three by Hebdomadal Council, of whom one was to be nominated by 'the Board of the Faculty most directly concerned with the Study of Social Problems'. The Chancellor of the University was to make the Donor's appointments upon Lord Nuffield's death. To secure the independence of the Trustees not more than one of those appointed by Council could be a member of the Committee of Council administering the College, or be Warden or a Fellow of the College. At least two of the members appointed by the Donor were not to be resident holders of any teaching or administrative post in the University or any College. The first Chairman was William Goodenough in whom Lord Nuffield reposed a great deal of trust.

The Trustees had the duty to consider the objects proposed to be financed out of the Trust Fund and the estimates of income and expenditure of the Fund in order to determine whether any of the objects proposed to be so financed were inconsistent with the terms of the Deed. They were to receive the annual accounts of the Trust Fund and of other moneys arising out of or otherwise subject to the Trust together with an annual report on the work carried out under the Trust and were required to report to the University on them. Thus the Trustees were to be the watchdogs to ensure that the Donor's intentions were not ignored. The 'watch dog' element would be particularly strong during Lord Nuffield's lifetime for the Chairman and three others, i.e. half the Trustees, were appointed and removable by him. In the event, as the narrative will show, he lived long enough to approve the winding up of the Trustees by Order of the Court in June 1958.

7 Social Reconstruction Survey

THE NUFFIELD COLLEGE COMMITTEE

A Nuffield College Committee was appointed by Hebdomadal Council on 29 October 1937, the original ten members being: the Vice-Chancellor (A. D. Lindsay); President of Magdalen (G. S. Gordon); Principal of St Edmund Hall (A. B. Emden); Principal of Lady Margaret Hall (Miss L. Grier); President of Corpus (R. W. Livingstone); Master of University (Sir William Beveridge); Sir Arthur Salter (Gladstone Professor of Political Theory and Institutions); Warden of All Souls (W. G. S. Adams); the Senior Proctor (C. R. Morris, Fellow of Balliol) and W. C. Costin (Fellow of St Johns). The Committee appointed two standing Sub-Committees each under the chairmanship of the Vice-Chancellor; a Residential Sub-Committee to prepare estimates of income and expenditure in connection with the residential part of the College and a Research Sub-Committee to consider for what research provision was to be made in the College. The Committee was not given any executive powers until 11 March 1944 when a Scheme of Delegation came into effect. Until then it could only make recommendations to Council and was referred to as the 'Interim' committee.

The Committee had two immediate tasks, to secure an Architect and a Warden. For Architect, they recommended Austen St B. Harrison, FRIBA, aged 47, until recently Architect to the Public Works Dept of the Palestine Government, all of whose work was in Palestine. He started in the summer of 1938 and produced a design that was approved by Hebdomadal Council on 16 January 1939. Lord Nuffield was abroad at the time and was not shown the design until late in June and immediately expressed his disapproval. On 15 August 1939 he told the Vice-Chancellor that he thought the design to be un-English, and out of keeping with the best tradition of Oxford architecture and that he would not allow his name to be associated with it. Harrison proposed an alternative design which was accepted by Lord Nuffield late in March 1940. By now, however, the war was well under way and there was no chance of construction being started.

The Nuffield Committee were not much luckier with their choice of Warden. They recommended Harold Butler, aged 55, the Director of the International Labour Office. Born in Oxford, son of a Fellow of Brasenose, he was a Brackenbury Scholar at Balliol, obtained a first in Greats and a Fellowship at All Souls, entered the Home Civil Service, became Deputy Director of the ILO in 1920 and Director in 1932. He took up his appointment as Warden on 1 January 1939. However, in September, at the outbreak of war he became Regional Commissioner for the Southern Region based on Readng. He managed to get clear of this in January 1942 but in May 1942 was again called away by the Government, this time as a Minister at the Embassy in Washington. His resignation from the Wardenship was accepted in June 1943 by which time he had spent little more than a year in the post.

The University Statute governing the College provided for not more than 12 Official, 8 Faculty, and 20 Visiting Fellows. There could also be Honorary and Professorial Fellows. Lord Nuffield was declared to be an Honorary Fellow in the Trust Deed. Lindsay was anxious to make early appointments of Visiting Fellows for these, being from the world of practical affairs, were essential to provide the special feature of the College – co-operation between the academic and non-academic worlds. The Statute, however, laid it down that the number of such Fellows could not exceed the number of Official and Faculty Fellows. There was, however, insufficient income available to pay the stipends of many Offical Fellows who were to be full-time. It was, therefore, more feasible to appoint Faculty Fellows who were to be part-time. In any case Lindsay saw that to associate Fellows of other Colleges as Faculty Fellows with Nuffield would fit in with the ideas about the role of the two sub-Faculties and ease some of their misgivings. As a result six Faculty Fellows were elected from 7 June 1939. They were G. D. H. Cole, R. C. K. Ensor, J. S. Fulton, R. F. Harrod, R. L. Hall and Margery

Perham. This enabled six Visiting Fellows to be elected from the same date. They were Lord Cadman (Chairman, Anglo-Iranian Oil); Sir Walter Citrine (Secretary, TUC); Sir George Etherton (Clerk of the Lancashire County Council); Lord Hailey; Geoffrey Vickers (Solicitor, Slaughter and May); and A. P. Young (Manager, Rugby Works of British Thompson Houston). Margery Perham was appointed Reader in Colonial Administration as from 1 October 1939 and gave up her Faculty Fellowship to become the first Official Fellow on that date. Professor Reginald Coupland became the first Professorial Fellow on that day.

The outbreak of war in September 1939 found the College little further on than when the Benefaction had been announced almost two years earlier. Lord Nuffield's letter of August 1939 rejecting the design for his College put back the building for at least a year and it was hardly to be expected that much progress could be made with the country's resources being diverted from civil to war purposes. The newly elected Warden went off to his wartime post and three of the five Faculty Fellows became full-time civil servants. Many other members of the Social Studies Faculty joined the Armed Forces or Whitehall. A few remained in Oxford, the most active being G. D. H. Cole. Lindsay also remained and the running of Nuffield's Benefaction largely passed into their energetic hands without, one suspects, receiving more than an intermittent interest from the rest of the University.

Lindsay wrote to Sir Frederick Leith-Ross (who at that time carried the imposing but somewhat misleading title of Chief Economic Adviser to the Government) in September 1939. He suggested that perhaps Nuffield College 'might get together a group of outstanding persons not eligible for service in Government Departments who would undertake special tasks for the Government'. Leith-Ross let it be known that a scheme of that kind might be of very great service. If a group were got together in Oxford of refugees or persons not British subjects by birth, he would undertake to see that problems were suggested to them, for example reporting on the economic state of the various European nations. The College would not, however, have any official mandate nor receive Government money, 'But,' as Lindsay told the Vice-Chancellor 'we could be assured . . . that we should be told what problems we could most usefully deal with; we could be sure that our results would get to the right quarters and that our suggestions would be listened to'. The Nuffield Committee invited Lindsay and Perham, and any other of its members, to submit concrete proposals.[1]

The Committee agreed, subject to the concurrence of Council and the Trustees, to put a sum of £1300 at the disposal of the Wartime Research Committee for political research during the eight months ending 31 July 1940 and to allocate a £2400 over two years to Miss Perham for the Colonial Project. The Trustees authorised expenditure up to £5000 in all on the two research projects during 1939–40 but warned that, if a similar application were to be put forward next year, Council ought to take account of the possible rise in the cost of building after the war.[2] These decisions look well on paper: in practice little or no research was undertaken during 1939–40.

Early in May 1940 the Warden prepared a memorandum expressing his belief that the College ought to be making some contribution to the problem of social and economic reconstruction, however difficult it might be to do so under present conditions. Had the College been in existence when the War broke out there was no doubt, he claimed, that its constitution and equipment would have given it a special qualification for dealing with the problem. The possible field for research was vast, but he suggested that the College should concentrate on the transition from war to peace. He hoped to get sufficient time from his official duties to be able to devote a good deal of it to the inquiry and, for the rest, the Institute of Statistics, and in particlar Professor A. L. Bowley, its Acting Director, should play an important role.

Veale tried to get a quick decision on this paper in view of 'Lord Nuffield's obvious dissatisfaction with the complete stagnation of the College for so long a period'.[3] With the same point in mind William Goodenough, Chairman of the Trustees, started to urge that the College should undertake some war-time research. Though at their November 1939 meeting the Trustees had taken the view that expenditure on war-time work should be restricted in order that funds might be conserved against a possible increase in the cost of building after the war, by April, Goodenough was writing to the Vice-Chancellor and Veale saying he would ask the Trustees to modify their views and was strongly supporting Butler's proposals.

The Warden's memorandum was discussed by the Finance Sub–Committee of the Nuffield Commitee on 25 May 1940, with the Vice-Chancellor, Warden, and Robert Hall present. They felt that in the existing circumstances it would be difficult to secure adequate staff for ambitious programmes. They recommended, therefore, that consideration of the Warden's scheme be deferred until the Autumn and that Council should advise the Research Committee to restrict its expenditure as rigidly as possible and to undertake no new commitments until the time came when the co-ordination of the programme could be considered.[4]

On 13 June 1940, therefore, the Trustees decided to inform Council that they agreed with the Warden's view that the College should play a valuable part in the investigation of certain cardinal problems of social and economic reconstruction. The planning of such investigation could most efficiently be done by one man, and should be started at the earliest possible moment. They suggested, therefore, that the Government be at once requested to release the Warden from his engagement as Regional Commissioner as soon as the immediate urgency of his national defence duties was over.[5]

On 17 June 1940 Council asked the Vice-Chancellor at a suitable opportunity to approach the Government for the release of Butler. They thought the suggestion of the Trustees was a good one.[6]

Goodenough continued to pursue his point. Writing to Veale on 26 July 1940 he said that recently he had been at 'certain interesting private gatherings listening to pronouncements from responsible people, including Labour Members of the present Government'. He had been struck with the way some of these people were 'thinking ahead and developing in their minds the lines on which every kind of development and reconstruction may be proceeded with after the War'. This had brought home to him again the fact that 'the present time, of all others may be *the* opportunity for Nuffield, and that unless work is done now and all the political interests kept in touch anything that is attempted later may be hopelessly 'behind the Hunt' and, therefore, useless from the point of view of trying to put the College in its right place as a leader of thought'. He appreciated the difficulty of obtaining Butler's return in the present circumstances but if Butler intended to stick to the post *sine die* 'I think the answer is that somebody else ought to be found to tackle the Nuffield problem'. This was all for Veale's private ear and he added 'the responsibility of the Trustees to the University in this matter is a real one which we ought not to avoid'. Veale 'unreservedly' shared Goodenough's views.[7]

On 10 September 1940 Lord Balfour of Burleigh wrote to *The Times* announcing the establishment of a '1940 Council' of which he was Chairman. Its work would have two sides – research and publicity. The former would be concerned with an analysis of the environmental needs of the community and the study of the means by which these needs could be fulfilled. In its Leader *The Times* thought there was ample evidence that Balfour's initiative was not premature though it might appear to be so in the midst of a life and death struggle. Goodenough used the letter and leader to stress to Veale once again that the activities of the College should not be neglected 'whatever the circumstances of the moment may be'. He intended to have a word with Halifax about the possibility of Butler's release.

Veale now thought that Butler should never have been allowed to accept the Regional Commissionership. The Nuffield Committee (but not the Trustees) knew before the War that Butler had accepted the post though he was not sure that the University had been consulted. 'We ought to have had enough vision to take a line then, when it might have been effective'. Veale thought Butler the ideal man for the job to be done at the College, but Butler would strongly resist any attempt at the moment to dislodge him from the Regional Commissionership: he would be supported by the Home Office, and the Nuffield Committee would be divided on the issue. Veale agreed that the best thing was to get the move to come from the Government side 'Something between an invitation and an order from the Government to mobilize the resources of Nuffield College at once to recall Butler, to work out a programme.'[8]

Goodenough saw Halifax on October 9, stressing that the University was under an obligation to Lord Nuffield not to neglect any effort to make the best use of the opportunity. Halifax said he was generally in accord with Goodenough's views.

Goodenough continued to write to Veale about the matter. On 25 October 1940 he wrote: 'the ideal solution is to engineer that Nuffield College should be virtually asked to do certain work for the Government. That would put everything right both with the politicians and with Butler.'[9] He thought that the meeting between the Vice-Chancellor and Halifax was 'fairly satisfactory'.

But he was not entirely convinced that the College activites should be shelved agan in the event of the Government not being able to give much direct help or encouragement to Butler: 'the obligation on the University to Lord Nuffield is so great that a start ought to be made as soon as possble'. He thought that in their Annual Report to the University the Trustees should re-affirm their opinion that the College activities should be proceeded with and that if 'we let the opportunity for doing so slip, we are, in fact, failing to meet our obligations to Lord Nuffield'. He finished his letter to Veale, 'I am afraid you will think I am something of a maniac on this subject'.[10]

In the meantime, on 23 November, the Warden's memorandum was discussed by the Nuffield Committee. They agreed that the College ought to make its contribution to research on problems of reconstruction and decided to ask the Government what place there was in its plans for such a contribution. Meanwhile a sub-committee, composed of the Vice-Chancellor, the Warden, Lindsay, Cole and the Principal of Lady Margaret Hall were asked to work out a plan of research which would be feasible in the altered circumstances since the Warden had written his memorandum.[11]

When this Sub-Committee met on 11 December 1940 the Vice-Chancellor was able to report that he had received two letters from the Chancellor. In the first Halifax said he had conferred with the Departments on whose work research organised by the College might be expected to have most bearing. He had not been encouraged to hope that they would be able to do much in the way of providing facilities. It also seemed improbable that Departments would be willing to give the College any special status in the matter of advising on policy or that the Warden would be released from his duties as Regional Commissoner in present circumstances. However, in a second letter Halifax said he had seen Sir Horace Wilson and was now inclined to think that his first letter might have been too discouraging. Wilson had expressed a wish to discuss the matter with the Vice-Chancellor.

The Sub-Commitee came to the conclusion that, in previous deliberations, eyes had been fixed too intently upon the post-war period. In fact post-war England was in the process of being made and the study of current events had a dual importance. Local authorities and voluntary agencies were tackling unprecedented problems and unless the history of their activities was written now it could never be accurately written at all. In the second place, whatever influence on the course of events was to be exercised by the College and similar bodies must be exercised immediately, otherwise the structure of post-war society would have been too completely moulded by current happenings. Cole volunteered to give time to the organization of research in consultation with the Warden.[12]

The Vice-Chancellor saw Sir Horace Wilson shortly before Christmas. Wilson told him that the Cabinet Committee on Reconstruction, of which Attlee was Chairman, had not so far made much progress. Wilson vividly remembered the experience of the Ministry of Reconstruction at the end of the last war when Departments found themselves hampered rather than helped, for the Ministry had pursued its work without much contact with Departments. He had suggested, therefore, that the Cabinet Committee ought to have a permanent secretary. Sir George Chrystal had been appointed to this post and, with his knowledge of the working of the Civil Service, would be able to keep in touch, at one end, with the research oganisations, and at the other, with the Departments. One of Chrystal's duties would be to see that proper access to materials required for research was given by the Departments. Wilson, therefore, wanted the Vice-Chancellor to see Chrystal. When the question was raised of 'digging Butler out of his Regional Commissionership' Wilson made it quite clear that that process must be subsequent to the making of arrangements for recognition and the provision of material.[13]

Butler took part in these discussions, indeed he produced, along with Cole, a proposed scheme of research. But he showed no inclination to return as Warden. Towards the end of December he told Goodenough that though he was initiating a limited programme of research for the College 'he himself would not be able to pay much attention to it'. Neither this statement nor the research now proposed by Butler, into the future distribution of population, pleased Goodenough. He would not be satisfied unless the Warden himself took charge of some major operation which would provide a full-time job for him and his helpers. He told Veale (1 January 1941) 'I am bound to keep on returning in my mind to the question of whether I shall not have to raise this matter again with Lord Nuffield in a rather heavy-handed way. I do not in the least want to do so but it may still be necessary, much as one would dislike it.'[14]

Three weeks after talking with Warren Fisher and Harold Hartley, both Trustees, Goodenough asked Veale, as Secretary of the Trustees, to inform the Vice-Chancellor that he would have no choice but to resign the Chairmanship of the Trustees 'unless the Warden is willing to throw himself with vigour into the work of the College or make way for someone else who would'. Had he done so Fisher and Hartley would almost certainly have resigned at the same time. Goodenough also thought that Lord Nuffield would be outspoken in his public criticism of the way in which the University had used his great benefaction.

Veale minuted the Vice-Chancellor on 21 January 1941. The University must either recall Butler or convince Lord Nuffield and the Trustees either that the future of the College and the present public interest would best be served by some sort of improvised programme not requiring the stimulation which the Warden's presence could give or that it had a defence for its inaction which would carry conviction to the public against the criticism which would be focussed upon it by these resignations. However convincing that answer might be 'its failure to convince Lord Nuffield would be a lamentable fact'.[15]

Shortly after this Butler offered his resignation. The Nuffield Committee (on 8 February 1941) refused to accept it on the grounds that it was impossble for him to give up his Regional Commissionership and resume his duties as Warden while heavy air attacks were still probable and the threat of invasion continued and that it would be impossible either to replace him or to find a deputy.[16]

Lindsay had already on 20 November 1940 proposed that the College should undertake an enquiry into the social work of Local Authorities and voluntary agencies, including collecting documents and other materials relating to it. In their joint report of early January the Warden and Cole took up this suggestion but proposed that the enquiry should be focussed on a single problem which touched on almost every phase of local social activity, namely the social effects of the redistribution of population which was taking place as a result of the War.[17]

Chrystal met the Vice-Chancellor, Registrar, the Warden, Lindsay and Cole when he visited Oxford on 17–18 January 1941. He suggested that College representatives should explore the matter with the Royal Institute of International Affairs who were already engaged on work for his Committee. Though the primary concern of Chatham House was international affairs it had established a Social and Economic Reconstruction Committee which it was anxious should not overlap the work done by the College. The College representatives explained that the work proposed for the College fell into two sections:

(1) Work already begun independently by the Institute of Statistics: analyses of national income – expenditure and war finance.
(2) Contemplated new work which would be concentrated first on such matters as the redistribution of population due to the war and how far this was likely to be permanent. Miss Perham's interest in African problems was also mentioned.

It was agreed that the next step must be to define the respective spheres of the two bodies. One point of possible difficulty was the number of aliens working in the Institute of Statistics, which might prevent the College having access to confidential material.[18]

In February 1941 the scheme of research suggested by Lindsay and Cole was agreed and placed under a Social Reconstruction Survey Committee.[19]

THE SOCIAL RECONSTRUCTION SURVEY

Writing in May 1942, Cole[20] explained that for the first 18 months of the war the College was practically in abeyance. During the latter months of 1940, however, a number of Fellows, and the Trustees, began to have an uneasy feeling that in doing nothing 'we were guilty of a dereliction of duty', But the Nuffield Committee found itself under very severe handicaps. The Warden was absent on war service and could give no more than occasional advice. The Fellows, academic and non-academic, were scattered far and wide in war jobs. There was hardly anyone left to give either time or serious attention to the problems of the College. 'The Committee was in a dilemma, when by a pure accident I was able to make the suggestion on which the Social Recontruction Survey was based'.

Towards the end of 1940 the national Man-Power Survey, in which he had been helping Beveridge, finished its work. Cole had been in charge of co-ordinating the local side and for that purpose had built up a series of Local Surveys covering most of the country and based on the remaining staffs of the appropriate departments of the Universities or extramural staffs in the areas. 'The men and women who helped me with these Local Man-Power Surveys had done . . . a remarkably fine piece of work; . . . and it seemed to me a great pity that they should be disbanded, if there was further useful work waiting to be done'.

Cole, therefore proposed to the Nuffield Committee that if he were entrusted with the work he would try to organise a Social Reconstruction Survey, using as much of the Man-Power Survey as possible. This offer was accepted. It was, however, thought out of question to proceed unless the Government was prepared to give its support and endow the Survey's workers with some measure of official recognition. A high proportion of the facts and figures accessible in time of peace had, under war conditions, passed into the category of secret information. The research workers would also have to have access to 'busy people who were up to their eyes in important jobs'. The requisite status was secured, it being arranged that 'we should work, unofficially but with official backing, primarily for the Reconstruction Department'.

Cole became Director and the Chairman of the Social Reconstruction Survey Committee. By June 1941 the other members were: Lindsay, Miss Grier, Professors A. G. B. Fisher, D. H. Macgregor, G. N. Clark and A. L. Bowley, R. C. K. Ensor, Agnes Headlam-Morley, C. H. Wilson, C. S. Orwin, Margery Perham, Montagu Harris and Patrick Abercrombie.

On 1 April 1941 the Minister without Portfolio (Arthur Greenwood) who was Chairman of the Cabinet's Reconstruction Committee at the time, was asked in the House of Commons whether he would take steps to ensure that the experience and knowledge at the command of independent organisations such as Nuffield College would be utilised to the full in connection with the preparation of reconstruction plans. He replied:

> Yes, Sir. Full advantage is being taken of public spirited offers of co-operation from independent organizations in connexion with the preparation of reconstruction plans. The authorities of Nuffield College have been good enough to collaborate with my Noble Friend the Minister of Works and Buildings and myself in conducting an inquiry into certain problems of reconstruction and the transition from war to peace conditions.

We expect the result of this inquiry to be most valuable, and we hope that the investigators will be given all possible assistance.[21]

Cole agreed with the Ministry the following terms of reference.[22]

The subject-matter of the inquiry to be conducted by Nuffield College will be:

(a) The redistribution of industry and population brought about by the war, and the extent to which, in view of the probable industrial situation after the war and the changing conditions affecting the location of industry, this redistribution is likely to persist. (This part of the inquiry includes an investigation into the working of the local and regional organization of industry which has been evolved by the supply departments.)

(b) The effects of war conditions on the working of the public social services, both national and local, and the social services provided by voluntary agencies. (The working of the emergency hospital services is excluded from the scope of this part of the inquiry.)

(c) The human effects of evacuation, industrial migration, and other war-time changes in the conditions of living, and their bearing on the problems of social reconstruction.

(d) The bearing of all these factors on the general problem of social and economic reorganization and on the practical efficacy of democractic institutions, including both Government and voluntary agencies.

The investigators have been specifically instructed that they are not to conduct anything in the nature of a house-to-house inquiry into the views of private individuals on the subject-matter of the investigations.

It was originally intended to include the future of Local Government but this was struck out at Mr Greenwood's suggestion for fear of objections from the Ministry of Health. When, however, Sir William Jowitt succeeded Greenwood in December 1942 he specifically included Local Govenment within the Survey's terms of reference.

Under Cole's vigorous direction the 'Survey' rapidly widened in scope and complexity. In addition to the enquiry into the probable future distribution of population and location of industries, national studies were started of particlar industries, e.g. building and physical reconstruction, and in the general areas of education, social services and local government. The headquarters of the Survey was 17 Banbury Road, taken over in the summer of 1941, but some work continued to be housed in the Indian Institute. There was also a London Office under the Chief London Investigator, G. R. Mitchison. Cole was even given an office in the Ministry of Reconstruction and in the Ministry of Works and became a member of several official committees of these two Departments. An important by-product of the programme came to be the holding of Private Conferences. These are dealt with later.

The Survey was a considerable feat of organisation on the part of Cole. Two Sub-Committees were quickly set up under the main Committee; one on Education under Miss Grier's chairmanship and one on Social Services under Lindsay, with Cole a member of each. A third Committee – on Local Government – was then set up under C. H. Wilson, with Cole again a member. There was also a special committee for the international aspects of the Survey's work composed of three represenatives from each of the Survey Committee, Chatham House and the Institute of Statistics. Cole was chairman.

Cole's report for 1941-2 shows a total of 26 full-time staff. That report listed four reports submitted to the Government with a further three promised in the near future; two industrial reports; three reports for the Central Council for Works and Buildings and three for the Scott Committee (Land Utilisation in Rural Areas); three other reports prepared at the request of the Government and twenty memoranda on a variety of subjects, e.g. reconstruction of devastated areas in France and British Export Trends. This was an exciting time for those engaged in this work. Cole was in every activity, stimulating and organising.

Work on this scale cost quite a large sum in terms of the circumstances of the time. For the full year 1941–2 Cole estimated his expenditure at £8000. A Treasury grant of £5000 for the period April 1941 to April 1942 was swallowed up mainly by the expenses of the local survey teams and did not reduce the cost to the College. An application to the Rockefeller Foundation for a large annual grant (including £8000 a year for the Survey) was not successful. The income of the College's endowment from dividends interest and rents was rising, being £9500 in 1940–41 and £11500 in 1941–42, but expenditure othr than on the Survey had to be met out of that. More important, a growing concern about rising building costs led to a strong demand for putting part of the income into a Building Reserve Fund.

The level of expenditure was not the only aspect which caused alarm in some quarters. Harold Butler was very immersed in his duties as Regional Commissioner and was unable to exercise any supervision or oversight of developments. The Survey was in effect G. D. H. Cole, recruiting whoever was available, working with feverish energy and creating, overnight as it were, a large, varied and expanding research programme. Goodenough told Veale in November 1941 that Cole had talked with him about 'the inevitability ... of the scope of the Survey increasing'. It struck Goodenough that Cole was 'a little over-excited about it and disposed to try and take anything and everything that might come in his stride'.[23]

Some of this concern was expressed at the meeting of the Hebdomadal Council on 10 November 1941. A resolution carried *nem. con.* that Council could not approve the Social Reconstruction Survey in its present form was referred to a Committee which was authorised to submit its views direct to the Trustees for their meeting on November 15 and to ask for Council's approval on November 17.[24]

They recommended that Council should, when returning the Estimates to the Nuffield Committee, assuming they were approved by the Trustees, express the general view:

(1) That any further development of research should aim at concentration rather than diffusion and that the Survey should concern itself with the range of questions which were included in the programme as it stood in May rather than with those on the periphery of the subjects in which research was then being conducted.

(2) That the work of the Survey would be much helped if the Warden or an Acting Warden were immediately installed. If an Acting Warden were to be appointed he should not be personally immersed in research, but should be able to look objectively at it and further, should be of a standing to ensure that proper attention were given to the Survey reports by the authorities to whom they were sent.

When the Report came to be discussed on November 17 Council was divided, voting 12 to 7 that it be received. Voting in Council is a rare happening and so the feeling on both sides must have been very strong. Unfortunately the Minutes of Council are uninformative about the views expressed and who expressed them. However, Council agreed to inform the Nuffield Committee that they were glad to endorse the Trustees' expression of satisfaction with the steps taken to organise the Survey and with the progress made but considered that any further development should aim at concentration rather than diffusion. They also agreed to ask the Nuffield Committee to appoint representatives of the Survey Committee or of the War-time Research Committee to meet a committee of Council to discuss the future development of the programme.[25] The Trustees made the point about the need for the return of the Warden, or should that not prove possible, for the appointment of an Acting Warden.

Both comments could only be seen as directed at Cole. Indeed, briefing Goodenough before the meeting of the Trustees on 15 November, Veale speculated on the possibility of Cole resigning. The name of Hailey as a possible Acting Warden was being discussed and, if Cole were to resign, should that appointment be made, his resignation 'would be put down to pique and jealousy'.[26]

It perhaps did not surprise anybody, therefore, that Council's comments produced a somewhat emotional letter from Cole to the Vice-Chancellor, dated 21 November 1941. He could not help, he said, resenting the censure implied in the resolution 'a resolution passed in ignorance of essential facts and without any *prior* consultation with those in the position to know the facts'. In a note dealing with the accusation that the Survey had been guilty of dissipating its energies over too wide a field he said 'I cannot remain at my post unless the imputation contained in this resolution is withdrawn'. He then reverted to his earlier threat to resign if an acting Warden were appointed over his head. There was, he said, no question of personal objection to any particular individual. 'The matter is one of principle and of practical bearing on the work'. No similar issue would arise if the Warden were to return. 'I would most gladly be relieved of a very onerous charge which I assumed only because of his absence'. Cole said that, were Butler to return he would bring the work to an interim point, probably by the end of the year and hand over to him and would then be free to return to the previous arrangement under which he carried out part-time academic duties in Oxford and combined them with his other work in London. He concluded:

> If I observe that the work I have done for the Survey has cost me a large part of my normal income, and that on this ground I should be glad to be quit of it at the moment I feel free to go, I hope I shall not be regarded as mercenary – for I remain willing to carry on unpaid as long as the conditions remain the same as they were when I undertook the work. Only if the conditions are altered do I claim the right to be relieved of obligations which have proved in practice very much more onerous than I contemplated when I agreed to undertake them.[27]

The tension was relieved by Butler's announcement at the meeting on November 22 that the Home Secretary was willing to release him on December 31 and he would, therefore, be able to take up full-time duties as Warden on 1 January 1942. At that meeting the Nuffield Committee considered it inexpedient that Council should control the research of the College in a way which their comments suggested. They thanked Cole for his successful exertions during the Warden's absence and expressed the hope that he would not resign from the Chairmanship of the Survey and Cole agreed.[28]

The stage was thus set for a fresh start. In May 1942 however Butler went off to the United States. Cole was again in sole charge with the question of the appointment of an Acting Warden still in the air. The Vice-Chancellor felt it would be increasingly difficult to deny Cole the post and reasonable remuneration for it, there being a growing feeling in the University that his work was bringing credit to the College. When the Vice-Chancellor had met Lord Nuffield recently he had found him much more favourably disposed to the College. Lord Nuffield 'did not explode at all on the subject of Cole's being in charge of the Survey'. He agreed with Veale that there was something to be said for leading Nuffield gently up to the idea that Cole might be made Acting Warden. Lord Portal (Minister of Works) or Brendan Bracken (Minister for Information), or both might be persuaded to hint to Nuffield that 'in view of the importance of the Survey it would be rather a happy thing if Cole were appointed Acting Warden'.

Veale, however, told Butler that there was 'unhappily a further complication'. The appointment would have to be made by Council and there was certain to be some opposition there. Some members of Council had been offended by 'the overbearing tone of a letter for which Cole was known to have been responsible. It would not be safe, therefore, to assume that a recommendation from the Nuffield Committee to appoint Cole as Acting Warden would pass Council without question'. Veale could imagine 'nothing more untimely than a controversy between Council and the Nuffield College Committee on this question'.[29]

The Sub-Committee appointed to consider the position created by the absence of the Warden pointed out that it was usual in Colleges for there to be a deputy for the Head who automatically took over his duties when he was absent or incapacitated. This office was usually held in rotation among the Fellows and this system should apply in Nuffield. They recommended that an office of Sub-Warden should be created and Cole should be appointed until 30 September 1943. The sub-committee added that it was known that Cole had made great personal sacrifices to enable him to achieve the remarkable work which he has done, and therefore, should be paid a proper salary as Director of the Social Reconstruction Survey. His academic income at that time was £900 and it was recommended that an additional £1100 should be paid to him from College funds: The proposals were agreed.[30]

On 27 May 1942 Lord Nuffield wrote to the Warden, who had informed him of the decision:

> I had already heard of the proposal to appoint Cole to be Sub-Warden of the College and I am pleased to be able to say the Goodenough and myself, after full consideration, are in agreement with this course. I must confess that when I first heard of the suggestion that Cole should deputize ... I was caused a little uneasiness by a thought that his past ideas and activities might to some extent reassert themselves, but on this point I have gained assurance from the knowledge that the Vice-Chancellor [now David Ross, Provost of Oriel] will be associating himself personally with the development of the College as he will be taking care of its interest in the Hebdomadal Council.[31]

Some members of Council, however, were still worried about the size of the demands of the Survey on the endowment income. On 22 June 1942 a proposal that Council stated its unwillingness to sanction expenditure on the Survey beyond £8000 (the 1942-3 estimate was £9730) was only narrowly defeated by 9 votes to 8.[32]

Nuffield's contentment with Cole did not last long. Early in November 1942 he called on Veale 'boiling with rage about the College, saying that he was thinking of publicly dissociating his name from it, and making it plain that the University must never expect to get another penny of his money'. His rage was principally directed at Cole having been appointed to look after the Social Reconstruction Survey. Veale pointed out that this was an accident, the original intention being that it should be run by the Warden and Cole. Veale also told Nuffield that so long as it was known that he viewed the College with disfavour he would find plenty of people to decry it to him. If, however, it became known that he was eminently satisfied that the idea of the College was sound and that he did not mind a considerable number of mistakes being made by the University so long as the same mistake was not made twice, he would get a very different account. At the end of an hour and a quarter's conversation Veale thought that some good might result but he subsequently learnt from Goodenough that this had not been the case. (One result of the interview was that Veale's stock with Nuffield sank 'lower than its previous low level').[33]

At their meeting on 12 December 1942 the Trustees agreed to inform Council that they thought the time had come to find out from the Government Departments for whom the Survey had been working whether the material supplied to them had been of the quality and nature and in the form required. The Vice-Chancellor, who as usual was present, said that, if the proposal were adopted by Council, he would personally undertake the necessary enquiries and would welcome the assistance of the Chairman of the Trustees. Council agreed to the suggestion and the Nuffield Committee formally heard the news on 24 December.

Veale explained to Butler that the idea was not to send a carefully worded official letter which would elicit a carefully worded official reply but that Ross and Goodenough should make personal enquiries. 'This should enable us to dispose of the critics one way or the other. Either the report will be favourable and the critics will be blasted or . . . unfavourable and the Survey will be blasted'.[34]

The report of Goodenough and Ross was received by Council at the end of March 1943. They said they had undertaken their inquiries because 'during the Michaelmas Term various rumours unfavourable to the Social Reconstruction Survey had reached some of the Nuffield College Trustees, and had also reached Lord Nuffield, who had expressed serious perturbation about them'. The result, they said, might be summed up in the statement that the Chancellor of the Exchequer, after consultation with the Minister without Portfolio and with other Departments to which the Survey had provided memoranda, had decided not to renew the Treasury grant. Any Department in future desiring the College to undertake a particular inquiry would have to pay for it by way of a fee. So far as they could ascertain no Department, with the probable exception of the Board of Trade, had any inquiry in prospect which it wished the College to undertake.

The result, they claimed, was very disappointing. The attitude of Departments was partly to be explained by the fact that those which were too hard pressed in the anxious days of 1941 to find time to think about reconstruction were now more able and more inclined to conduct their own surveys. Appreciation was expressed of the energy with which the Survey had been conducted. At the same time, they had received 'criticisms which particularly when addressed to an academic body, must be regarded as severe ... The reports were said to be too diffuse, and sometimes rather superficial ... quality had been unduly sacrificed to quantity.'[35]

When Council came to discuss the report on 8 April it was told that the Survey Committee had already decided not to continue working for the Board of Trade because of the conditions laid down by the Department. Council decided, therefore, that, if the Survey was going to fade away naturally, it would be injudicious to try to kill it.[36]

Council had, however, misjudged the reactions of the Survey Committee and of Cole. Cole with his usual fluency produced several lengthy 'Notes' on the work of the Survey and on its future.[37] These, along with the views expressed by Council, but not the report by Ross and Goodenough, were before the Nuffield Committee at their meeting on 15 May 1943, a meeting which, according to Margaret Cole was 'painfully stormy'.[38]

The Nuffield Committee asked for a copy of the Ross-Goodenough report and appointed a committee composed of Professors A. L. Bowley, G. N. Clark and D. H. Macgregor 'to consider the material accumulated by the Survey and to report on the practicability and value of publishing those parts to the publication of which no objection could be raised on the grounds of secrecy'. They concentrated on the 'academic value' of the work, which might, of course, have little bearing on its value to the Departments. The Nuffield committee also decided not to provide money for the whole of 1943-4 but instead to provide for the first six months to allow the completion of Surveys still outstanding for Departments; the working up of material still to be published; the continuance of certain of the Sub-Committees of the Survey, e.g. Education, Social Services and Local Government; and the continuance of the Conferences. The Survey staff were to be warned that they must not count on their services being continued beyond that period, i.e. beyond 31 January 1944.

Cole told the meeting that, under doctors' orders, he would at the beginning of June, have to take two or possibly three months' sick leave. He asked that it be put on record that he did not wish to receive any salary for directing research after the close of the financial year. However he still had the energy to write further notes and memoranda. He addressed a long letter to the Vice-Chancellor[39] dated 21 May 1943, saying that, as a member of the Nuffield Committee, he had just seen the memoradum of 31 March. He did not believe the charges to be justified, but, if they were, would clearly make it impossible for him to remain as Director of the Survey or to retain any connection with the research work of the College. He was fully aware that the reports submitted to the Government were of varying quality, this being quite inevitable in the circumstances under which the Survey had to work, including shortage of personnel and difficulties in securing disclosure of essential material. But, after allowing for these factors, he did not admit that the reports were superficial or unduly diffuse or that quality had been sacrificed to quantity. Cole denied that the cessation of the Treasury grant was the result of dissatisfaction with the quality of the work: it was against the advice of the Reconstruction Secretatriat, who had pressed strongly for its renewal. The reason he understood arose from the decision to deal with reconstruction policy through the separate Departments, future work should take the form of a contract between the Survey and a specific Department.

Bowley, Clark and Macgregor reported on 8 June in what Margaret Cole called 'a rather muted document'. While their primary purpose was to advise on publication they also had something to say about the value and quality of the work undertaken. They excluded from their attention the materials accumulated by the sub-committees for Local Government, Education and the Social Services, as none had reported to Government Departments. 'The reports' they said, 'are unequal in the number of subjects covered and in the intensity of their treatment; but within their range and having regard to the limitation of information they are in the main scholarly and valuable'. Later they commented that the work done by the local investigators was of unequal value. Some of the reports were of very little value, others were important contributions to research. In their opinion two volumes of public interest might emerge from the labours of the Survey, but nothing should be published which did not set a high standard for the future of the College.[40]

Circulated at the same time as this report was a statement[41] by the War-time Research Committee of which Lindsay was again Chairman. They claimed that it had been made clear to them from the beginning that the idea of the Survey carrying out independent investigations had been unwelcome in certain quarters in Government Departments and that the views of those who did not believe in the Survey, or indeed any independent body doing research about reconstruction, might at any time prevail. This was true whatever the merits of the Survey, although they knew that the kind of work which the Survey was asked to do was bound to have defects which could be used by Departments as an excuse to conduct their own surveys. The tendency of Departments to keep research of this kind to themselves was not in the public welfare. The assumption that Departments only adopted this policy because of defects in the independent research with which they were dispensing was as unfortunate as it was unwarranted.

The cessation of the Treasury grant and the terms under which Departments could pay for work undertaken in future meant the complete winding up of the machinery of local investigation. The cost, estimated at £7000 for 1942–3, had been met out of the grant. Though, in future, Departments could pay for a particular piece of work this would not involve a contribution to the basic cost of the Survey. Moreover the bulk of the Survey's work had been stimulated, and in some cases only made possible, by being undertaken for a particular Department. Though at first Cole claimed that notwithstanding the alleged critcisms of the quality of the work several Departments were still commissioning work from the Survey even this faded. The Board of Trade's proposal could have been met only by keeping the teams of local investigators and in any case was 'hedged about by such restrictions as to make it unacceptable'. The Ministry of Town and Country Planning only wanted the Survey to complete its series of regional reports which could be done only if the local investigators remained in existence.[42]

The Nuffield Committee met on 12 June 1943, but Cole did not attend. It was agreed that Cole should be informed that the Committee appreciated the value of the work he had done and desired that the working up of the material collected by the Survey, as recommended by Macgregor's Committee, should go on for six months after the end of July 1943 and that he should continue to supervise it.[43]

Consideration of the proposed estimates to enable the Survey to carry on for a further six months led to another vote in Council on 21 June. A motion by P. Landon (Trinity) that the question should be referred to a special Committee was defeated by 11 votes to 4. And so the financial proposals were approved and sent to the Trustees.

Landon then gave notice that at the next meeting he proposed to ask the Vice-Chancellor whether he had any reason to believe that 'Lord Nuffield is dissatisfied with the decision of the University to associate Nuffield College with the subject of Social Studies'. On 28 June the Vice-Chancellor replied that it was laid down in Lord Nuffield's original offer that the College should be associated with Social Studies and this was included in the Trust Deed. The Minutes went on: 'Rumours had come to his ears to the effect that Lord Nuffield now regretted this decision and it was known that Lord Nuffield felt serious misgivings about the Social Reconstruction Survey. But he had reason to think that Lord Nuffield would feel reassured by the appointment . . of a not less able Warden [Henry Clay] who would be in a position to give continuous attention to the work of the College.'[44] (After some persuasion Henry Clay had agreed to accept the offer of the Wardenship in April 1944).

Cole refused to stand for re-election as Sub-Warden claiming that he had accepted the appointment originally only with reluctance. He agreed to remain, however, as Director of the Survey until not later than 31 January 1944. The Nuffield Committee passed a resolution thanking him for his self-sacrificing labours in connection with the Survey. Lindsay was appointed Sub-Warden temporarily.[45]

SOME EXPLANATIONS

There is no single explanation for the remarkable rise and fall of Cole and the Survey: several factors, taken together, probably led to the final result.

First, neither the Reconstruction Secretariat nor the Ministry of Works with which Cole had close relations, carried much weight in Whitehall. Moreover there was little or no active interest in post-war reconstruction among top Ministers and Civil Servants until the Allies began to win victories. All the effort was on winning the war, indeed there was annoyance in many quarters at those who worked on the assumption that the war had already been won and only the post-war world needed attention. This in part goes some way towards explaining the change in attitude between 1941 and 1943. In this connection it must be borne in mind that Whitehall was full of academics quite capable, when the time came, of doing the work that Cole was doing. Cole was probably not held in the highest esteem as a scholar by these Whitehall academics. Though he carried the title of Reader in Economics it is doubtful whether he considered himself as an economist. He was regarded as a prolific writer on Labour Party Policy and social history. Any doubts therefore which the permanent Civil Service might have had about the usefulness of his work were not likely to be put at rest by the academic temporaries in their Departments.

Second, Cole probably asked for more status for the Survey and more recognition from Departments than would have been normal even in peace-time. Oxford, with an arrogance based on its links at the top of Whitehall rather than on its academic record in the field of economic and social research, was not content to undertake useful research within the limits of war-time conditions. Cole, and no doubt others in Oxford, wanted to be assured that their views on policy carried weight. He also wanted those engaged on his research to be given a special, almost official status.

His relations with the Ministry of Labour, of which Ernest Bevin was Minister, were particularly bad. The Ministry laid it down from the outset that its divisional and local offices were much too busy with war work to afford time for the Survey and the Investigators were specifically forbidden to get in touch with them. The Ministry also refused to disclose, except to Cole, the employment figures which were treated as secret. Even the central office of the Survey was refused access to the local figures.[46]

Third, Cole both gained and lost from being a one man band. Butler could not get released until 1 January 1942 only to be taken away again after four months. So, for most of the time, Cole was Sub-Warden, Director of the Survey and Chairman of the Survey Committee. Veale wrote to Butler early in December 1942:

> I have come to the conclusion that what is wrong with the Survey is that it does not carry out the fundamental idea of a College. It is a one-sided, one-man production such as would be more appropriate to say a Department of Economics than to a College. Cole ought to have had associated with him in the final production of his documents, politicians [politics dons], and many other brands of scholar who could point out the consequences in this field of the adoption of his economic proposals.[47]

There was, however, nobody who had the time or authority or expertise to share the burden, nor even to keep a check on what was being produced. The Nuffield Committee met infrequently and until the trouble at the end of 1942 appears to have concerned itself with the Estimates and a few issues of principle raised by Cole. Several of the Visiting Fellows were very attracted by Cole, e.g. Sam Courtauld, but in large part this flowed from the success of the private conferences.

Veale minuted the Vice-Chancellor in May 1942 *a propos* of the Agenda of the Nuffield Committee: Cole says 'no reduction of any kind possible in his estimates . . It is quite useless to argue with him and [he] knows perfectly well that he can sink us by walking out on us. We can only therefore submit with a good grace covering up the surrender by asserting the need for expanding in other directions since the Warden is away'.[48]

The strain of trying to run a large show on his own in the face of much criticism seriously affected Cole's health. He had been a diabetic since 1930 and for the rest of his life worked under this physical handicap. According to his Doctor, Cole walked on a knife-edge between an excess and a deficiency of blood sugar and so finding himself in a coma. Margaret Cole[49] says that it led to him developing 'a certain feverish activity, a nervous condition which from time to time affected both his work and his judgement'. She continued:

The urge to write at top speed . . [became] firmly estblished; and though this was agreeable for the many associations and periodicals which asked him for pamphlets and articles and received them almost by return of post, there is little doubt that it affected the quality of his output. Most of the complaints . . of 'dull, dead level writing' date from 1930 onwards . . One other result was that he became more unwilling to revise or correct, and gradually less ready to accept serious criticism . . (because revision would have involved delay) and less easy as a collaborator; his own pace was now so rapid that he became impatient with those who could not keep up with him.

More seriously, the nervous strain . . did result from time to time in an uncertainty of judgement or a reaction of quick irritation which made him take sudden unpredictable actions or refuse to play.

Cole resigned his Faculty Fellowship by scribbling a note to the Registrar during a meeting of the Nuffield Committee on 4 March 1944: 'I resign my Fellowship of Nuffield College from the end of to-day's meeting.'[50]

These observations of his wife are echoed in the comments of Veale who in November 1942, wrote:

I should, I confess, look to the immediate future with a bit more confidence not only as regards Lord Nuffield but as regards the reputation of the College if Cole were a wiser man. My criticism of him is that he pours out endless memoranda, containing much which is pure gold and a great deal which I could see for myself on the subjects I understood, and which I am told by Civil Servants who are expected to use his memoranda, is just dross. He has a fatal gift of being able to dictate perfectly grammatically and with a lucid flow of argument apparently for hours on end. If he had less facility for writing and would provide less stuff, all of the best quality, which he is capable of producing his position would be absolutely unassailable. As it is, the attitude of many departments, though not all, is that they pray to be spared from his memoranda.[51]

These were not the qualities on which to build a sound academic reputation. Nor were they the qualities to carry through successfully a vast enterprise which the Survey turned out to be, involving delicate and difficult relations with a variety of Government Departments.

Fourth, the decision-making machinery with which Cole had to deal was extremely complicated. Neither the Social Reconstruction Survey Committee nor the War-time Research Committee which were largely under the control of Cole and Lindsay had final authority for expenditure. Above them were the Nuffield Committee, Hebdomadal Council and the Trustees. Recommendations were passed up and approvals or decisions passed down these three bodies. Their only common elements were the Vice-Chancellor and the Registrar, and even the former changed every three years. Cole was a member of the Nuffield Committee, along with other Fellows, but had to rely on Lindsay and Miss Grier to tell him about what was being said in Council. According to his Secretary (Mrs Broadley), two very important members of the Nuffield Committee were hostile to the Survey from the beginning. If everything had gone well the machinery would have worked. But it always offered an opportunity for obstruction and in difficult times it needed somebody with greater diplomatic skill and a less touchy person than Cole to make it work smoothly and produce the decisions he wanted.

Finally, and probably least significant, there was Lord Nuffield's attitude. As we have seen in the early stages he was ready to accept the wisdom of appointing Cole as Sub-Warden after some misgiving. Had the Survey been successful and widely approved it is probable that Nuffield would have remained of that opinion. But once criticisms came to be voiced, and there would be many to feed him with stories, his doubts returned greatly multiplied. As Veale wrote on 4 December 1942:

> Nuffield is out of humour with the College. We failed to keep alive, perhaps even to realise, the burning ardour with which he founded it. All his enthusiasm cooled during the months when nothing overt was happening and he heard nothing from us. From the time you came [he told Butler] you must share the blame for this with the rest of us, though, in fairness to you, I must add that if you had found the practice in existence you would undoubtedly have carried it on. If that had been done I believe Cole could have preached the class war from the steps of the College and Nuffield would have borne it.[52]

Veale was rather carried away in his last sentence. True, relations with Lord Nuffield would have been friendlier had there been somebody in the College, or even in the University, who had had his confidence, and had kept him informed and explained what was happening. But he did not like those who advocated socialism. This must have been a factor in his relations with Lindsay particularly after Lindsay had stood against Quintin Hogg at the Oxford By-Election of October 1938 as an Independent with Labour and Liberal support. Cole was openly political, having been associated *inter alia* with the Daily Herald, the New Statesmen and the Fabian Society; His political views received a good deal of publicity. On 19 October 1940, for example, the Oxford Mail had printed a long report of a talk Cole had given to the University Democratic Socialist Club. It was headlined 'Mr G. D. H. Cole urges Socialist methods. Tells Oxford capitalism is unable to conduct war well'. There is a story that Nuffield was greatly incensed when Montagu Norman said to him 'How is that little Kremlin you have set up?' Remarks like these and the impression that the money he had given to foster research into social and economic problems was being used to further left wing doctrines, combined with the troubles about the building, turned him against the College.

In his last memorandum to the Nuffield Committee,[53] circulated on 15 September 1943, Cole referred to Lord Nuffield's role. He recalled that the inquiry by the Vice-Chancellor and the Chairman of the Trustees was due in part to the fact that Lord Nuffield 'had expressed serious perturbation' about certain rumours unfavourable to the Survey. He made no complaint against Lord Nuffield on this score, but claimed he should have been clearly informed about the attitude of Lord Nuffield and the nature of the rumours and should have been given an opportunity of discussing the matter with the Trustees and of seeing any adverse comments on the work of the Survey. He added that on grounds of academic independence and freedom of research, the Vice-Chancellor had acted improperly in citing Lord Nuffield's perturbation to Hebdomadal Council in his report.

On grounds of fair dealing it is difficult to deny his first point. In part, however, what happened reflected the isolation of Cole in the University. As Margaret Cole wrote later: 'he did not realise, buoyed up as he was by the enthusiastic loyalty of his staff and the remarkable attendance at conferences, how serious the opposition was becoming'.[54] Politically, Cole was to the left of the great majority of those who held leading positions in the University. Of those only Lindsay and Miss Grier seemed to have been in close contact with him. Lindsay gave him general support in public but because their political views were so similar, was hardly the best to advise about the criticisms of those with opposing views. Miss Grier, who was Chairman of the Survey's Education Sub-Committee was a strong supporter certainly in the early days, for she helped to persuade him not to resign in the summer of 1941.

His second point is more debatable. The University had already displeased Lord Nuffield with the building they had proposed to erect. He had been a great benefactor and might well, if properly handled, continue to be one. Council were, therefore, entitled to be told of Nuffield's 'perturbation'. In any case the worry was widespread and the cessation of the Treasury grant would have caused some inquiry to be made. It should also be remembered that the approval of the Trustees was required for the College's expenditure. The Chairman of the Trustees, William Goodenough, was respected in the University and had close links with Lord Nuffield.

Questions of academic independence and freedom of research always rouse strong emotions. At no point is there any evidence that Lord Nuffield tried to exert any influence on the work being undertaken by or the policies being advocated by Cole. Being as Veale wrote 'out of humour with the College' he was readily shocked to hear strong criticisms of the character and quality of that work. Clearly Nuffield did not like Cole and his political views but the same could be said of many senior University members. Cole would never have been appointed Warden or even Acting Warden. Perhaps the lesson was that research into social and economic problems is difficult to separate from beliefs about the social and economic system. It is easier to separate them the less one is involved in party political controversy. At the same time there was no suggestion that memoranda prepared by the Survey were weak or unsatisfactory because they contained particular political views.

CONFERENCES

During his short period as Sub-Warden Cole produced a series of memoranda about matters other than the Survey for consideration by the Nuffield Committee. They are a testimony to his feverish energy and his fluency.

'As the Survey gets underway', Cole wrote in June 1941 'it becomes clear that the drawing up of any practical plans for social reconstruction involves making certain presuppositions of a broadly political or sociological character'. After making three assumptions about the likely post-war situation and then reflecting on the likely political set-up, he argued that from the viewpoint of the Survey the important thing was to know how far one could assume 'a broad basis of immediate consent among key persons drawn from different parties or representing different long-run points of view'. By bringing such persons together at week-end conferences Cole hoped to discover whether there would emerge 'anything in the nature of a common basic attitude to the underlying problems of social reconstruction'. The method would be less to discuss what precisely ought to be done in this or that particular field than to consider how the problem of deciding what was to be done could most fruitfully be approached. Those attending would speak more freely if they knew their words would not be quoted.

Cole therefore urged the holding of a series of small, very private conferences to be held in Oxford at week-ends, at which a few people drawn from different walks of life and from different parties and ideological groups, could frankly exchange views. The Nuffield Committee approved on the understanding that Cole would ensure that all documents were marked confidential and that publicity was avoided.[55]

The first conference was held on 4–5 October 1941 and was concerned with reconstruction problems generally. It was followed by:

2. 13–14 December 1941:
   The building industry:
   (a) The machinery and areas of planning; land acquisition and other problems.
   (b) Labour supply, training, and conditions.
   (c) The organisation of the building industry and the supply of materials.
3. 28–29 March 1942:
   The prospects and policy of British export trade in the post-war period.
4. 27–28 June 1942:
   Educational problems:
   (a) The common school.

(b) Education in relation to industry and vocation;
(c) Relation of education to other community services.
5. 26–27 September 1942:
Industry and education.
6. 12–13 December 1942:
Post-war employment policy in Great Britain.
7. 27–28 March 1943:
To what extent should girls' and boys' education follow the same lines?
8. 3–4 April 1943 (Continuation of 6th Conference):
Problems of employment and of the relations between the Government and industry after the war.
9. 11–12 September 1943:
The international aspects of post-war employment policy.
10. 25–26 September 1943:
Local Government areas.

Several Conferences were held by the College in conjunction with another body.
1. 18–19 April 1942 (with Institute of Statistics):
General Conference on international reconstruction problems.
2. 16–17 October 1942 (with Institute of Statistics and Chatham House (London)):
International agencies for economic reconstruction.
3. 10–11 April 1943 (with Institute of Agrarian Affairs):
The agricultural import policy of the United Kingdom.
4. 29–30 January 1944 (with Dartington Hall Arts Inquiry):
The place of visual arts in post-war education.

The Conferences started after tea on a Saturday, usually in the Junior Common Room at Balliol. A second session was held after dinner. On each occasion two or three were asked to open the discussion and after that anyone who wished could join in, the sessions usually lasting about two hours. Cole, as Chairman, was always careful to see that those holding different views had a chance to air them. A third session was held on the Sunday morning, usually lasting from 10 to nearly 1 o'clock. Cole summed up in the last session held immediately after lunch. There were usually 40 to 50 present, many of them staying in Balliol. Each person who spoke at any length was sent a typescript of his or her remarks and asked to approve or change them. The final 'Statement' was then worked on by Cole in consultation with one or two who had attended the Conference and sent round to all concerned for signature.

In 1943 the outcome of the proceedings of Conferences on two matters were published by the Oxford University Press as Statements: Industry and Education, and Employment Policy and the Organization of Industry after the War. The signatories, 45 in the case of that on Industry and Education, made it clear that they were not committed to every detail but strongly supported the general tenor of the recommendations and associated themselves with the underlying attitudes. The Statements studiously avoided party doctrines matching themselves more on the reports of departmental committees. They were pamphlets for the time and were widely bought.

The general verdict of those who participated was that the Conferences were a considerable success. Sir Raymond Streat, (who became a Visiting Fellow on 6 June 1944) was convinced that the College had 'discovered a new technique or procedure in the approach to social and economic problems. The bringing together of business men, administrators, and economists in the way which Nuffield College had done . . has already produced remarkable results . . .'[56]

The success was due almost entirely to the skill and enterprise of G. D. H. Cole. He was the instigator, the Chairman and the drafter of the minutes and the reports. Cole had a remarkable capacity for converting a somewhat rambling and diffuse discussion into a coherent, readable, even impressive statement of views. Margaret Cole quotes Mr Samuel Courtauld, a Visiting Fellow and an admirer of Cole: 'We have marvelled at the almost magic skill with which he produces a sentence embodying a common measure of agreement in a few lucid words in the midst of a crossfire of suggestions. His perfect fairness and suppression of any personal views have been equally remarkable'.[57]

The Conferences satisfied a need by providing a platform for thought about the post-war outside the overwhelming mass of the official machine. They were not particulary liked by Ministers or senior Whitehall who were touchy at attempts to produce a policy for the post-war world whilst they were spending all their time in winning the war. In October 1942 the Treasury decided that Civil Servants should not accept invitations to attend conferences of this kind. But this ban was never wholly operative. The conferences concerned with full employment policy became a platform for Beveridge and so came within the conflict between him and the Government about who should produce such a policy.

8 Emergence of Nuffield College

Though Lindsay, Cole and others referred to Nuffield College as though it were a recognisable and effective entity it did not really come into existence until 1944–45 after the Scheme of Delegation had been put into operation, Henry Clay had been appointed Warden, and several full time Official Fellows had been elected.

THE SCHEME OF DELEGATION

The Trust Deed vested the College and its endowments in the hands of Hebdomadal Council. Nothing was vested in the hands of Warden and Fellows, which by tradition would have been the governing body of the College. It was appreciated, however, that Council was not the most suitable body to manage a College and its research activities. The Trust Deed, therefore, provided that Council could delegate all or any of its powers under the Trust to a Committee or to the Warden or to the Warden and Fellows but not, however, divest itself legally of its ultimate responsibility. The Nuffield College Committee gave early attention to preparing a Scheme of Delegation. In one sense the problem was quite limited – it was to decide to which body or bodies should be delegated Council's powers, and in particular what powers should be vested in the Warden and Fellows as the potential governing body of the embryo College. To Lindsay, however, the Scheme had to take account of the wider purposes of the Benefaction, as he saw it. Lindsay remained as Vice-Chancellor until October 1938. For almost a year, therefore, by virtue of office, knowledge of the subject, and the major voice in the terms of the Benefaction, he was well-placed to lead the discussions and to influence the University's thinking. Even when he ceased to be Vice-Chancellor he remained a major figure in any discussion of the development of the College and the carrying out of Lord Nuffield's Benefaction.

Lindsay's general ideas about the role of the Benefaction and of the College in the provision of teaching and the research in social studies emerged in February 1938 when he circulated a Memorandum on Financial Policy to the Nuffield Committee.[1] It was estimated that the annual income of the Benefaction, after the buildings had been completed, would be about £21 000. Of this, £7550 had already been allocated, e.g. £2200 for a Warden and £2000 for Students, leaving £13 450 for further consideration.

In deciding how to allocate this substantial sum Lindsay stressed, as a fundamental consideration, that Lord Nuffield had not intended the College to be used 'merely to enlarge the opportunities for the kind of research which is at present carried on in the University'. In the field of social research the College, he claimed 'will be used for two complementary and distinguishable purposes... most easily distinguishable by the source of the direction of the research'.

The first purpose was to enable the University teachers and others to research more effectively, i.e. the College would provide the equipment and help to enable them to do more comprehensively the kind of work which had been done during the last two and a half years under the Social Studies Research Committee. The second purpose would come from the non-academic Fellows who would ask the College to undertake pieces of research for which, by its equipment and its powers of effecting co-operation between academic and non-academic persons, it would be particularly fitted. The Warden was certain to be particularly concerned with this part of the College's work and he suggested £4000 a year should be kept in hand for it.

This left £9450, of which he estimated £1000 would be needed for the maintenance, heating, lighting, etc., of the non-residential part of the College. The remainder he proposed to allocate as follows:

(a) £1000 over and above the current cost for an Institute of Statistics 'which would be available for all branches of studies carried on in the College, though naturally it would be most used by the Economists'. This followed a recommendation of the Standing Sub-Committee on research that the Institute should be included in Nuffield College.

(b) £1250 a year for library staff of the College.

(c) £3525 to be available to the Economists and £2675 for the Politics teachers who, through their appropriate organs, were to suggest how the money might usefully be allocated in detail. They were to be told that they would find provided by the College: (i) a fully furnished library and staff; (ii) a statistical institute with computing equipment and a staff to work it; and (iii) research rooms, conference rooms and common rooms.

Each group would be expected to include in their proposals provision for: (i) Fellows, including a certain minimum number of Visiting Fellows (he suggested five each); (ii) books; (iii) research assistants and clerks; and (iv) special equipment not provided as part of the basic services.

It was tempting, he said, for Politics Fellows to suggest that the £6200 should be divided equally between Economics and Politics. But Politics would be able to rely on the Bodleian for library facilities to a far greater extent than the economists. The Politics side also had just benefited by an extra £3500 a year provided by the Rhodes Trust Endowment. As the cost of books for the economists had been estimated at £1700 per annum he proposed to allocate them half (£850) more than for Politics otherwise they would absorb the total cost of books needed in the College.

Each group would have to consider which posts now provided out of the grant from the Rockefeller Foundation, must go on and which new posts should be added at this stage. So the Social Studies Board were invited to appoint two consultative committees — one for Economics and one for Politics — to confer with the Nuffield Committee. That for Economics was composed of Professor D. H. Macgregor, G. D. H. Cole, R. L. Hall, R. F. Harrod, and Redvers Opie and that for Politics, Professors Sir Alfred Zimmern and R. Coupland, Lucy Sutherland, R. C. K. Ensor, J. S. Fulton, R. B. McCallum and J. P. R. Maud. The Research Sub-Committee of the Nuffield Committee had various discussions with these two consultative bodies from which emerged the views of the Economics and Politics sides of the Faculty on such matters as the number and character of appointments to Fellowships.

A similar two-level approach occurred in the discussions about the kind of and amount of accommodation required in the building. The resulting schedule covered both College and University needs. The College requirements took account of its special features, e.g. 16 visitors sets of two rooms each, a conference hall to hold 250 in addition to a dining hall to hold 120; forty research rooms, and sets for Fellows and Students. The Architect was also asked to provide accommodation for an Institute of Statistics (thirty to fifty rooms being mentioned at various times) and for part of the work of Barnett House (about four rooms).

There was a certain air of unreality in these early discussions. The Benefaction was being paid in thirteen equal half-yearly instalments and so would not reach its full amount and yield until the end of 1943. Assuming the building of the Physical Chemistry Laboratory and of the College went ahead quickly the early instalments would be needed for that purpose. In the event, as a result of the rejection of the Architect's plans and the War, the first small part of College accommodation was not available until 1950, by which time the financial situation had greatly changed. The discussions in the Nuffield Committee during 1938–39 are interesting as evidence of the interplay of ideas stimulated by the Benefaction rather than as the shape of things to come.

The Scheme of Delegation took well over a year to prepare and get agreed, being approved, but not implemented, by Hebdomadal Council on 19 May 1939. There was a clash of opinions on the extent of the powers which should be delegated to the Warden and Fellows and on the role which the sub-Faculties of Economics and Politics should be given. In the end the agreed Scheme contained three features.[2]

1. A Nuffield Committee was to continue to be appointed by Council and was to be composed of the Vice-Chancellor and the Warden of Nuffield, six members of Convocation, of whom at least three had to be members of Council, and at least two had to be members of the Board of the Faculty of Social Studies, and three Fellows nominated by the Warden and Fellows of whom at least one had to be a Visiting Fellow. It was stressed that the Warden and Fellows should always be in a minority on the Committee.

The powers of Hebdomadal Council under the Trust Deed were to be delegated to this Committee except for the duty to submit estimates to the Trustees, and Council retained the power to appoint the Warden. The Nuffield Committee was empowered to appoint Fellows of the College after consultation with the

Warden and Fellows and to consider and approve for submission to Council the annual estimates submitted to it by the Warden and Fellows.
2. The Scheme empowered the Warden and Fellows to appoint Students, the Bursar, the Librarian and other necessary officers and servants but their appointment of the Chaplain required the confirmation of Council.

The point which proved most troublesome arose out of Lindsay's opinion[3] that: 'The two-fold character of Nuffield College as a novel experiment in social research and an extension of the research already done by the University' could best be safeguarded in the constitution by the 'co-operative experiment being the special concern of the Warden and Fellows and general care of social research in the University the concern of the [Nuffield] Committee' which would take the place of the Social Studies Research Committee. The two bodies would 'interpenetrate' but the two rather different jobs were likely to be better done if there was that sort of demarcation of functions. The primary job of the Nuffield Committee, once the Warden and Fellows were appointed, would be the allocation of finance to the several parts of the whole scheme. This was the reason why he proposed that a fixed annual sum of £4000 should be made available to the Warden and Fellows.

The proposal brought strong comment from Harold Butler,[4] the Warden elect. He said

> The distinction between the use of Nuffield College for cooperative research with the aid of the 'outside world' and its use as an instrument of research by the University does not appear to be tenable. There cannot be two kinds of economic research going on in Oxford simultaneously and independently 'Nuffield research' and University research, the former perhaps eyed askance by the University and the latter regarded as theoretical by the 'outside world'. All economic research ought to be University research, planned and carried out in accordance with the highest scientific standards.

This implied that the Economics Faculty should be 'strongly represented in Nuffield itself and on whatever body is set up to control and direct research'.

Butler thought that there seemed 'some distrust of the "Warden and Fellows", which is natural seeing that they are still an abstraction'. There also seemed to be

> some mistrust of the intrusion of non-academic persons into an academic institution, which the College must be if it is to be anything at all. These distrusts are no doubt largely responsible for the tendency to divide the College into two watertight compartments, one controlled by the University and removed from the purview of the Warden and Fellows, the other relegated to the latter, for whose activities the University would only assume a secondary and mitigated responsibility.

He went on: 'If such a conception were to be carried into practice, it would largely frustrate Lord Nuffield's aim of fostering co-operation "between the scholar and the man of affairs". There was no real danger that the non-academic element will overshadow the academic element. On the contrary, owing to the limitation of time from which the former will necessarily suffer, the converse is much more likely. But unless dualism can be avoided at the start' he doubted 'whether the essential purposes of the foundation can ever be achieved'.

Lindsay's distinction was, however, retained. The Scheme agreed by Council in May 1939 envisaged an annual sum of £4000 being placed at the disposal of the Warden and Fellows 'for the promotion of co-operation between the academic and the non-academic elements in the College and the support of research . . .' The Warden and Fellows could in addition submit estimates for expenditure on research in Economics and Politics after consideration of the proposals of the sub-Committees on these two subjects appointed by the Faculty Board.

3. The first draft of the Scheme required the Nuffield Committee to appoint three sub-committees (1) for an Institute of Statistics, (2) on Politics, and (3) on Economics. However in view of the insistence of those concerned with the Institute that it should be managed quite independently of the College, the sub-committee proposed for that purpose was dropped. The Warden of Nuffield was to be Chairman of the sub-committees which were also to contain at least two Fellows of the College (one of whom had to be a Visiting Fellow) and three elected by the sub-Faculty. Their duties were (a) to submit to the Warden and Fellows estimates for expenditure on research, including the purchase of books and

periodicals and (b) to advise the Warden and Fellows an matters relating to teaching or research and on the use of the Institute of Statistics as an instrument of research in Economics or Politics.

Though Council agreed the Scheme in May 1939 it was not brought into operation. The Interim Nuffield Committee was, however, reconstituted to include the Warden and the dozen Faculty and Visiting Fellows first elected in July 1939. They outnumbered the Vice-Chancellor and the six members appointed by Council. But the Committee still only had the power to make recommendations, Council retaining the final authority.

In November 1941 the Nuffield Committee decided to ask Council to put the Scheme of Delegation into operation with such qualifications as the special circumstances of the war might make necessary. They had been annoyed by Council's comments[5] that 'any further development of research should aim at concentration rather than diffusion'. They resolved that while they were willing to make any arrangements which would enable Council to understand more in detail what the College was doing they considered it 'inexpedient that Council should control the research of the College' in a way which Council's comments suggested. They invited Council to appoint three representatives to discuss with three members of the Committee 'the questions of principle and procedure relating to the conduct of research raised by Council's communication'.[6]

The representatives reported in May 1942.[7] The Nuffield Committee representatives were now inclined to suggest that Council should now delegate to them the entire supervision of research seeing that they were a committee of Council and contained members specially appointed by Council to represent it. Nevertheless they agreed that definite limits must be set to the delegation even of such functions. This followed from the duty of Council under the Trust Deed to submit estimates to the Trustees and this could not be delegated. 'Indeed, it was part of the original intention that the College should be a University instrument of research, and it must, in that case, be subject to the same kind of financial control as [was] exercised over Departments by the General Board of Faculties, the control of the College being somewhat stricter because of the terms of the Trust Deed'.

The two sets of representatives agreed, however, that the subjects with which the College dealt were both technical and controversial and as Council was less of a technical body than the General Board it was of great importance that the College should have freedom in research. Council in carrying out its duties in approving the programmes of the College should bear this in mind. The joint committee were convinced that some of the difficulties which had arisen in respect of the Social Reconstruction Survey might have been avoided if Council members of the Nuffield Committee had been more fully prepared with the answers to the questions raised in Council. They suggested that any enquiries which Council wished to make about the work of the College or the execution of its programmes should normally be made through its representatives on the Committee.

The issue was examined afresh by another joint committee which reported in October 1943.[8] They seized on the 'curious provision' in the Trust Deed which imposed on Council the duty of preparing draft estimates for submission to the Trustees. 'Control of finance means control of policy, and if Council is to control policy through finance, how can there be any autonomous research'. The answer they saw in the Scheme of Delegation whereby a sum of money was placed at the disposal of the Warden and Fellows for certain general purposes. Once that was settled the amount of any interference possible through the estimates was inconsiderable.

The joint committee recognised that as long as the war lasted the College could not even begin to take its final shape. Nevertheless, particularly having regard to the conspicuously successful organisation of Conferences, the College had started work on lines intended by the Founder. They recommended, therefore, that the Scheme should be brought into effect at once except for those parts relating to the Institute of Statistics.

The Nuffield Committee gave their support. On 27 February 1944 Council agreed to bring the Scheme into operation subject to two modifications.[9]

(1) It was made clear that the appointment of the Warden remained in the hands of Council. It was also decided that appointment of an acting or sub-Warden should remain with Council until a Warden was appointed.
(2) It also seemed reasonable that during some interim period Council should be free to appoint its six members of the Committee without the limitation that two of them should be members of the Board of the Faculty of Social Studies. As Lindsay explained to Austin Lane Poole[10] at the time,

The Board ... is extremely attenuated at the present time, as is the Faculty, and the retention of that clause ... might easily involve that the representatives of the Warden and Fellows would be in a majority and not – as the scheme of delegation clearly intended – a minority on the Statutory Committee.

The Scheme of Delegation came into operation on 4 March 1944 and, with a few subsequent changes the College entered into a formal structure of government which was to last until June 1958. The Nuffield College Committee was reconstituted and was now composed of eleven members: two were ex officio – the Vice-Chancellor and the Warden; six were appointed by Council, of whom at least three had to be members of Council; and three were nominated by Warden and Fellows, of whom at least one had to be a Visiting Fellow.

THE WARDEN AND FELLOWS

Henry Clay became Warden on 1 October 1944. He read Greats at Univ. but failing to gain a First he did not at first seek an academic appointment. He had attended Professor Edgeworth's lectures and was amused to recall that there were only three present at the first lecture, two at the second, and only himself at the third, whereupon Edgeworth invited Clay to his rooms to talk Economics. He was Fellow of New College, 1919–21, and became Stanley Jevons Professor of Political Economy at Manchester University in 1922. He exchanged this post for a new Chair of Social Economics which relieved him of administrative duties, resigning in 1930 to become an adviser at the Bank of England. He was unpretentious and clear-headed and had a wealth of experience of Universities, the City, and Whitehall. He also had the great advantage of not having been involved in the quarrels and in-fighting that had bedevilled the early years of Nuffield's Benefaction.

After six months' experience in office Henry Clay asked the Nuffield Committee to reconsider two provisions of the Scheme.[11] The first was that which empowered the setting up of Sub-Committees on Politics and Economics to advise the Warden and Fellows on matters relating to research in their fields and on the use of the Institute of Statistics. He understood (not quite accurately) this was originally incorporated when it was intended to merge the Institute of Statistics in the College. This was no longer intended. Even without that change the arrangement would have been inconvenient 'since it would have involved the executive and research staff of the College acting in the same field for two independent directing committees'. It being understood that the Social Studies Board agreed, the Nuffield Committee recommended Council to delete the Section which set up the two Sub-Committees.

In that same connection Clay suggested the deletion of the provision, held over until his views had been obtained, whereby at least two of the six members appointed by Council should be members of the Social Studies Board. 'Technical questions calling for the expert knowledge of members of the Faculty will normally be settled by Warden and Fellows, and the Faculty can make its wishes felt at that level through Faculty and Professorial Fellows; at the level of this Committee [i.e. the Nuffield Committee] discussion will turn on matters of general principle, and a repetition of the technical discussions at the earlier level is on the whole undesirable.' This was also agreed.

The second provision was that which drew a distinction between expenditure on 'the promotion of co-operation between the academic and non-academic elements in the College' and 'expenditure on research after consideration of the proposals submitted' by the Politics and Economics Sub-Committees of the Nuffield Committee. While recognising the value of leaving the Warden and Fellows a field in which to spend at their discretion he saw practical difficulties in carrying out the College's work in two compartments. The type of research was not sufficiently differentiated by reference to co-operation with non-academic elements in the College. Visiting Fellows were not likely to be expert in the actual work of research. But their help would be invaluable in giving access to fields of practical experience and commenting on questions in the light of their own experience. This help should be available for any work done by or through the College. Clay's 'expectation and hope' was that 'the planning of research programmes' would in practice 'be left entirely to Warden and Fellows, who will only have to satisfy the [Nuffield] Committee that the programme is within the terms of the College's Trust and the proposed expenditure both within the College's capacity and reasonable in itself'. The Nuffield Committee agreed to recommend that a new sub-section would be substituted to the effect that the Warden and Fellows should include an estimate for expenditure on research among other items in the budget they were submitting to the Committee. Council agreed to the changes. Some months later doubts were expressed, whether under the Statute Council could legally delegate the power of the appointment of Fellows. In view of that doubt the Statute was amended in Congregation on 19 November 1946. This stated that 'Council shall appoint the Warden and Fellows' then went on 'Council may delegate the appointment of Fellows to the Committee referred to in Clause 14(a) [i.e. the Nuffield College Committee]. The Committee shall in that case consult the Warden and Fellows'.[12]

Henry Clay was not dissatisfied by the position thus attained by the College. In March 1945 he said he could not judge whether any other changes were needed 'until the College has acquired a larger number of Official Fellows, and, with their advice available, has framed its policy'. But, he went on, it did not seem that the Scheme, revised as he had suggested

> would restrict or obstruct the development of the College in any desirable direction. The [Nuffield] Committee would still be able to discharge its responsibility to Council for the general oversight and control of the College, through its power to approve an annual budget and to appoint Fellows. The Warden and Fellows, on the other hand, could frame their own programmes and policy freely within the limits set by the income available and the restriction of the College by its Trust Deed to post-graduate studies and research primarily in the social sciences. The relation of the College with the Institute of Statistics, if this is not to be absorbed, has to be re-defined; but this must wait on a decision by the University on the future of the Institute. There may be a need arising out of the same change of plans to define relations with the Faculty of Social Studies; but this also must wait, and in any case need not involve fresh legislation.[13]

When the Scheme of Delegation was put into operation there were 19 Fellows: one Official, eight Faculty, six Visiting and four Professorial. The Warden and Fellows held their first formal meeting on 19 March 1944 but had already met informally in

January and February. At the February meeting the difficulty of the Visiting Fellows having the time or inclination to attend meetings in Oxford concerned only with the day to day running of the College was recognised. It was decided that the 'Resident Fellows' should form an Executive Committee. By June this was referred to as an Executive and General Purposes Committee to deal with finance, staff, publications and general purposes subject to the approval of the Warden and Fellows.

The next development was brought about by the election of a number of Official Fellows: Michael Fogarty in August 1944, David Champernowne in February 1945; D. N. Chester in November 1945; J. R. Hicks and A. Loveday in 1946. In July 1946 therefore the Executive Committee was reconstituted; in future it was to be composed of the Warden and the Official Fellows with one Professorial and one Faculty Fellow. This was an important shift of power to the full time Fellows, a shift that was emphasised as more Official Fellows were elected: P. W. S. Andrews and T. Barna (1947); Hugh Clegg, Michael Oakeshott and Kenneth Robinson (1949), and P. M. Williams (1950).

Increasingly the government of the College passed into the hand of the full-time Fellows, a development reflected in the relations between the Warden and Fellows and the other three bodies which legally had a voice in the conduct of the College. Though the Warden and Fellows were in a minority on the Nuffield College Committee it was their recommendations which came to constitute the main business of the Committee and which came to be approved with little or no questioning. The same attitude came to be adopted by Hebdomadal Council and the Trustees.

The problems encountered with the Social Reconstruction Survey had shown that neither Hebdomadal Council nor its Nuffield College Committee were suited to bear responsibility for or even generally control the diverse activities of a College. These bodies were only too glad to rely on the judgement and advice of Henry Clay. He on his part was clear that the College could be effective only if it could attract an able body of full-time scholars who would be left free to develop their own affairs. In May 1944 when asked for his comments on a proposal to increase the number of Faculty Fellows permitted by the Statute Clay replied that he would be sorry to see the balance of Faculty and Official Fellows altered. Faculty Fellows were at that time normally fellows of other Colleges. He went on: 'the Official Fellows must constitute the core of the College . . . and it would be running the risk of failing to secure adequate consideration of the College's needs on occasion if this core is reduced further'.[14] His policy and attitude were continued by his successors A. Loveday (1950–54) and D. N. (Norman) Chester (1954–78), and indeed to the present day.

The terms and conditions of the Official Fellowships were attractive to scholars of all ages. There was no obligation to teach undergraduates, give lectures or seminars or supervise graduates. The primary obligation was to undertake research and the College provided secretarial and research assistance and other facilities not usually provided by Colleges nor for that matter adequately provided by the University in the immediate post-war years. It became usual, however, for these Fellows to engage in a limited amount of tutorial teaching and to hold seminars. They were, therefore, a welcome addition to the resources of the Social Studies Faculty, particularly at a time when most Tutorial Fellows were heavily loaded with undergraduate teaching.

Inevitably the College developed a reputation for research in certain areas, for example, Trade Union Studies and Industrial Relations started by Hugh Clegg, Electoral Studies developed by David Butler, African Studies by Margery Perham, and Social and Occupational Mobility by John Goldthorpe and Chelly Halsey. The work of the distinguished group of Economists did not lend itself to particular programmes or themes, their work covering a wide range of topics as they applied their analytical tools to different aspects of the Economy.

The academic resources of the College were strengthened by the occasional election to Professorial or Faculty Fellowships of a few of the University appointments in its field. But unlike as envisaged in the early years of the Benefaction these were seldom also Fellows of other Colleges, indeed after 1958 dual allegiances were no longer permitted by the College Statutes.

The election of Visiting Fellows from the world of practical affairs, Parliament, Civil and Local Government Service, Trade Unions, Commerce and Industry, continued to be a feature of the College. It cannot be claimed, however, that this worked in the way originally envisaged by Lindsay. It is very useful for an academic engaged on a particular piece of research to have ready access to those with practical and inside knowledge of that subject.

To have these 'insiders' as members of the College makes such access easier. But the circumstances of the 50s and 60s were very different from those apparently obtaining in the 30s. Then it seemed to be accepted that Oxford teachers lived rather in an Ivory Tower, with little knowledge of and contact with the world of government and industry. The War changed that, for a large number of academics became temporary civil servants, and some remained permanently in Whitehall. Ministers, civil servants, banks and many organisations turned to academics for advice. The problem, so far as the College was concerned, was not to bring the Fellows into touch with the world of practical affairs, but to prevent them becoming completely immersed in that world.

A major feature of the College with a significance not clearly seen in the discussions at the time of its founding has been the small body of graduate Students. The provision of accommodation in College, and of a variety of research facilities, together with the opportunity to be a member of a small group, about fifty, of graduates in social studies enabled the College to attract many very able candidates. The success can be seen in the substantial number of Oxford Fellowships and teaching posts in other universities gained by former Students. The College also had the initial advantage of being the first mixed Oxford or Cambridge College.

The building of the College proceeded slowly owing to the tight licensing control. Though the Foundation Stone was laid in April 1949 it was not until July 1955 that work could commence on the greatly reduced Hall and the Library block at which date five staircases and the part originally envisaged as the Warden's lodgings were available for occupation. The first meal in the Hall was served on 6 June 1958. The College became residential for men students in October 1958 and for Students of both sexes a year later. In 1956 the Nuffield Foundation accepted a suggestion from Lord Nuffield and made a grant of £200 000 to enable the building to be completed by 1960. At that date it provided accommodation for a Warden and some 25 Fellows and for some 33 graduate Students as well as a Library for some 30 000 volumes, including G. D. H. Cole's large collection of books, which the College had purchased in 1949, a dining hall and kitchens, seminar and lecture rooms.

The growth of the building went along with moves that

increased the independence of the College. In 1956 Hebdomadal Council agreed that proceedings should commence to give Nuffield the status of College in the Oxford meaning of the term. To achieve this various steps had to be taken of which the most difficult was to set aside the Trust Deed of October 1937. As explained earlier this placed the endowment and the College in the hands of Hebdomadal Council whereas to be a College this and other matters had to be vested in the governing body of the College. The High Court had to agree to such a transfer, in effect setting aside the machinery of the Trust Deed though not, of course, its objects. The path was smoothed by the Founder, still in vigorous health, giving his full support to the change. On 29 July 1957, Mr. Justice Upjohn agreed that, should the College be incorporated by Royal Charter, the Court would approve an Order authorising the transfer to it of the property and powers vested in Council by the Trust Deed. Hebdomadal Council applied to Her Majesty in Council for the grant of a Royal Charter which was granted on 14 March 1958, the Charter being dated 18 April 1958. The Court Order was made on 5 June and the College then took its place beside the independent Oxford Colleges, many of them of ancient foundation. The change relieved the College of a good deal of complicated machinery (the Trustees, for example, disappeared) and placed fairly and squarely on the shoulders of the Warden and Fellows responsibility for its continued success and development. The College could now matriculate students whereas hitherto it had to reply on other Colleges to perform this essential admission procedure.

The status granted to the College reflected in part the new interest in the concept of the 'graduate college'. In his Oration of October 1945[15] the Vice-Chancellor, Richard Livingstone, said the postgraduate studies might be expected to increase in coming years and take new forms. The University had long felt the want of a centre which might do for postgraduate students what Rhodes House did for Rhodes scholars. Colleges, he went on, were centres for undergraduates and for those of their graduate members who stayed on for further study. 'But those who came from outside to do post-graduate work in Oxford ... are apt to have little share in the life of the Colleges of which they become members, and no ready opportunity of contact with students pursuing advanced work in the same field ...' He announced that the University had purchased 62 Woodstock Road (a Convent) which it proposed to use as a postgraduate centre. The centre became known as Halifax House.

In 1948, however, Antonin Besse, an Aden business man, offered to found a College primarily for graduate studies to be entitled St Antony's College. Originally envisaged as being housed in Wytham Abbey, it ultimately came to take over the Convent buildings and site in the Woodstock Road, Halifax House moving to 6–7 South Parks Road. It is noticeable that the University had learnt from problems created by vesting a College in Hebdomadal Council. From the earliest stage it was made clear that the intention was to found an academic institution which should in due course acquire the full status of a College. Formal arrangements were therefore made for the College to be managed in its early years by a Council on which the University was represented. In May 1950 St Antony's was given the status of a New Foundation and in April 1953 received a Royal Charter. Its reception was greatly eased by the founder making £250 000 available for distribution among the poorer men's Colleges.

It is noteworthy that both Nuffield and St Antony's were commented upon favourably by the Report of the Commission of Inquiry under the Chairmanship of Lord Franks in 1966. They had, the Report said, 'been the pace-setters for the whole body of Colleges. What they do has immediate repercussions upon the "traditional" Colleges'. Nuffield, it said, had 'developed special techniques for dealing with post-graduate work and the whole range of Social Studies; its seminars have brought Oxford social scientists into touch with each other and with men of distinction from outside Oxford to their mutual benefit'. St Antony's, the Report said 'has shown how specialization on particular areas (e.g. European Studies, Latin American Studies) can enable a College to stimulate minds in every part of the academic community'.[16]

And so notwithstanding the early troubled years of its origins Nuffield College developed into a major element in the Social Studies Faculty. It is pleasing to be able to record that its Founder came increasingly to appreciate the contribution which his College was making. When he died in August 1963 he made the College his residuary legatee, leaving it his home and personal effects and the still substantial remains of his wealth.

9 Training for Social Work

The first move to provide a course of training for social workers came in October 1913 from the Social and Political Studies Association, composed of dons and others interested in social problems, such as Sidney Ball, W. G. S. Adams, W. M. Geldart, L. R. Phelps, Miss C. V. Butler and A. J. Carlyle. A Certificate was awarded by the Association to candidates who had taken the Diploma and had pursued a course of training for at least twelve months to the satisfaction of the Committee of the Association. The course was in two parts. First, the study and observation in Oxford, for not less than two terms, of the working of such institutions as the Oxford City and Oxfordshire County Councils, the Poor Law Guardians, the Courts, local Friendly and Co-operative Societies and Trade Unions. Second, either (a) a course of supervised practical work in connection with a Settlement or some organisation engaged in social work and a report thereon or (b) a special enquiry and report as to some problem of rural or urban conditions.

THE ROLE OF BARNETT HOUSE

This arrangement was very soon overtaken by the establishment of Barnett House. It is indeed impossible to write about the development of training for social work at Oxford without dealing with the major contribution made by Barnett House.

When Canon Barnett died in 1913 his many friends and admirers felt that his life and the ideas for which he had worked should be commemorated. He had inspired the Settlement movement and had been Warden of Toynbee Hall. He had been active in every campaign for improving the conditions and education of the working classes. In February 1914, therefore, an Appeal was launched for money for (a) a centre in Oxford and

(b) a Fellowship attached to Toynbee Hall. The former resulted in a house at the Exeter College corner of Broad Street and Turl Street, called Barnett House. This was to have three objects. The first was to advance social and economic studies at Oxford by the provision of better facilities: the Appeal was headed 'Social Studies in Oxford'. 'A specialised library, collecting and co-ordinating material for study and investigation' was required and could be provided in a set of rooms that would be available in the House. Second, the House would become a permanent centre in Oxford for the Settlement movement, and would be in close touch with the opportunities afforded by Settlement life and work in different centres. The third object was to further the work of the Tutorial Classes Committee in Oxford.

It is not surprising that the Appeal echoed some of the ideas in the report of the joint Committee on Oxford and Working Class Education for it was signed by three members of that Committee: T. B. Strong, Dean of Christ Church; Sidney Ball and A. L. Smith. Other signatures were of dons active in developing the Diploma, e.g. Professor W. G. S. Adams and L. R. Phelps.

Barnett House was formally launched in the Hall of Balliol College by Lord Bryce, in June 1914. He said that one of the most noticeable features of modern Oxford was the increasing interest taken by senior and junior members of the University in social problems. It was the home of living causes. On undergraduate bookshelves Blue-books were found side by side with Herodotus and Thucydides.

The Appeal had hardly been launched when war broke out. It raised sufficient to buy the house but there does not appear to have been much money available for other things. By the time Peace returned no doubt memories of Canon Barnett had been obscured by more recent happenings. Anyhow a small but useful library was provided and rooms were available for various activities. Increasingly Barnett House became associated with the training of social workers.

Early in 1917 the Social and Political Studies Association agreed to merge with Barnett House, the latter agreeing to carry on the work of the Association's Social Training Committee providing satisfactory arrangements could be made about the Certificate.

It is, of course, unusual in a University for an academic award, if only a Certificate, to be granted by a body not part of the University. The obvious University body that might perform this function was the Diploma Committee and in 1918 this announced that the Barnett House scheme of training had received its approval. In the following year the University granted the Committee power to issue a Certificate in Social Training to candidates considered to have pursued a satisfactory course of training.[1]

The qualifications required for admission to the award of the Certificate were somewhat vague at first. The Diploma Committee were probably more concerned to encourage people to take the course than to put high entrance qualifications in the way. In 1924, however, a new Regulation stated that the course consisted of:

(1) three terms' work in Oxford under Supervisors approved by the Committee for Economics and Political Science; and
(2) either (a) a period of supervised practical work in connexion with some approved organization or organizations for social or industrial work, or (b) an inquiry into some problem of rural or urban conditions or administration in a selected district with a report thereon.

Also for the first time candidates were told that they must possess the Diploma in Economics and Political Science. In 1926 the possession of Honours in the Oxford Schools of either Modern History or Philosophy, Politics and Economics, were made alternative basic qualifications.

The number awarded the Certificate was quite small, two or three a year in the pre-1939 period. In 1933 the University agreed that the Certificate could be awarded with a Distinction.

The Diploma was extended in 1936 to meet the needs of another group – principally officials in local and central government. The Hadow Report on the Training and Recruitment of Local Government Officers had in 1934 emphasised the value of Diploma courses in public administration and many Universities were providing such courses. Manchester University even had a degree in Public Administration which could be taken in the evenings and so was attractive to local government officers. In Oxford John Maud was particularly interested in providing such training and had the support of senior City and County officials. It was also thought that a new Diploma in Public and Social

Administration would provide a better alternative to the confusing and unattractive combination of Diploma in Economics and Political Science and Certificate in Training for Social Work.

As and from October 1936[2] there were to be two Diplomas – in Economics and Political Science and in Public and Social Administration. They were covered by the same Regulations. These listed six General Papers and nine Special Subjects and prescribed which combination was required for each Diploma and for the Certificate. The six General Papers were:

(a) British Social and Economic History from 1760.
(b) The Constitutional History of England from 1688; and Modern Political Organisation.
(c) Theory of the State.
(d) Economic Theory.
(e) Modern Economic Organisation.
(f) Public and Social Administration.

The Special Subjects included Public Finance; Local Government since 1760; Statistical Method; Currency and Credit; Social and Industrial Psychology and Administrative Law.

For the Diploma in Economics and Political Science candidates had to take the first five General Papers and one Special Subject. A Special Subject not listed could be taken with the Committee's approval. Also in lieu of a Special Subject a Candidate could offer a dissertation not exceeding 12 000 words. For the Diploma in Public and Social Administration they had to take (a), (b), (c) and (f) of the General Papers and a Special Subject. In addition candidates for this Diploma had either to submit a thesis of between 10 000 and 20 000 words on a first-hand investigation into some problems of public or social administration and to satisfy the Committee that they had undertaken a short period of approved work; or to undertake 3 to 9 months of supervised practical work in connection with some approved organisation or organisations and to submit a written report on the work showing power of observation and analysis. For the Certificate in Public Administration candidates had to take (b) and (f) of the General Papers and Local Government since 1760 of the Special Subjects and submit and essay of about 5000 words on some current problem of public administration. Successful candidates for the Certificate could subsequently qualify for the Diploma by taking two further General Papers (a) and (c) and by complying with the requirements as to practical work and thesis or report.

As the majority of the candidates for the new Diploma and Certificate would be living in or around Oxford they did not need residential accommodation. For this and other reasons they were quite unlike the ordinary undergraduates admitted by way of one of the Colleges. It was therefore agreed that Barnett House should be given the right, which Ruskin College had enjoyed since 1913 and the Catholic Workers (now Plater) College since 1926, to enter names on the University Register of candidates for a Diploma or Certificate and become responsible for the preparation of these particular candidates.

First examined in June 1937 the new Diploma did not reduce the demand for the old one, there being 41 and 40 candidates for the latter in 1938 and 1939. In the former year there were 14 candidates for the Diploma in Public and Social Administration and 7 in 1939 all of whom passed. Of these 21 candidates 9 were put forward by Barnett House. There were 7 candidates for the Certificate in Public Administration in the same two years, all except one being prepared by Barnett House.

Barnett House, like Ruskin and the Catholic Workers College, did not receive any money from the University: they were voluntary bodies not under the control of the University. But Barnett House had closer links with the University than had the other two. Its Memorandum and Articles of Association provided for its affairs to be administered by a Council appointed by various bodies including one each by Hebdomadal Council and the Committee for Economics and Political Science. The Drummond Professor of Political Economy and the Gladstone Professor of Government and Public Administration were members ex-officio. Though these members served in their individual capacities and not as representatives they provided a link with the University.

Until 1935 Barnett House and the training of social workers did not cost the University a penny. The library was maintained mainly out of annual donations, most of which were made by Colleges. Miss Violet Butler, strongly imbued with the traditions of middle-class voluntary service, directed the courses for some 20 years without any payment. In 1935 the University allocated £300 a year out of its Rockefeller grant to Barnett House for social training work. In that year the original house at the corner of Broad Street and Turl Street was sold and 14 years lease of 34–5 Beaumont Street was purchased and so provided a new home.

In 1936 the Council of Barnett House decided to undertake a study of the social services both statutory and voluntary in Oxford and adjacent areas. They established a Survey Committee with Warden Adams as Chairman, Miss A. F. C. Bourdillon as Editor and Organising Secretary and Miss (later Dame) Elizabeth Ackroyd as Research Assistant. The work was made possible by a grant of £1500 made by the University out of the Rockefeller grant.

The Survey produced two main volumes, in 1938 and 1940.[3] Chapters were contributed mainly by various Oxford dons, for example, by Robert Hall on Unemployment; and R. F. Bretherton on Local Government Finance. Small sub-committees were responsible for the Sections on the Personal Health Services and for Town and Country Planning. The enterprise was a triumph for Barnett House and another sign that, at least so far as Social Studies were concerned, the University was actively prepared to use its learning for the benefit of the everyday world.

These contributions from the University were in part a recognition that some of the work done at Barnett House was properly a University function. In part, however, they reflected the harsh fact that the Council of Barnett House were finding it increasingly difficult to finance its activities. This point came up when the University considered the large Benefaction made by Lord Nuffield in October 1937. It was suggested that it would be advisable to include in the new College, the Library, the Survey, and the University side of the work of Barnett House.

When the proposal was put to them the Council of Barnett House replied, in June 1938, that 'the greater part of the work for which Barnett House is at present responsible should be transferred to accommodation within the College'. It hoped that any rent to be charged would be of a nominal character. The Council contemplated 'retaining for the time being at any rate its autonomy in carrying out the work it is now doing; at a later date, however, it might well seem desirable that direct responsibility for certain parts of the work should be transferred to the College'. It pointed out that Barnett House was a corporate body holding property under trusts and any important change of status would therefore need consideration from the legal point of view.

The main current activities of the Council according to the letter from its Secretary included the maintenance of the Barnett Library, both reference and lending; the organisation of Lectures and Conferences and of the Social Training course and of work for the Diploma and Certificate in Public Administration. He said that six rooms would be needed, two being for the Library, for which ample space for future growth should be available. The Nuffield Committee thereupon agreed to inform the Architect to make provision for this accommodation in his plans.[4]

In the absence of any progress with the College building the matter rested there until November 1942 when the question arose of establishing an Information Bureau dealing with the Social Services. The idea had been discussed before the War and Barnett House had been interested in it. By now, however, the Social Reconstruction Survey had blossomed vigorously and G. D. H. Cole felt that an attempt by Barnett House to establish such a Bureau would necessarily involve a great deal of duplication with the Survey in the collection of material, etc., and that it would be much better if the Nuffield Survey, when it had completed the present range of its work, felt able to establish a Bureau, at any rate on a small scale, in readiness for the post-war period. According to Cole, when the proposal had first come up, strongly supported by Lindsay and Miss Grier, it had not been anticipated that it would make much difference whether the Bureau was started by Nuffield College or by Barnett House, as the inclusion of this side of the latter in the College was definitely contemplated. However, the future relations between the two bodies had been left unsettled. The Nuffield Survey had developed quite independently of Barnett House, and its work on the Social Services clearly altered the situation and made it expedient that, if the Bureau were to be started at all, it should be begun at the College rather than at Barnett House. Cole favoured this idea. It did, however, raise the whole question of the future relations between the two bodies. When the matter had been recently discussed by the Council of Barnett House the general feeling, according to Cole, (who was also a member of the Council of Barnett House) was that the Council would like the College to take over not only the proposed Information Bureau but also the Library and responsibility for the Social Training Department, leaving Barnett House to develop itself as a community centre and a point of contact between the University, City, and County.

Cole said he had consulted the Social Reconstruction Survey Committee which was in favour of proceeding with it, subject to the agreement of the Nuffield Committee.

The Nuffield College Committee [5] did not, however, think that social training, though a proper academic activity, was a suitable activity for the College. But, they asked Cole to continue discussions and as a result meeting took place between representatives of the two bodies on 5 February 1943.

The meeting examined the question in terms of the various activities. Social training had already been ruled out as a College function and its future was seen as being in the hands of a University Delegacy. There was a difference of opinion about the future of the Library. This had been opened at the same time as the House in 1914. Colleges had subscribed to it since 1921, but the House had always had to subsidise it and the Library had never paid any rent. Warden Adams, supported by Professor D. H. Macgregor, thought there were strong arguments for keeping the Library and Social Training in the same place. Even if the Social Training Department moved elsewhere the provision of a Library in Barnett House would still be required. Cole thought the Library mainly served undergraduates reading Modern Greats who would find it far more convenient if the libraries of Barnett House, the College and the Institute of Statistics were in the same building. He even suggested that Barnett House should keep the books needed for Social Training and allow the books in more general demand to go to the College, but was told this was impracticable. In the end it was agreed that as the Library was the property of Barnett House it was for the Council of that body to say whether any part should move to Nuffield. For the rest, Warden Adams suggested that a room in the College should be allotted to Barnett House for the use of the Secretary or Director. It was felt, however, that such provision was not really necessary and that in view of the many other demands on space in the College it would be difficult to keep such a room for occasional use by an outside body. Personal links might be established through admission of members of the House to the College Common Rooms.

In the end Warden Adams (Chairman of the Barnett House Council) agreed that the House did not require any accommodation in the College. Turning to wider matters, the two sides agreed that Barnett House reserved the right to initiate surveys and hold conferences, but that overlapping might be avoided by consultation. The Council of Barnett House endorsed the views of its representatives on 19 February and on 13 March the Nuffield Committee agreed to inform the Architect that no accommodation was required for Barnett House.[6]

The discussion about the future responsibility for Social Work Training and the decision of the Nuffield College Committee that it was not a suitable function for the new graduate College caused the Council of Barnett House to decide in March 1943 that the time had come for the responsibility to be transferred to a committee or delegacy directly under the University. The number of those registered to read for the Diploma and Certificate had reached 50 in 1938–39 and the demand was expected to increase after the War. The House could not continue its work without financial assistance. It was also desirable to establish more definitely the University status of the course. The Council would be glad to continue the existing provision of accommodation and even provide more in the future. There was also a feeling in some quarters that the standard of training needed raising and that this could be achieved only by placing responsibility in the hands of a University body.

The Social Studies Board agreed that the social training scheme had reached such dimensions as to make it desirable for it to be officially administered through a Delegacy or similar body. They also agreed that, as a centre for such a Delegacy, Barnett House offered the advantages of its library and suitable accommodation in a central position.

A Delegacy of Social Training was established by the University early in 1946[7] and took over the training functions performed by Barnett House. It was composed of the Vice-Chancellor and Proctors, one member appointed by Hebdomadal Council, three by the Social Studies Faculty Board, one by Nuffield College, one by the Delegacy of Extra Mural Studies, one by the Department of Education and seven by Barnett House. Its function was to make arrangements for the training in social work of members of the University and others, including the arrangements for the supervision of the practical work of candidates for the Diploma in Public and Social Administration and for the Certificate in Social Administration. Control of the examinations and the award of Diplomas and Certificates became a responsibility of the Faculty Board for Social Studies. The allocation of seven places out of fourteen to the Council of Barnett

House probably reflected pre-war memories of the extent of its contribution. In May 1948, however, the Council asked that the number should be reduced to two. The University agreed and the reduction came into effect in October 1949.

Barnett House Council remained in possession of the Library, which, in 1946, received for the first time a grant from the University of £200. It proved impossible, however, for the Council to maintain the library and early in 1949 they agreed to hand it over to a new body to be called the Barnett Library Trust, two of the six Trustees being appointed by the Social Studies Board. The cost continued to rise and in August 1955 the Trustees handed over the library to the University. It became the Social Studies Lending Library and in 1978 was housed in the newly established Social Studies Centre in George Street. The Council of Barnett House remained in being until it was wound up and its assets transferred to the University in 1957.

RAISING THE STANDARD

Early in 1958 Hebdomadal Council appointed a committee to carry out a general review of the activities of the University in order to see whether radical economies could be achieved in expenditure, particularly in activities peripheral to the University's main functions of teaching and research. The Committee on Radical Economies suggested that the work of the Delegacy was a peripheral activity which needed examination and justification. At that date the cost of the Delegacy to the University, after allowing for fee income, was around £13 000.

No doubt the case for such an appraisal reflected the view long held in the Social Studies Board, and indeed more widely, that the Delegacy catered mainly for candidates of a much lower level of ability than were admitted to read for one of the Honour Schools. The Committee were, therefore, questioning the intrinsic value of the work of the Delegacy and whether it was the kind which ought to be done in Oxford under the auspices of the University. A subsidiary question was whether the activities of the Delegacy should be integrated more closely with other activities in the field of Social Studies, partly for academic reasons and partly for the possible economies that might thereby be achieved.

In the discussions the major new fact that emerged was the

recent change in the admission policy: the Delegacy's new policy being to cut down the number of non-graduates. In 1950, 46 candidates had been admitted to the Diploma in Public and Social Administration, 20 men and 26 women of whom 9 men and 12 women did not already possess a degree. By 1955 the total admissions had fallen to 36 of which only 3 men and 6 women were not graduates. In October 1959 only graduates were admitted: of the 37 (21 men and 16 women) 14 held an Oxford degree, 5 a Cambridge degree, 12 came from other British universities, and 8 from overseas universities. The new admissions policy had raised the status and value of the Diploma. As an earnest of the Delegacy's intentions the Certificates in Training for Social Work and in Public Administration had been abolished in 1957. At the same time the title of the Delegacy had been changed to the Delegacy for Social Administration, not Social Training, to bring it into line with the practice of other universities and no doubt to indicate the wider scope of the Delegacy's activities.

The other factor which influenced the Committee in favour of the University continuing this kind of work was the recent report of the Younghusband Committee on Social Workers employed by Local Authorities. They had stressed the need for more highly trained social workers and envisaged a top level group of social administrators with a degree, a postgraduate qualification and specialised training. The Delegacy and the Social Studies Board felt strongly that Oxford should concentrate on training candidates for these top level posts.

It was generally agreed, therefore, that training for social work in future would be provided by a postgraduate Diploma in Public and Social Administration with the usual arrangements for practical work. The Diploma in Economics and Political Science would continue in being but mainly for non-graduates or for those who were not seeking employment in public and social administration.

The enquiry revealed that the half-dozen teachers employed by the Delegacy were rather isolated from the Faculty of Social Studies, an isolation fostered in its early days by the feeling on the part of College tutors that the Delegacy were largely concerned with training women social workers not up to Honour School standard and by a general ignorance of their specialised work. For this and other reasons it was agreed that the Delegacy should be wound up and its work undertaken by a Department of Social and Administrative Studies under the full control of the Board of the Faculty of Social Studies. The change came into operation in May 1960.

Though by its admission policy the Department was able to limit its entrants to the Diploma in Public and Social Administration to graduates, the terms of the Statutes still left both Diplomas open to non-graduates. From 1967, however, there were to be two separate awards or courses: one strictly confined to members of the University with at least a second-class Honours Degree and the other open to non-members, principally from Ruskin and Plater Colleges. The former retained the title of the Diploma in Public and Social Administration but with a very changed content. It was assimilated academically to the B.Phil. with two of the papers in basic social studies drawn from the B.Phils/M.Phils. in Economics, Politics, Sociology or Management Studies. There was a short essay on a professional subject not exceeding 20 000 words based on supervised research or field work and two papers on a professional specialism. Vocationally the new Diploma aimed at the top levels of the social welfare professions and satisfied the requirements of the relevant professional bodies.

The Board's original intention was to designate the other qualification as a Certificate. This would have been in line with the growing practice of other universities to confine the title of Diploma to postgraduate work and to use Certificate for non-graduate awards. However Ruskin and Plater Colleges protested against the proposal, their candidates having over the years established a vested interest in the title of Diploma. The Board, therefore, proposed 'Diploma in Social Studies for Mature Students'. The General Board of Faculties were not happy with this, for the Diploma would still be open to undergraduates. On the assumption that Hebdomadal Council would be willing to allow the title of Diploma to be used for an award to be taken mainly by non-graduates the General Board suggested the title of Special Diploma in Social Studies. This was agreed. It was first examined in 1968, the other Diploma being first examined a year later.

Thus the Diploma in Economics and Political Science, established in 1903, came to an end after 64 years of useful service. It had not produced any outstanding economists but had in the course of its life performed several useful functions now met in other ways. As a basic qualification for training in social work, combined with a Certificate, it had been replaced by the Diploma in Public and Social Administration. There was PPE for those who wished to specialise in Economics or Politics at the undergraduate level and the choice of several B.Phils. for those who already possessed a Degree. There remained, however, the candidates prepared by Ruskin and Plater Colleges, who had been among the main candidates of the Diploma, the former since 1910.

During the inter-war years the Diploma in Economics and Political Science had attracted some 30–40 candidates each year. The number from Ruskin was around 10–12 each year and after 1926 there were usually 3 or 4 candidates from the Catholic Workers' College. As might be expected there was a high failure rate: in June 1923, there were 17 failures out of 49 candidates, in 1925 there were 13 out of 31. A 25 per cent failure rate seems to have become usual. Also fewer Distinctions came to be awarded. In their Report for 1927–28 the Diploma Committee said:

> The provision for the study of Economics and Politics has been greatly extended since the establishment of the Honour School of Philosophy, Politics and Economics, and the Committee is thus enabled to publish from time to time a much fuller list of lectures than was possible formerly; and this has made it both easy and reasonable that the standard required to obtain a Diploma, and even more, distinction, has been steadily rising.[8]

Some of the entrants from the Ruskin and Catholic Workers Colleges with an inadequate formal education undoubtedly set problems for the Examiners. In their Report on the June 1934 examination they said they continued 'to feel a difficulty in the relatively low standard which now admits to the mark of Distinction . . . in the past this standard may have been set through a desire to reward a candidate whose work seemed specially deserving when considered in relation to his educational background;' They went on 'but though in one year it seemed only fair to reckon in one candidate's favour his conquest of difficulties, in the next it would seem hard to pass over another whose marks had attained the same level, simply because he was not known to have suffered from the same handicap.' They considered that 'even should they in any year find it possible to raise the standard, the situation which prompted the original lenience might well recur.'

But if there was academic weakness at one end of the entry there was ability and strength at the other. From 1925 onwards some products of Ruskin were thought good enough to read for one of the Final Honour Schools. An Extra-Mural Delegacy was established in 1924 and soon began to give financial support each year to a few adult scholars. Between 1925 and 1941, 46 were awarded scholarships and admitted to the University under the Delegacy's powers, 31 of whom read for Honours and 6 took the B.Litt. Modern Greats was the popular School, attracting 19 of the adult scholars of whom 4 gained Firsts and 11 gained seconds. George Woodcock, General Secretary of the TUC 1960–69, after taking the Diploma in Economics and Political Science as a student of Ruskin was admitted by New College, obtaining a first in PPE in 1933.

There was a big increase in the numbers prepared by Ruskin College after 1945. In 1950 Ruskin put forward 25 of the 43 candidates for the Diploma in Economics and Political Science and in 1960 put forward 42 of the 52 candidates. This was in addition to the handful of candidates it put forward for the diploma in Public and Social Administration. There was also an increase in the number of candidates from Plater College.

The disentangling of the two Diplomas clarified the role and academic status of the Department of Social and Administrative Studies. It was no longer a matter of admissions policy, as it had been in the Barnett House days, whether non-graduates were allowed to take the Diploma. In 1972 any element of ambiguity that might have lingered disappeared when the Diploma was redesignated as an M.Sc. in Applied Social Studies.

The development, accelerated by the appointment of A. H (Chelly) Halsey as Director in 1962, were greatly helped by, indeed was a major factor in, the expansion of sociological studies in the University. By 1980 the Department could draw upon sixteen Lecturers, two of whom were part-time. Nine of these were concerned with Applied Social Studies, two with methods of Social Research and one with Industrial Sociology. In addition to teaching candidates for the M.Sc. they were available to teach and supervise candidates for other degrees. In recent years the Department has undertaken several major pieces of research, for example, the study of Social Mobility made in collaboration with Nuffield College.

10 The Institute of Economics and Statistics

The impetus for the establishment of an Institute of Statistics came in the 1930s from the small group of economists, most of whom had been quite recently elected to College Fellowships. At the time of the discussions which led to the grant from the Rockefeller Foundation this group set out their reasons and detailed proposals.[1]

They claimed general agreement that economic studies could be advanced by a further analysis of statistical evidence in the light of the system of thought provided by economic theory. Such research was usually dependent upon the use of equipment, whether in the assembling of sources or for computation, facilities not available to the economist in Oxford. The last decade had seen the appointment of some thirteen College tutors in ecnomics, all relatively young. The foundation of an Institute giving facilities for statistical studies could also meet a need already felt by senior economists. Such an Institute would not suffer lack of work. In 1933 the special subject 'Statistics' had been examined in the Honour School for the first time and instruction in the subject would benefit if the facilities of an Institute were available. There had also been an increase in the number of graduate students engaged in research in economic subjects. While economic studies would have priority, the facilities of the Institute would also be available for statistical work in connection with, for example, social anthropology and psychology.

The Institute should obtain and house the chief statistical sources and acquire the back numbers of periodicals and provide equipment for computing. It should have the services of a Secretary, who would supervise the arrangements of the Library and the use of the machines. An initial outlay of £1175 (of which

£750 was for stocking of the library) was envisaged and an annual outlay of £515.

Congregation agreed on 22 October 1935 that an Institute of Statistics be established under the direction of the Social Studies Research Committee.[2] The Decree did not define the purpose or scope of the Institute. Shortly afterwards it was decided that the Institute should be managed by a Standing Committee. Jakob Marschak had already been appointed to the new Readership in Statistics for 5 years from 1 October 1935. He was also appointed Director of the Institute for the same period.

The Institute was first housed in 46 Broad Street. When that building had to be demolished to give place for the Bodleian Extension the Institute moved at the end of 1936 to 74 High Street. These premises, which were a great improvement, consisted of eight rooms: five in the basement provided an office for the Director, a small Calculating Room, two rooms for researchers and a 'Lower Reading Room'. There was an 'Upper Reading Room' on the first floor along with the office of the Librarian-Secretary and the second floor provided a large room for researchers. In September 1939 the Institute moved into the St Catherines Building in St Aldates but in January 1940 moved again into the Bodleian Extension, only to move into Balliol in October 1943.

At their second meeting on 29 July 1935 the Social Studies Research Committee asked the Registrar to consult Bodley's Librarian informally as to whether permanent accommodation could be provided for the Institute in the Bodleian Extension, about to be built, and whether in the meantime, if permanent accommodation could not be so provided, the Bodleian Curators would be likely to agree to the deposit of statistical works in the Institute.

As it was part of the initial conception of the Institute and in accordance with the Curator's policy at the time, agreement did not take long to reach. A Decree[3] was approved by Congregation in March 1936 empowering the Bodleian to deposit in the library of the Institute such periodical and serial publications as were approved by Bodley's Librarian after consultation with the Social Studies Board. In February 1937 Bodley's Curators went futher. They deposited temporarily the duplicates of some 120 selected 'fundamental works' on Economics, which were ultimately to be housed in the Radcliffe Camera Reading Room for Undergraduates. At the same time the Curators extended their list of periodicals and serial publications deposited in the Institute. Their action resulted from a resolution of the Social Studies Board on 27 November 1936. The Board 'holding that it is undesirable to divorce the study of statistics and statistical method from the cognate studies of Economic Theory and Organisation' stated that it regarded the Institute's Library as 'the most appropriate centre for the development of a Library of Economics' and emphasised the importance of providing in it 'adequate facilities for the study of Economic Theory and Organisation as well as of Statistics and Statistical Methods'. On the recommendation of the General Board of Faculties the University made a non-recurrent grant of £500 to help fill some of the gaps.

The interest of the Institute in Bodley was more than a question of books, it was also very much a question of accommodation. The researchers, whether senior members or graduate students wanted to be able to work as close as possible to the research material. In March 1937 the Curators had agreed to house the library of the Institute in the new Extension on the understanding that funds were provided for subscriptions to duplicate sets of periodicals etc.[4] In November of that year the Institute's Standing Committee set down their accommodation needs. They pointed out that they already used what they called 16 'window units', covering seminar and reading rooms, offices for the Director and Librarian-Secretary as well as accommodation for the work of such people as A. J. Brown, H. Phelps Brown, R. F. Bretherton, G. L. Schackle and P. W. S. Andrews. A joint committee composed of two from the Social Studies Board, two from the Social Studies Research Committee and two from the Institute's Standing Committee was established to deal, on behalf of these bodies, with all matters concerning the accommodation to be provided for social Studies in the new Bodleian. This joint committee was empowered to consult with the very recently established Nuffield College Committee of Council.[5]

Aided by grants specifically for the purchase of books and periodicals the Institute quickly accumulated a working library for economics and statistics. At 31 July 1937 it contained 4530 books, of which 3953 had been presented or exchanged, and had 292 current and 1593 annual volumes of periodicals.

Thus, in October 1937, when Lord Nuffield's new benefaction

was announced the Institute had been in formal existence for two years. It had a Director and a Secretary-Librarian and some rooms in 74 High Street. It had secured a special arrangement with the Bodleian Library, being treated as a kind of departmental repository for books and reports on statistics and to some extent on economics. It had also purchased from its own resources or otherwise acquired a largish collection.

It was not, however, until its third year that the Institute was financially able to employ any research staff. In 1937 the Rockefeller Foundation made a grant of £3400 to be spent over some two years on research relating to trade cycles. This provided the salary for one full-time and one half-time research assistant working for the Institute under the supervision of the Director (mainly on Labour Mobility and on the capital Market); an additional assistant for the Economists' Research Group (on studies of Public Works and the Trade Cycle and on Company Accounts); a research assistant for Henry Phelps Brown (on Monetary Circulation) and additional computing, and clerical services. This grant was due to come to an end in July 1939, one year before the main Rockefeller Grant would end. Moreover All Souls had not committed themselves to finance the Readership in Statistics beyond 1940.

Lord Nuffield's large new benefaction appeared both as an opportunity and as a problem to the Institute and its supporters. On the one hand it might solve the financial future. Though the benefaction was not a direct response to the appeal it was for Social Studies which had featured prominently in the Appeal. On the other hand, the Vice-Chancellor had told Congregation that Nuffield College was to be 'the University's instrument of research in social studies'. The Institute, however, regarded itself as the University's chosen instrument, at least in statistical and economic studies. But the new instrument was also to be a College and though the Vice-Chancellor and others might say that Nuffield was to be a somewhat unusual College, and under the control of Hebdomadal Council, nevertheless anybody who knew Oxford was well aware that Colleges were not like Boards or Departments or University Institutes.

It is not surprising, therefore, that the relations between the embryo Institute and the future College received very early consideration. The Co-ordinating Committee of the Social Studies Research Committee decided that it was desirable that the

Institute with its Library should be placed in Nuffield College. If that were done it was desirable that (a) the present arrangement for the deposit of Bodleian books should be continued and (b) the Library at the College, or the Institute's part of it, should not be a dependent library of the Bodleian. They considered that the expense for library purposes thrown upon the funds of the College, if the Institute were put into it, should not be more than (a) the cost of the building; (b) salaries of Library staff (£1250 per annum) and (c) purchase of books etc. £1700 per annum. This was on the assumption that the loan of periodicals from the Bodleian (estimated at £300 per annum) would continue. The cost of back publications in order to make an 'efficient Economics Library' was estimated as £7000. The Committee pointed out that if the Institute's Library were to be housed in the Bodleian the expenses under (a) and (b) would be avoided, as would a considerable amount on the purchase of publications. But there would still remain a considerable sum under (a) and (b) for the College Library. They had not taken into account the saving in work and capital expenditure which would accrue to Bodley if the Institute were placed in Nuffield College.[6]

On the same day the Research Sub-Committee of the Nuffield College Committee recommended that the Institute of Statistics should be included in the College on the understanding that:

(1) every endeavour would be made to obtain outside financial support for it; and
(2) its services would be available for all branches of studies carried on in the College, though naturally it would be most used by Economists.[7]

The Standing Committee of the Institute agreed, early in February 1938, that it desired the Institute to be housed in the building of Nuffield college on the understanding that an adequate library for economics and economic and political (including local government) statistics would be provided. This assumed the amalgamation of the Institute's Library with that of the College and the joint use of the facilities by the Institute's researchers, the Fellows and Students of the College and other interested members of the University. They estimated that by 1940 the Institute's stock would be 15 000 volumes and that of the College 10 000 volumes. From then on there would be an annual intake of 5000 volumes so that by 1970 space would be needed for 175 000 volumes. They asked for 12 carrels in the book store, 30–40 rooms for researchers and a reading room for 40 readers.[8]

The Committee pointed out that Bodley's Librarian was awaiting a reply to his letter about the future allocation of space in the Bodley Extension. The reply would depend on whether the Nuffield College Committee could meet the requirements set out in the memorandum. Before, however, the Nuffield Committee could decide or even comment on the Institute's claims for space and library facilities in the College buildings the Standing Committee submitted a general memorandum[9] on the character of their relations with the College. Starting with the Vice-Chancellor's statement that the College was to be *the* University organ for research in the field of the Social Studies it pointed out that the Institute already existed as *a* University organ of research in substantially the same range of studies, though not formally confined to them, the approach being by the use of statistical material. There appeared, the Standing Committee claimed, to be common agreement that the two organs should be combined as the two approaches they represented to their common problem – of statistics and fieldwork – had to be combined if results were to be achieved: therefore, 'when Nuffield College is established the Institute of Statistics should be housed there'.

The memorandum stressed that the financial position of the Institute was precarious. Total expenditure was estimated at £3940 per annum and income at £3503, of which some £3000 was from two Rockefeller Grants due to end in July 1939 and 1940. The committee envisaged an annual expenditure of £5000 a year (excluding the cost of the Readership). As regards the constitutional position, the Institute's Committee stated that transference to the College should not involve the disappearance of the name or of the organism which was growing up as a unit under that name. 'The natural course will be to make the Director a Fellow of Nuffield College and to establish the Institute there, with a set of rooms definitely assigned to it, a budget and power to receive grants, and its own notepaper'. They stressed that the Institute should be available to serve any qualified member of the University whether or not he had any connection with the College. It should continue to be the meeting place of all economists and politics teachers wishing to use statistical methods and not only for those who became Offical or Faculty Fellows or

Students of Nuffield. In the same way it was desirable that conduct of the work of the Institute should be divided in accordance with the work of social scientists in the University as a whole and not be disproportionately affected by the projects undertaken in the College. The Sub-Faculties of Economics and Politics should be given special powers in relation to the Institute. The Committee preferred that the Institute should be regarded as a Department of the University rather than a Department of the College. If it were to be decided that the main body of books in Economics and Politics should remain in the Bodleian there would apparently be no reason, according to the Standing Committee, for the College itself to have any substantial library. A Nuffield research student would find the books he needed on economic or political theory in Bodley just the same as any other graduate student.

In a revised version of his Memorandum on financial Policy circulated at the same time the Vice-Chancellor left aside for the moment the consideration of the constitutional questions. He did, however, suggest an allocation of £2255 for the Institute to be met out of the income of the College.[10]

The Nuffield Research Sub-Committee agreed in March 1938 that no decision could be reached on the constitutional question until the constitution of the College had been settled. In any case they wished to hear the views of the consultative committees for Economics and Politics.[11]

The Economics Consultative Committee was anxious that the Institute should not lose its identity since it was nervous about the Institute's continued usefulness if it were to be directly under the control of Council, as the College would be. If the College were to be the University's instrument of research in Social Studies the Committee felt that the teachers in that field should be in a position to impress their views effectively on the Governing Body. It was pointed out to them that Nuffield College would be somewhat in the position of a Delegacy and that, in practice, Delegacies did not find that they were hampered by Council's control. They were unanimous in wishing the name Institute of Statistics to be retained. The Research Sub-Committee of the Nuffield Committee considered these views and, while deferring consideration of the constitutional position until the recently-elected Warden was in Oxford, seemed ready to agree that rooms should be allotted to the Institute in the College and would be called the Institute of Statistics; the Reader in Statistics would be ex officio the Director, and a fixed annual sum of £2255 should be allotted out of the Nuffield funds for purposes of the Institute. They stated 'Whatever objection there may be to calling an integral part of the College an Institute, is almost certainly outweighed by the value of the connexions established by the present Institute. These might be broken if the name disappeared'. The Politics Consultative Committee do not appear to have expressed any distinct views about the Institute.[12]

The relationship had to be settled in order for the Scheme of Delegation referred to earlier to be formulated. The first draft of July 1938[13] provided that the Nuffield College Committee should appoint a sub-committee for the Institute. The Warden of Nuffield College was to be chairman, three members should be elected by the Social Studies Board (two of these on the recommendation of the Sub-Faculties of Politics and Ecnomics) and the other members should be the Director of the Institute, two elected jointly by the Boards of the Faculties of Literae Humaniores and Modern History, and by the Boards of the Faculties of Medicine, Physical Sciences and Biological Sciences respectively, at least one Official or Visiting Fellow of the College, and not more than three other persons appointed by the main committee. The duties of the sub-committee would be to allocate rooms, recommend appointments, submit estimates of expenditure, and to apply the revenue grants for the purposes prescribed. It would replace the Standing Committee.

Harold Butler began talking to people in the University, including Marschak, before taking up the post of Warden. On 27 May 1938 he wrote to Lindsay[14] that the Institute of Statistics was really an Institute of Economics. Not more than 10 per cent of its books were statistical books and Marschak had admitted that he could not confine the activities of the Institute to the purely statistical field. From that Butler had drawn two conclusions. First, if the Institute were to continue in existence as if it were a separate entity, it would inevitably clash before very long with the other portions or persons of the College who were engaged in economic research. Second, that it was impossible to do effective economic research without a library on the spot. The present library of the Institute was quite inadequate for the purpose of social and economic research. He could not see how Nuffield could become a real centre of research unless it possessed a sufficiently good working library, both on the economic and the political side. Lindsay replied on 3 June 1938: 'The problem of the Institute of Statistics is one of the most difficult which we are considering'. He thought 'on the whole, that the view taken here is that the 'Institute of Statistics' ought not to be an "Institute of Economics".'

Butler thought that it would be a mistake at this stage to reach any definite decision. The precise place of the Institute, if it were to be incorporated in the College, could be settled only when the whole scheme of the College was clearly worked out. He did 'not like the idea of an *imperium in imperio*' though he did not doubt that it would be possible to make such arrangements for the incorporation of the Institute and to give it all the autonomy which it required. There seemed, however, to be some uncertainty as to the Institute's precise nature and functions. If it were not to be an 'Institute of Economics' then the present scope would undergo some contraction, as it was clearly engaged in more than statistical study. If, however, it were to retain its present scope, overlapping and constant friction with other parts of the College were likely to arise. He was already afraid that the arrangements for the management of the Institute might remove it from all control and all organic connection with the College. He therefore hoped that no decision would be taken about the constitution of the Institute until that of the College had been worked out.

The views of the Warden-elect must have reinforced the unease that Lindsay and others may have felt about the strong claims being put forward by the Economists and the Standing Committee of the Institute. The revised draft Scheme of Delegation circulated in September 1938 omitted a Sub-Committee for the Institute of Statistics and made responsibility for the Institute a function of the Warden and Fellows of the College afforced by the Director of the Institute and not more than two persons co-opted for this specific purpose.[15]

An alternative draft circulated on 24 November 1938 provided that the Director should be a Fellow of the College, but made no reference to either a sub-committee for the Institute nor to the Warden and Fellows having any specific duties in respect of the Institute.[16]

A new draft circulated on 12 December 1938 drew on both drafts. The Director of the Institute was to be appointed by the Nuffield Committee after consultation with the Warden and

Fellows and become a Fellow of the College. The Warden and Fellows were to be responsible for appointing the staff of the Institute, fixing their remuneration and conditions of service and for granting permission to work in the Institute or to have statistical investigations made. The sub-committees on Politics and on Economics, of which the Director of the Institute was to be a member ex officio, had among their duties advising the Warden and Fellows on the use of the Institute as an instrument of research in their respective fields.[17]

The Consultative Committee of Economists were not happy. They could not 'but regret that this Institute, which has been a University institution of great importance to economists, should now entirely disappear as a distinct body'. It would be difficult and undesirable for its work to be divided sharply into separate departments of Economics and Politics, 'without any single Committee being in charge of the general supervision of the work'. It seemed likely, they claimed, that the Warden and Fellows would want to set up such a committee in any case, and therefore they suggested a third sub-committee with the Warden as ex officio chairman, the Director, two appointed by the Warden and Fellows four from the Faculty of Social Studies and not more than two others chosen for their special knowledge of statistics. Their duties would be to supervise the administration of the Institute, to advise the Warden and the Fellows on the appointment of staff, etc., and on the admission of persons to work there, etc. The Standing Committee of the Institute, with a rather similar membership, took the same line and made the same recommendation.[18]

The Nuffield Committee did not accept the views of the Economists. On 9 March 1939 Robert Hall, on behalf of the Economics Consultative Committee reiterated the demand for a separate sub-committee for the Institute and a meeting of the Standing Committee of the Institute held on the same day took exactly the same view.

It is perhaps difficult now to understand the fervour with which the status of the Institute was pursued. Writing in the Oxford Magazine[19] for 27 January 1938 Robert Hall stated 'The Institute of Statistics has become indispensable in the short time in which it has been in existence.' It was imperative, he argued, that the University should be able to guarantee its future when the Rockefeller grant came to an end in 1940. Yet the Institute at that time mainly consisted of a Director who as Reader in Statistics would have been available anyhow. The very small research staff was financed by a two-year grant not for the general activities of the Institute but mainly for a particular research project and here again could have been available had the Institute as an institution not existed. The major attraction of the Institute to the Economists was as a centre providing rooms and readily accessible and adequate statistical and economic periodicals, year books and reports. These might have been provided in the Bodley Extension.

The problem facing these enthusiastic lobbyists was to find the money to finance the Institute after 1940 when the Rockefeller grant ran out. The University did not have any spare money available, hence the attraction of Lord Nuffield's benefaction. But if an Institute and its library were to be financed from that source and housed in the College could this be done without giving some control to the Warden and Fellows? And, in so far as the Institute was in effect an Institute of Economics, there was an added reason for College participation.

Robert Hall and others had, however, a legitimate worry. Were the Institute to be housed, financed and managed by the College they feared that members of the College would have the first claim on its services. The College might indeed come to monopolise or at least have an unfair advantage in the field of applied economic research.

The fears of the Economics and Politics Tutors were to some extent lessened by the decision in November 1938 to appoint five members of the two Consultative Committees (Cole, Hall, Harrod, Ensor and Maud) to Faculty Fellowships in the College, so giving them a direct say in its government.

Discussions between the University and the Rockefeller Foundation were going on during the summer of 1939. As a result the Foundation extended their grant of £5000 for a further year and then on a year-to-year basis. From 1940 to the end of 1944 the £600 a year provided by All Souls for the Readership in Statistics was, in the absence of a holder, made available for general research purposes. The Institute was the major claimant for this money, the research undertaken by the College being financed out of its endowment or from a Treasury Grant. During the War therefore the Institute was enabled to increase its expenditure substantially: from around £2500 in 1939–40 to around £5500

The Institute of Economics and Statistics

in 1941–2 and to some £6000 in 1943–4. In that year it was spending over £4000 on research and administrative staff.

At the outbreak of War the Standing Committee and the Economists Research Group revised their scheme of research. Where specific pieces of work were almost completed it was decided to finish them but more comprehensive or less far advanced studies, e.g. of Company Accounts, were abandoned. Instead it was decided to concentrate on the impact of the War on the economic system. A Diary was kept by Ian Bowen and, along with any memoranda on current problems, were circulated to Oxford economists and to certain Government Departments. In September 1940 it was decided to publish, by Blackwells, the diary and a Bulletin at three weekly intervals and put it on a subscription basis. A substantial part of the Institute's work came to be published in the Bulletin.

Professor A. L. Bowley, until recently Professor of Statistics at London University, became Acting Director of the Institute in February 1940 with Frank Burchardt as his right-hand man. The research staff was greatly strengthened by the appointment of T. Balogh, M. Kalecki, E. F. Schumacher, and G. D. N. Worswick.

Two features of this war-time development should be noticed. First, the Institute became the main, indeed almost the sole, centre of economic research in the University. Most of the College tutors in economics had gone into Whitehall or the Armed Forces. The Social Reconstruction Survey of the College was largely concerned with social and administrative issues. There was little contact between the research of the College and the Institute except for one joint arrangement.

In 1941 following discussion with Chatham House an International Committee was set up to co-ordinate the studies of recent developments in Germany and German-occupied Europe. The Committee was composed of representatives of the Nuffield College Survey, the Institute of Statistics and the Economic and German Departments of the Foreign Research and Press Service of the Royal Institute of International Affairs. So far as Oxford was concerned the work was carried out in the Institute, Nuffield College contributing £3500 in 1942–3; £1200 in 1943–4 and £1000 in 1944–5. In 1943, however, Chatham House withdrew from the arrangement upon its work being absorbed into the Foreign Office. The Joint Committee came to an end in July and the volume of work was reduced.

Second, the research staff of the Institute were largely refugees from Hitler. They were treated as enemy aliens by Government Departments and were not allowed access to statistics and other information available only in those Departments. This precluded them from taking part in the Social Recontruction Survey, much of which had been commissioned by Whitehall and which obtained data from the Ministries. Much of the work of the Institute had perforce to be concerned with economic events in Germany and the occupied countries or with projects which could be studied from readily available, published figures or with theoretical issues.

These two features meant that by the end of the War the Institute had emerged as a main centre for economic studies separate from and quite independent of Nuffield College, financially and constitutionally.

The relations between the College and the Institute came up when Council once again looked at the Scheme of Delegation and the possibility of putting it wholly or party into operation. A joint committee of Council and the Nuffield College Committee reported[20] in October 1943. They pointed out that the proposed union of the Institute with the College had never taken place. The Institute was constitutionally separate from the Reconstruction Survey and from the college. What was perhaps more important, the Institute was largely carrying on its own programme of research and publishing regularly a Bulletin which had already won recognition, not only in this country. They recommended, therefore, that though the 1939 Scheme of Delegation should be brought into effect at once, those parts which related to the Institute of Statistics should be excluded. This exclusion was accepted by the Nuffield Committee and by Council. Thus, in the Scheme which came into operation in March 1944, the Warden and Fellows were given no powers in relation to the Institute. The Director no longer was to be ex officio a Fellow and presumably there was no obligation on the College to house or finance the Institute.

In October 1944 a joint committee of the College and the Institute spelt out the possibilities. They thought that the Institute must always have a special relation to the College since their fields of activity overlapped and it had originally been contemplated that the Institute should provide the research undertaken by the College with the services of a specialised statistical organisation. This service the Institute should continue to provide and constitutional expression should be given to the special relation of the two bodies. It was not, however, desirable to merge the Institute in the College. The Institute provided a University common service for research workers in fields other than those with which the College was specially concerned. It had stood in a special relation in the past to the Economics Research Group and might well hold a similar position to other University bodies in the future. The Insitute, moreover, had important functions in a field from which the College, as a college of postgraduate research, was excluded, viz. undergraduate teaching. It followed, therefore, that the Institute should remain independent, administered by a separate committee working under the direction of the Social Studies Research Committee or some other University body, and drawing the income needed to perform its basic functions from general University funds. The special relationship should be recognised by the representation of the College (normally by the Warden) on the Committee of the Institute and the election of the Institute's Director (and at times other members of the staff) to Fellowships in the College. The College should also be prepared to make an annual grant or grants to the cost of research undertaken by the Institute. There would be great advantages in having the Institute physically located in the College when the buildings were complete, particularly in making readily accessible to students the specialist libraries of both institutions. However, the University should continue to make itself responsible for providing accommodation for the Institute's work. Pending the building of the College this was a problem of some urgency.[21]

Early in 1944 the University decided that the Readership in Statistics, vacant since Marschak's departure in 1939, should be filled. The Social Studies Board recommended that the next Reader should also be the Director of the Institute though this should not necessarily apply to his successor. About the same time the Joint Advisory Science Committee supported a proposal for the creation of a Lecturership in the Design and Analysis of Scientific Experiment but thought this ought to be considered in relation to the existence of an Institute of Statistics. They asked whether the Institute was concerned only with Ecnomic and Social questions and suggested that the General Board should be asked to advise on its work. This the General Board did. Bowley, who was a member of the Board's Committee which considered the matter, said that the Institute was concerned only with Economic and Social questions, and rightly so. He thought that in addition there was a need for a Lecturer in Statistical Methods concerned primarily with the techniques of biological, agricultural and, to some extent, physical investigation. The General Board recommended that for the immediate future, the work of the Institute and the position it held in the University should remain unchanged but that a Lecturership in the Design and Analysis of Scientific Experiment should be created.[22]

Council asked All Souls whether they were prepared to revive their earlier contribution of £600 a year for the Reader and the Nuffield Committee whether they were prepared to meet £400 a year out of the College income for the stipend of the Directorship. Both were willing and so the post of Reader was advertised tenable with the post of Director. David Champernowne was appointed and took up office in April 1945. He was also elected to an Official Fellowship in the College.

In February 1945 the Nuffield Committee asked Council to consider urgently the future of the Institute. Council referred it to a committee which included Clay, Lindsay, and Hubert Henderson. In an Appendix, Henderson, now Chairman of the Standing Committee, dealt at length with the organisation of the Institute and the range of inquiries it covered. It was a very friendly and persuasive appraisal.

The Committee reported[23] that Council would see from Henderson's statement 'how important a place the Institute has taken in economic studies in the University and the reputation which it has made outside Oxford'. The Committee agreed that the work should be maintained at least at its present volume. This, they said, was in accord with the views of the newly appointed Director who was 'anxious to maintain this work on much the same lines ... as well as to expand gradually the Institute's work in other fields, including applications of statistical methods in the natural sciences, which will be the chief subject of his personal researches'.

As for the government of the Institute, the Committee pointed out that the functions of the Social Studies Research Committee had long ceased to be more than formal: practical control of the Institute was in the hands of 'a special, and to a large degree, self-constituted Committee'. If the Institute were to become a permanent part of the University some regular machinery should be established for its government. They thought it undesirable to increase the number of independent committees concerned with social studies and, therefore, recommended that the Institute should be governed by the General Board through a Committee appointed by the Board. They concluded their report: 'It has already been decided that the Institute shall be located ultimately in Nuffield College and the Committee sees no reason to disturb that arrangement.'

The General Board consulted the Faculty Boards of Biological Sciences and Social Studies late in 1946 and then Council sent a draft statute to the Boards for their consideration. Clause 1 provided that 'the work of the Institute shall include the study of the development and application of statistical methods to

(i) economic social problems;
(ii) problems in the natural sciences, including agriculture and forestry.'

Neither the Biology Board nor the Social Studies Board liked this definition of the scope of the Institute. The former felt that the clause extended the field of the Institute too widely and might lead it to undertake work which was more appropriate for the Lecturer in the Design and Analysis of Scientific Experiments. The Social Studies Board disliked it because it compelled the Institute to undertake the study of the problems of the Natural Sciences. The clause was therefore replaced by one defining the Institute's work as including 'the study of the theory of statistics and the methods of statistical analysis' and 'the application of statistical methods to ecnomic and social problems'.

The Social Studies Board also took strong exception to the powers and role of the Director accorded by the draft Statute. These had been assimilated to the practice prevalent in the Science Departments and gave the Board no control over him. The Social Studies Board contended that 'it was desirable that the role of the Institute as a service for the assistance of those engaged on economic research in the Colleges or in the University should receive recognition in the constitutional arrangements'. This object had hitherto been achieved through the Standing Committee and the draft was revised to give general supervision of the work of the Director and the Institute to the Social Studies Board, including approval of the research programmes.[24]

The Statute as revised was passed by Congregation in 1947. As a result in July the University took over responsibility for the financing of the Institute, the grant from the Rockefeller Foundation having come to an end in June.

David Champernowne became Professor of Statistics in October 1948 but continued as Director until the end of that year, Frank Burchardt taking over in January 1949. The research staff of the war years soon scattered and it did not prove easy to retain able people for long. The Institute was, however, a major beneficiary of the earmarked 'Clapham' money for the development of the social sciences. As a result its budget and its number of established posts expanded quite markedly. It proved advantageous both to the Institute and to some Colleges to link a research post at the former with a teaching Fellowship, in say Economics, at the latter.

In recent years most of the research undertaken has been done by individuals rather than by teams. For a time the Institute was interested in formulating an Econometric Model of the UK Economy but in the 1960s there was an emphasis on the Economics of Developing Countries. The main value of the Institute to Oxford economists in general has been the rapidly expanding library. By 1980 this contained over 87 000 books and some 2000 periodicals and serial publications.

After a period of uncertainty in which it had a succession of temporary homes the Institute moved into a fine new building in 1964. Assisted by a substantial grant from the Rockefeller Foundation the University decided to build a Law Library at Manor Road and, on the same site, to erect an English Faculty Library and to provide accommodation for the Institute of Statistics as well as for the Faculties of English and Law. Work started in 1961 and the Institute moved into its new home in January 1964. The Institute's quarters included a reading room and gallery with space for 75 readers, two seminar rooms, a staff common room and twenty-five research rooms. It was formally opened by Harold Wilson, then Prime Minister, who recalled that, as Lord Beveridge's assistant, he had worked just before the war in one of the Institute's temporary homes. The Institute was renamed the Institute of Economics and Statistics from 1 October 1962 with substantially the same terms of reference.

11 General Developments after 1945

THE B.PHIL./M.PHIL.

At their meeting in February 1945 the Social Studies Board appointed a Committee to discuss every aspect of PPE and to report what alternative possibilities there were for the future. The members were Professor H. J. Paton, Chairman of the Board, Professor H. H. Price, and D. M. MacKinnon (philosophy); Professor Cole and R. B. McCallum (politics) and H. D. Henderson and R. L. Hall (economics). They made three main recommendations:[1]

(i) The institution of a postgraduate course for each of the three subjects of the School leading possibly to a Bachelor of Philosophy (B.Phil.).
(ii) Changes in the entrance requirements involving a Preliminary Examination with papers closely related to the scope of the Final Honours School.
(iii) The possible introduction of an Honour Moderations for Social Studies of six papers, two from each side of the School. This would be taken after five Terms and would in effect turn PPE into a four-year School, comparable with Lit. Hum. It might be possible, however, to allow candidates who had taken the new Honour Moderations to take the Final School in four Terms, i.e. 9 Terms in all. Candidates who entered the Final Honour School after taking Honour Moderations might well be allowed to drop one subject. In the Committee's mind this development was linked with the possibility of reducing the scope of the School.

The ideas were discussed by the three Sub-Faculties in October-

November 1945.[2] All were in favour of the new postgraduate Degree. The Philosophy Sub-Faculty unanimously agreed that the existing arrangements for the B. Litt. were unsatisfactory and that a new postgraduate School in Philosophy should be created, analogous in some respects to the BCL. The Economics Sub-Faculty were also strongly in favour and the Politics Sub-Faculty agreed in general principle.

The proposal for a Preliminary Examination related to the subjects of PPE also got general support. There was, however, little or no support for the introduction of an Honour Moderations leading to PPE. The Philosophers thought three years was sufficient time. The Economists were not prepared to accept any reduction in the present scope of the Final Honours School which would turn it into a two-subject School. They thought, however, that advantage should be taken of the introduction of a B.Phil. to simplify the character of PPE by removing the specialist tendencies which were more appropriate in a postgraduate course.

Thus it was generally agreed in the Faculty to go ahead with the introduction of a new postgraduate Degree and a new First Public Examination. As regards the B.Phil. there were points of difference between the Sub-Faculties particularly as to whether provision should be made for an optional or a compulsory short thesis. On one matter the Philosophers got their way – the other two Sub-Faculties accepted their strongly held views that there should be neither Classes nor Distinctions in the B.Phil., but reserved the right to re-open the question at some date after the Degree had been established.[3]

In presenting their case to the General Board in January 1946 the Lit. Hum. Board argued that the B.Litt. system required candidates to be supervised and examined *ad hominem*, hence there was no concerted instruction for them in philosophy. Theses were on disparate and often excessively peripheral subjects which did not bring them in touch with each other nor create a demand for co-ordinated instruction in subjects other than those already covered by the Final Honours School. Consequently there was little utilisation of the expertise of the Oxford philosophy teachers. This was producing a tendency to multiply the alternative special subjects in Lit. Hum. and PPE.

The Philosophy Sub-Faculty proposed the introduction of a new degree comprised of a small thesis (say 80 pages); a paper on a Chosen Authority, e.g. the cardinal doctrines of some major philosopher or school; two papers out of Moral Philosophy, Political Philosophy, Metaphysics and the Theory of Knowledge and Logic and Scientific Method; and a serious *viva voce*. The results would be unclassified, to avoid 'alpha hunting'. The degree could be taken in one year by graduates who had done well in philosophy in Lit. Hum. or PPE. Graduates from other Universities or in some cases from other Oxford Honour Schools would have to take two years.[4]

Knowing that the Politics and Economics Sub-Faculties also favoured the proposal the General Board of Faculties arranged for the Statute to make the same provision for those subjects. However they adopted a proposal from the Committee for Advanced Studies to place a limit of five years on the Statute, as an experimental period. They insisted on this even when Hebdomadal Council struck out the limiting date and so Council had to agree to move an amendment to this effect in Congregation.[5]

The Statute first came before Congregation on 12 June 1946 and aroused considerable interest, support and opposition. It was steered through its successive stages by Professor H. J. Paton, the Chairman of the Social Studies Board. He called it 'a long considered attempt to meet a pressing need'. There were, he claimed, 'widespread complaints that while our Honour Schools have an outstanding reputation, our postgraduate degrees leave much to be desired'. Many students were unripe for the isolated work involved in a research degree and that method had been proved wholly unsuitable in more abstract subjects like philosophy. The present arrangements were discouraging graduates from Canada and the United States. Far from being illiberal the proposal sought to counteract the tendency to press highly specialised teaching into the Honour Schools. There was already a considered scheme to lighten PPE if the proposal were accepted.[6]

The preamble was passed in an atmosphere of anticlimax: the expected opposition failed to act, through misunderstanding the procedure and a lack of organisation. However on 22 October 1946 a crowded Congregation heard an amendment which, while approving the course of study and the examination, objected to its leading to a new degree: it should lead to the B. Litt. The amendment was lost by 58 votes to 45. The move to restrict the new degree to an experimental period of five years was also defeated (38 to 28). On 5 November 1946 the Statute was approved but by less than a two-thirds majority (66 to 46) and therefore had to be submitted to Convocation. Two weeks later a massed Convocation of some 400 passed it by 149 votes to 76.[7] It was first examined in June 1948.

The papers and requirements for Philosophy were as already indicated. Candidates for Politics were required to offer (a) General Social and Political Theory, (b) Political Institutions and (c) a General paper, plus two papers chosen from a list of nine subjects: Political Theories of Hegel and Marx, Modern Theories of Law from Bentham, History of British Political Thought 1760–1900, Social Structure, Procedure and Practice of Parliamentary Government in Great Britain, Comparative Local Government, Comparative Colonial Government, Federal Government and the Paris Peace Conference 1919. The Regulations specifically stated that a thesis might not be offered.

The requirements for Economics were (1) two compulsory papers on General Economics and (2) two from a list of five: Statistics, Theory and Economic Application; History of Economic Thought before 1914; Economic Developments between 1815 and 1914; and between 1919 and 1939; Economic Functions of Government; and International Economics. In place of one of the two papers under (2) candidates were free to offer a thesis of not more than 30 000 words. Very soon the thesis requirement was standardised at not more than 30 000 words but was optional for Economics and Politics and compulsory for Philosophy.

The introduction of the B. Phil. was a major landmark in the development of the University, probably more significant than the introduction of the D. Phil. after the first World War. To some it may have appeared to be simply a solution to the problems created by an Honour School combining three disciplines all of which had expanded in scope since the School was founded. For it opened the way for the clever PPE man to spend a fourth year concentrating on the subject in which he wished to specialise. But the conception was wider and more fundamental than that. Hitherto the only options open to those who had the means to do graduate work were to undertake the B. Litt. (Bachelor of Letters) or the D. Phil. (Doctor of Philosophy). Both these were awarded on a thesis, the former usually taking two years and the latter usually taking three years. Whilst the Statute governing the B. Litt. required the student 'to attend such courses of instruction and classes as his Supervisor may advise' the overwhelming emphasis was on the completion of a thesis. In the case of the D. Phil. the Supervisor was debarred from giving him 'systematic instruction'.

Increasingly it had come to be appreciated that embarking on a thesis immediately after taking a First Degree was in very many cases not the best form of educational development. The point was well made in a note submitted by some Professors of Toronto University to the Vice-Chancellor early in 1946 and circulated to Faculty boards.[8] The note stated that the war years had accelerated the process by which the influence of the American pattern of graduate work had impressed itself upon Canada. American Universities had realised the dangers of allowing students to specialise prematurely. Hence a Ph.D. candidate was required to take a number of graduate courses designed to extend the range and depth of his undergraduate work and to provide a broader background for the subject chosen for his thesis. In Oxford the major emphasis was on the Honour undergraduate courses with a close tutorial and collegiate residential system. In this pattern graduate work was hardly envisaged as a natural sequence and it was largely graduates from other Universities who demanded such studies. The Toronto Professors believed it would be better if their own graduates were required to take a limited number of advanced courses, preferably of the seminar type of instruction. They went on: 'it might allow some combination of the best elements in the honour undergraduate courses . . . with the work of the graduate school, just as the provision of a graduate centre (why not a college?) should do something to provide – what has hitherto been lacking – a common meeting place'.

Views of this kind had been expressed for some years, both from outside and increasingly from within the University. They are, however, worth quoting for they led the General Board of Faculties to ask the views of the Faculty Boards on the arrangements for teaching and examining of research degrees and on the desirability of a Graduate College.

The Lit. Hum. Board pressed for consideration of a new postgraduate College. It would offer many advantages to postgraduate students, it would make it easier to find College places for the desired increase in the number of Professors and Readers, and it would facilitate an expansion of the intake of highly qualified students. The Social Studies Board in supporting the idea added: 'In relation to the maintenance and development of postgraduate studies, both Nuffield College and the Institute of Statistics have an important part to play. Nuffield College in particular will in due course perform the functions of a Postgraduate College in the field of Social Studies'. It would be wasteful if the two were not used to their fullest extent and to achieve this their resources needed to be greatly augmented. Both Boards could virtuously point out that the new B.Phil. would meet precisely the needs mentioned by the Toronto Professors.[9]

In the haste to get the B.Phil. established little thought was given to its relations with the other higher degrees. In the field of Social Studies candidates for either the B.Litt. or the D.Phil. were first admitted as Probationer B.Litt. students. They had to indicate the field of their research interest, e.g. British Government, but not submit a precise title. Not later than their fourth Term they could transfer with the Faculty Board's approval, to either the status of B.Litt. student or of Advanced Student, i.e. for the D.Phil. They then had to state the precise title of the thesis on which they proposed to work. In some cases a candidate might proceed from Probationer status to B.Litt. status and then transfer to that of Advanced Student. At all these stages candidates had a Supervisor appointed by the Faculty Board.

The Statute establishing the B.Phil. contained no provision for transference of a candidate's residential qualifications to either B.Litt. or Advanced Student status. In October/November 1949 therefore the Lit. Hum. and the Social Studies Boards asked that transfers should be possible between B.Litt. and Advanced Student on the one hand and B.Phil. status on the other. In other words a person admitted to read for the B.Phil. might then, after two or three Terms, transfer to B.Litt. status or vice versa without loss of Terms. This was agreed and the amending Statute was passed by Congregation in May 1950.[10]. The new arrangement had the great advantage of enabling B.Litt. or D.Phil. candidates to secure a years tutorial teaching.

In 1954 the Philosophers and Economists raised a much bigger issue. The Statute governing the D.Phil. required the Examiners to exclude from consideration any part of the dissertation which had been submitted successfully for another degree. Thus a successful B.Litt. thesis could not be counted as part of a D.Phil. thesis. In Michaelmas Term 1954 the Social Studies Board, with the support of the Lit. Hum. Board, submitted a proposal whereby holders of the B.Phil. would be permitted to include in their D.Phil. thesis material which had formed part of their B.Phil. thesis. Such candidates should be allowed to submit for the D.Phil. after only three terms as an Advanced Student, not six as was the general requirement. In other words they envisaged a graduate spending two years on the papers and thesis for the B.Phil., then developing this thesis to D.Phil. standard in a further year.

More far reaching they asked that such candidates could be excused by the Board from spending these three Terms in Oxford. The D.Phil. Statute already enabled a Faculty Board to allow candidates to spend up to three of the six compulsory Terms of residence away from the University should their thesis subject warrant it. Thus a candidate engaged on a study of French politics might be given leave to spend three Terms in Paris, but would still have to spend three Terms in Oxford. The Philosophers wanted B.Phil. holders to be allowed to spend no further time in Oxford after completing their B.Phil. – an arrangement of obvious advantage to those who had returned to their own country and would find it difficult to spend a further year in Oxford.

The Philosophers did not believe that the D.Phil., with its emphasis on the thesis being an original contribution to knowledge, was the most suitable qualification for their profession. They wanted the B.Phil. to become the recognised credential for those who wished to secure University posts as teachers of philosophy. Originally, therefore, the Philosophers wished Examiners to be empowered to give a doctorate for specially meritorious work in the B.Phil. but could not get support for this proposal outside their own ranks.

The arguments used by the Economists in favour of the proposals turned primarily on the increasing emphasis on the refining of economic theory. As Professor John Hicks explained in a letter to the Committee for Advanced Studies, candidates for a D.Phil. in Economics usually chose a topic in what might be called contemporary economic history and wrote up an analytical account of a certain series of events. The Sub-Faculty did not wish to discourage theses of this sort but there was place for work which would be 'scientific in character rather than historical'. Such work would consist in the elaboration of methods and in the application of these methods to problems to which the methods were appropriate. Those who came to do postgraduate work in Economics were not ready to do analytical work of that sort. 'They do not know enough technique'. They should, therefore, pursue more general studies of an advanced character before undertaking research in the narrower sense. The Politics side of the Board favoured the principle underlying the proposals but did not expect themselves to make much use of them.[11]

The proposals were referred to the Boards of other Faculties for their views. Most were opposed, in particular there was strong opposition to the proposal which would have enabled B.Phil. holders to undertake all their statutory minimum Terms as an Advanced Student outside Oxford. It was argued at first that were B.Phil. theses to be allowed to count towards a D.Phil. the same concession would have to be allowed to B.Litt. and B.Sc. holders. It was appreciated however that these two degrees were awarded entirely on thesis work whereas the thesis was only a part of the B.Phil.[12]

In the end, in May 1955, the General Board agreed to accept the proposal of the Social Studies Board subject however to the requirement that the B.Phil. holder must work in Oxford for at least three Terms without any possibility of being granted leave of absence.

At first it was assumed that the Faculty's teaching responsibility for those registered for the B.Phil. would be satisfied by the provision of seminars of a graduate level. It was left to the College to provide other teaching. This proved inadequate in some instances and in 1958 each candidate was placed under a Faculty supervisor who taught him or sent him to someone else to be taught by the tutorial method traditional in the Honour Schools. Even so, the graduate seminar became an increasing feature of each Term's Lecture List, with 5 p.m. as the most favoured time.

The new Degree grew in popularity. In 1950 there were 18 candidates: 11 for Philosophy, 3 for Politics and 4 for Economics. By 1970 the numbers had risen to 51–27, 7, and 17.

Its success and the merits of the ideas underlying it led to the creation of B.Phils. in an increasing number of other disciplines. By 1960 there were B.Phils. in Greek and Latin languages and Literature; European History and the History of the British Commonwealth and Empire and of the United States of America. By 1970 there were B.Phils. in sixteen different disciplines. The great increase in the popularity of International Relations was recognised in 1971 by the introduction of a B.Phil. in that subject. The use of the term Bachelor came to be criticised. It gave a misleading impression to other Universities not familiar with the Oxford practice for at other Universities the term was confined to first degrees. As a result the B.Phil. and B.Litt. were redesignated from January 1979 as M.Phil. and M.Litt. except for the B.Phil. in Philosophy. Arrangements were made for existing holders of these degrees to have them redesignated.

THE HONOUR SCHOOL

Though increasing attention came to be paid to postgraduate studies the various Honour Schools continued to flourish and indeed, in terms of numbers, to dominate the scene. In 1958–9, excluding the postgraduate course for intending school teachers and other graduate courses in Education, they constituted over 80 per cent of all students in the University.

The end of the War brought a big increase in the number of undergraduates, there being 6159 first-degree students in residence in 1948–49 as against 4391 in 1938–9. By 1958–9 the number had increased to 7370. The numbers reading for the main Honour Schools in the Arts and Humanities were:

	1938–9	1948–9	1958–9	1968–9
Modern History	869	1148	1150	925
Literae Humaniores	584	454	774	587
PPE	495	798	751	769
Jurisprudence	464	535	703	565
Modern Languages	463	673	782	724
English	360	722	700	678

SOURCE *Oxford University Gazettes*

PPE had replaced Modern Greats as the term in everyday use for the Honour School of Philosophy, Politics and Economics. In passing it is interesting to note that PPE became far more popular than Cambridge's Economics Tripos. In 1938–39 there were 324 reading for the Tripos as against 495 for PPE. By 1954–5 the numbers were 327 as against 847.[13]

The Social Studies Board's Committee of 1945 had not suggested any changes in the structure of the School. Their proposal for more relevant entrance requirements was however implemented in 1949. A Preliminary Examination specially designed for Philosophy, Politics and Economics was introduced. Initially the papers, all of three hours, were:

(1) French or German or such other language as the Board might from time to time prescribe or Introductory Mathematics.
(2) Introductory Economics.
(3) The elements of Deductive and Inductive Logic.
(4) British Constitutional History from 1660 to 1914.

Candidates were required to offer the language paper together with any two of the other three subjects. Introductory Economics covered 'National Income and Distribution; elementary theory of supply and demand; elementary account of monetary mechanisms (national and international)'. The language paper was discontinued in 1968 and the Examination now consists of three Introductory papers: in Economics, Philosophy and Political Institutions.

The first change in the Final School came in 1949, following the introduction of the B.Phil. The number of papers was reduced from 9 to 8 and the special optional papers were rearranged. The reduction was achieved by omitting British Social and Economic History since 1760 from the list of 'compulsory' papers. The further subjects were divided into two lists from which candidates had to choose one from each. List I was quite short; (a) Philosophy of Kant; (b) Political History, 1871–1914; (c) British Social and Economic History since 1760; and (d) Statistical Method and Use of Statistics.

List II was subdivided into the three sides of the School. There were two further subjects in Philosophy: Logic and the Philosophy of Mind. The Politics choice was the largest: Political Theory from Hobbes; Local Government in England since 1830; Modern British Government; Labour Movements 1815–1914 (previously in the Economics list); Political Structure of the British Empire, and International Relations. The choice for Economics was Currency and Credit; Public Finance; Economic Theory; and Economics of Colonies and 'Under-developed' Societies.

These arrangements changed very little during the 1950s and into the 1960s. A few transfers took place between the two Lists –

for example in 1953 Political Theory from Hobbes and Currency and Credit moved from List II to List 1. The changes between Lists were usually made to enable candidates to secure a better combination of further subjects whilst ensuring that they took one of the main-line further subjects. Thus in October 1961 International Relations 1919–39 was promoted to List I in place of Political History 1871–1918.

In 1964 began a new development: some provision was made for those who wished to specialise in Sociology. A paper entitled Modern Social Institutions was added to List I and Social Theory from Comte was added to List II. In 1968 the latter paper was included in List I along with a paper on Political Sociology, Modern Social Institutions being transferred to List II. Within the tripartite structure of PPE that was the most that could be done. Sociology could not be put on a par with the three long established sides of the School by the addition of two compulsory papers without altering its whole character. And so, though those who wished to specialise in Sociology could now offer two further papers, they still had to take the six compulsory papers in Philosophy, Politics and Economics. Their needs were, however, catered for to some extent by the introduction of a B.Phil. in Sociology first examined in 1967.

The change reflected the growing interest in Sociology among teachers and undergraduates. By 1965 there were three University posts clearly in the subject, Nuffield College had made three appointments, several College tutors were interested in actively furthering the subject, and the Department of Social and Administrative Studies was beginning to expand. The Social Studies Board responded to the increase by establishing a Sub-Faculty of Sociology which met for the first time in October 1973.

In 1969 the issue which had divided the Faculty for many years was resolved. The original conception of the tripartite School had lost a good deal of its appeal. Right from the beginning there had been two complaints: that the School was overloaded and that it provided inadequate coverage for those who wished to be a specialist in, say, Economics. These criticisms gained increasing force as the scope of the papers, in terms of the reading available, increased voluminously. The B.Phil. was in part the answer but that normally required two further years' residence. The Faculty Board debated a wide range of alternatives and in the end one that found most favour was to allow candidates for

PPE the choice of concentrating on two of the three sides, in other words they were offered a bipartite option.

The changes were introduced in October 1970 so that the option first came available at the June 1971 examination. Candidates were still required to offer eight papers. The papers previously designated as compulsory were increased from six to seven with three in the field of Politics: Political Institutions, British Politics and Government since 1865 and Theory of Politics. At first the further papers were still divided into Lists I and II but with a larger choice in each List. In 1974 the two Lists were replaced by a series of choices for each of the three sides of the School.

Candidates can now either offer papers on the three sides of the School as hitherto or opt for two: Philosophy and Politics, Politics and Economics or Economics and Philosophy. For the tripartite option candidates are required to take the two compulsory papers in Philosophy and Economics, the Political Institutions paper and either British Politics and Government since 1880 or the Theory of Politics. They are also required to take two further subjects; eight papers in all. Candidates for the bipartite option of Philosophy and Economics are required to take the two compulsory papers in each of those subjects and four further subjects, at least one being from each side. Those opting for Philosophy and Politics or Politics and Economics are required to take the two compulsory papers on each side, with an option between British Politics and Government since 1880 or the Theory of Politics with four further subjects, at least one from each side. Thus the specialist is able to take five papers, out of eight, in his area of interest. Each side has a long list of further subjects, several with a regional interest, e.g. Latin America, and several in Sociology.

It had been evident for some time that even within the limited choice offered by the tripartite School a substantial switch had been taking place from Philosophy to the other two sides, and in particular to Politics. In June 1970 when there were 281 candidates only 19 concentrated on Philosophy whereas 133 did on Politics and 57 on Economics. Politics and Economics was the most favoured combination of Further Subjects attracting 46 candidates, 16 opted for Politics and Philosophy and only 10 for Economics and Philosophy. There was, therefore, every expectation that the offer of a bipartite option would reduce the demand for Philosophy, indeed before agreeing to its introduction the General Board asked for an assurance that it would not be followed by a request for more teaching appointments in Politics.

The option first came available in June 1971 when many candidates' choices would be influenced by the teaching they had already received. In June 1972, however, the trend was clear. Of the 269 candidates examined 68 took the tripartite and 201 the bipartite option. Within the latter 116 opted for Politics and Economics, 66 for Politics and Philosophy and 19 for Economics and Philosophy. The option of submitting a thesis not exceeding 15 000 words instead of a further subject was introduced in 1974 for an experimental period of two years, continued for a further three years and then indefinitely.

By 1983 the proportion opting for the tripartite School had fallen even further. In that year there were 281 candidates for PPE of whom only 37 opted for the tripartite option in contrast with 113 who opted simply for Politics and Economics, 96 for Politics and Philosophy and 35 for Economics and Philosophy. In that year the Examiners marked 2214 papers (i.e. 281 candidates x 8 less 34 theses): 1054 of these were in Politics, 674 in Economics and only 486 in Philosophy. Politics in this context covers a wide range, including International Relations and Sociology. Indeed any paper which is not clearly either Philosophy or Economics is counted as Politics.

In some measure the decline in the role of philosophy in the School reflects the shift of interest on the part of the Oxford teachers of the subject. The approach of Lindsay and most of his contemporaries linked readily with the study of politics and economics. With the increasing absorption in linguistic philosophy the link was less direct or obvious.

So, whereas in its earliest years the Philosophers had dominated the School, they now contributed the smaller part. Because of the increased size of the School there was still a great deal of philosophy teaching needed, indeed fresh opportunities had been created. The B.Phil. was quickly followed in 1947 by the establishment of an Honour School of Psychology, Philosophy and Physiology. This was followed in 1969 by Mathematics and Philosophy, in 1970 by Physics and Philosophy in 1971 by Philosophy and Theology and in 1976 by Modern Languages and Philosophy.

The decline in the role of Philosophy in PPE has been reflected in the decline in the influence of the Philosophers in the affairs of the Social Studies Board. But here other factors emphasised the decline. The work of the Board has become increasingly concerned with postgraduate students – their admission, approval of research subjects, appointment of supervisors and examiners, and the handling of ESRC awards and the allocation of scarce resources. In Philosophy these responsibilities fall on the Lit. Hum. Board. The Honour School, save when a major issue of principle is raised, occupies little of the time of the members of the Board. The changed status of Philosophy is evidenced in the Chairmanship of the Board. Until 1958 it was the well accepted custom that each of the three sides of PPE should provide the Chairman for two years in turn. Thus H. J. Paton, Gilbert Ryle and J. D. Mabbott, each did their stint after 1945. Nowadays it is recognised that the philosophy content of the Board's work no longer justifies a Philosopher taking on the Chairmanship. Indeed any business of concern to the philosophy representatives on the Board is taken at the beginning of the meeting so that they can leave once their business is done.

Late in 1962 a committee of the Social Studies Board recommended that 'higher management study' – the application of economic and statistical theory to management problems – could properly and profitably be pursued at Oxford as a self-contained academic study and by extending the principle behind the existing Oxford Business Summer School, i.e. by providing courses for people engaged in industry. It was generally agreed that as business and industry preferred to recruit suitable candidates from any of the Honour Schools there was little point in creating a new specialised first Degree. Instead two courses came to be offered.

The more significant was a B.Phil. in Management Studies first examined in 1968. This comprised two compulsory general papers; one to include questions on theories of organisation, sources of finance, appraisal of investment projects and management economics; the other to include questions on the economic, social and political environment in which the firm operates. There was a compulsory thesis, not exceeding 30 000 words and two papers to be chosen from a list of five: Operational Analysis, Statistical Methods of Econometrics, Economics of Industry, Industrial Relations and Industrial Sociology.

There was also established a Certificate in Management

Studies. This was designed to encourage those already engaged in the management side of industry to spend six months at the newly established Oxford Centre for Management Studies. It was awarded on the basis of a short dissertation of a practical kind and a favourable report from the Centre. It did not prove very attractive to British industry, there being many Management Schools offering less demanding courses. The Oxford Centre, however, began to make a name for itself as an institution which provided high level teaching in a variety of management techniques, sometimes tailored for the needs of particular firms. It is independent of the University but receives a grant for its contribution to the teaching needs of the University. In 1984 the Centre received a benefaction of $5 million from John Templeton and became Templeton College.

In 1965 a joint Honour School of Engineering Science and Economics was established and quickly proved popular. It was followed in 1970 by an Honour School of Modern History and Economics. Then in 1979 stimulated by the University Grants Committee there came an Honours School of Engineering, Economics and Management. Part II of this, first examined in 1981, requires candidates to present a report on a project carried out during a period of attachment to an industrial firm. An Honour School of Metallurgy, Economics and Management was founded at the same time.

This narrative has shown some concern in earlier years that Oxford was not making any contribution to the training of those seeking careers in the business and industrial worlds. Though this was one of the arguments used to support the introduction of the Diploma in the early years of the century that award did not achieve what its exponents anticipated. The attempt in 1909-14 to create a Diploma in Business Studies was not successful. However PPE was successful and formed a sound basis for the expansion of Social Studies generally and for the provision of management studies.

A high proportion of PPE men enter industry. A study[14] of the five years 1964-8, showed that 54 per cent of the 2291 who took their first Oxford degree in those years and whose first appointment was known took a job in commerce and industry. The figure for PPE was 69 per cent, for Modern Languages was 66 per cent and for Lit. Hum. was 55 per cent.

Social Studies is about the largest Faculty in the University, larger indeed than that in any other British University. The total numbers reading for Final Honour Schools either wholly or mainly within the field of the Social Studies Board in 1979-80 were:

Philosophy, Politics and Economics	855
Modern History and Economics	57
Engineering and Economics	24
Engineering, Economics and Management	41
Human Sciences	53
Metallurgy, Economics and Management	7
	1037

SOURCE: *Oxford University Gazette*, CX pp. 862-3

There were also the following number of graduates in residence working under the Board in that year:

	Politics	Internat. Relations	Economics	Sociology	Management	Total
M.Phil.	24(1)	20(1)	58(1)	8	17(1)	127(4)
M.Litt.		55(45)	39(10)	24(8)	7(3)	125(66)
D.Phil.		54(63)	21(32)	13(35)	6(1)	94(131)
M.Sc. Applied Social Studies			55			55
M.Sc. Social Research and Social Policy				6		6
						407(201)

SOURCE: *Registry*
NOTE: The figures in brackets are the number of students registered as working for the degree but no longer in residence.

FACULTY

Whereas in the inter-war years the bulk of the increased demand for teaching in social studies was met out of the resources of the Colleges, after 1945 teaching posts paid wholly or partly (e.g. CUF Lectureships) by the University came to dominate the scene. In part this arose from the changing character of the teaching needs. In the first twenty years of PPE the need was to teach the

General Developments after 1945

basic subjects of the Honour School to undergraduates, very clearly a College responsibility. This development continued with the very large post-war rise in the numbers reading for the School. Before long most Colleges had at least one Tutorial Fellow in both Economics and Politics. Nuffield College and, to a lesser extent, St Antony's College, also appointed a number of Fellows in Politics and Economics out of their own resources. Though these were mainly engaged on research they also contributed to undergraduate teaching and to the supervision of graduates.

The big increase in postgraduate studies, however, was primarily a University not a College responsibility: entrants to postgraduate degrees being admitted by Faculty Boards on behalf of the University and pay their main fees to the University. Moreover appointments came to be made in specialised subjects, e.g. Soviet Institutions and Criminology, for which no single College had a demand sufficient to justify or finance the appointment of a Fellow devoted solely to that subject.

There was however a deeper, all-pervading cause: the big increase in Government grants received by the University and not directly by the Colleges. Oxford received its first Exchequer money in 1922 and though the amount increased it was still by 1939 only the lesser part of the Oxford's academic expenditure. By the 1960s, however, it had become a major element.

Social Studies were particularly favoured. In 1946 the Government appointed a Committee under Sir John Clapham to consider 'whether additional provision is necessary for reasearch into social and economic questions'. Their general conclusion was that the existing provision in the Universities in this field was entirely out of relation both to its importance and to the provision made in the physical sciences. They recommended a large increase in the University grant for the provision of more Chairs and other teaching posts and for a much more liberal provision for libraries, calculating machines, computing assistants and similar facilities. They estimated that a further £250–300 000 a year was needed. As a result the University Grants Committee made available for all Universities a grant earmarked for this special purpose rising from £102 000 in 1947–48 to £400 000 in 1951-2 when it was merged into the general Quinquennial Grant received by each University.[15] Oxford's share rose from about £22 000 to about £30 000.

The Social Studies Board gave top priority to Chairs in

Economic Organisation and in Statistics, to either Readerships or Lecturerships in Local Government and Sociology and to several new posts in the Institute of Statistics and the Delegacy of Social Training. And so, in 1948, John Jewkes left Manchester to take up the Chair of Economic Organisation and David Champernowne was promoted from his Readership in Statistics to the Chair. In the same year B. Keith-Lucas was appointed Senior Lecturer in Local Government and D. G. MacRae to a Lecturership in Sociology.

When the earmarked grant came to an end in 1952 these posts became a charge on the Quinquennial Grant in the usual way. Each quinquennium the Board had the opportunity to propose the establishment of further University posts. In addition special benefactions made possible the creation of new Chairs, e.g. a Chair in Colonial Economics had been made possible in 1946 by a grant from the United Africa Company.

In 1939 the Faculty of Social Studies included 13 Professors and 3 Readers. Five of the Chairs were in History, three in Philosophy and one each in Economics and Politics. By 1946 two more had been added – one by the division of the Gladstone Chair in Political Theory and Institutions into Chairs of Social and Political Theory and of Government and Public Administration, the other being the Chair in Colonial Economic Affairs. By 1950 four more had been added: Psychology in 1947 and Statistics, Economic Organisation and Modern History in 1948. Though convenient from the viewpoint of providing a University definition of what constitutes a Faculty the allocation of Chairs to particular Faculties can give a misleading impression. The Professors of Geography and in Social Anthropology are not included in Social Studies though many would regard them as clearly part of the social sciences: their Chairs are allocated to the Faculty of Anthropology and Geography. The assignment of five History Chairs to Social Studies may give an equally misleading impression. Their holders do not become members of the Board ex officio, and they may play little or no part in the work of the Faculty. Their major role lies in the Faculty of Modern History.

With reservations of this kind the list of teachers entitled to vote in the election of any Faculty Board, is a broad indication of the number of teachers in that field. In July 1939 the list of members of the Faculty of Social Studies contained 87 names of whom 24 and 46 were listed as members of the Sub-Faculties of

Economics and of Politics. By April 1949 the list, which contained many philosophers, included 131 names, rising to 192 in April 1959 and to 235 in May 1969. The size of the Economics Sub-Faculty was 47 in 1949, 54 in 1959 and 72 in 1969, the corresponding figures for the Politics Sub-Faculty being 59, 77 and 97. By Michaelmas Term 1979 the list of members of the sub-faculties contained 100 names for Politics, 89 for Economics, and 39 for Sociology. Some of the names appeared in two lists, there being a particularly big overlap between Politics and Sociology. Altogether, however, some 200 teachers were covered by the three sub-faculties.

BUILDINGS AND FACILITIES

With the University getting back to normal the Social Studies Board began to consider ways of securing the future of two bodies wholly in their field: the Institute of Statistics and the Delegacy for Social Training and one in which they had a shared interest, the Institute for Colonial Studies.

As we have seen the war had strengthened the claims of the Institute of Statistics as a research body in its own right. The financial existence of the Institute was assured when the General Board took over responsibility on the expiry of the Rockefeller Grant on 31 July 1947. At the same time its constitutional position was clarified, it being placed directly under the Social Studies Board. In 1947–8 an ear-marked grant for the development of the social sciences following the Clapham Report encouraged a substantial increase in research staff. Yet the Institute was housed in the most temporary of temporary accommodation. In January 1947 the Institute moved from 72 Woodstock Road into huts in the gardens of St Hugh's College on a lease due to end in July 1951.

Social Training, which before the war had not been a responsibility of the Social Studies Board became so early in 1946 with the establishment of a Delegacy. Barnett House and the Barnett Library still remained in the hands of the Council of Barnett House, a voluntary body not part of the University. The council had a lease on 34–5 Beaumont Street.

Colonial Studies was another recent acquisition to the Social Studies empire. At the end of the war, the Institute only set up in 1943, was financed from the University's general funds, Miss Perham's salary and research expenses being met by Nuffield College. Housed first in 74 High Street it was moved to a series of temporary premises in Bardwell Road, South Parks Road, and Keble Road.

In the circumstances it is little wonder that in 1949 the Board turned their attention to the pre-war idea of using part of the Nuffield site for the general purposes of the Faculty. By then it was generally accepted that the earlier estimates of what might be achieved financially out of the Benefaction were hopelessly wrong. In 1939 it had been estimated that the whole building would cost about £250 000. Construction costs rose markedly after the war, being some two and a half times greater by 1949 and still rising. An estimate early in 1949 put the cost at £652 000, exclusive of library fittings, furnishings and architects' fees. At the same time the cost of salaries and wages, maintenance and other items of current expenditure had risen and had every prospect of continuing to do so. In contrast the value of the original endowment and the income derived from it had risen very little. There was, therefore, no prospect of completing all the buildings for to do so would take the bulk of the endowment and leave insufficient income to meet the costs of maintaining them let alone provide the number of Fellowships originally envisaged.

It was inevitable that the immediate post-war appraisal of future plans should cause the Warden and Fellows and the University to concentrate on the basic object of Lord Nuffield's Benefaction – to erect and maintan a College. It had been possible to go along with A. D. Lindsay's wide-ranging ideas when the money available seemed so ample. But once the circumstances changed it was accepted generally that the first claim on the funds available must be the College in the traditional sense of the term – a residential building housing Fellows and Students.

The fact that Lord Nuffield's Benefaction was now unlikely to provide finance for the Institute of Statistics and other general University purposes did not worry the Faculty for other sources had opened up. Attention therefore came to be focused on buildings and sites.

The original design for the College buildings had been rejected by Lord Nuffield in August 1939. He approved a new design in the Spring of 1940 but the war prevented a start being made.

The strict licensing of new building and the shortage of materials continued for seven or so years after the end of the war and the Foundation Stone was not laid until April 1949. Those with responsibility for the College were thus faced with two inescapable facts: there was not enough money to complete all the buildings envisaged and in any case, only a small amount of building work would be allowed by the government each year. The major issue, therefore, was which parts should be started first and which parts deferred, possibly indefinitely.

The decision was helped by the fact that the buildings had been designed for two different purposes: to house a residential College on traditional Oxford lines and to house a variety of University activities. The former had been mainly destined for the land east of Worcester Street and the latter for the land to the west. The College's attention focused therefore on the eastern site, the aim being to proceed with the Warden's Lodgings (to be used for general College purposes), the residential staircase, the Hall, Kitchens and Common Rooms. This still left the 'College' library to be built on the western site where it had been placed along with the library for the Institute of Statistics and other general Social Studies purposes. If, however, room could be found for the library on the eastern site the whole of the buildings needed for the College could be concentrated on that area. The solution was found by abandoning building the Chapel on the eastern site and using the space for a library, the tower becoming a bookstack. This meant that the College had no immediate need of the western site.

Discussions between the College and the Social Studies Board began about the middle of 1949 with the broad approval of Hebdomadal Council and the Nuffield College Committee. In November 1949 the Accommodation Committee of Council reported in favour of using the western part of the site for University purposes 'congenial to Nuffield College, provided that the necessary buildings would be suitable for later incorporation in the College'.[16] The Social Studies Board put forward their 'maximum possible needs'. The Institute of Statistics would require 24 research rooms, a large common room that could be used for seminars, accommodation for a library and sundry other rooms. The Delegacy of Social Training would require, in the long run, accommodation for the Barnett Library, 20 rooms for research workers, a lecture room and possibly a common room.

For the Institute of Colonial Studies, 14 research rooms and offices and a room for a library would be needed. The Faculty Board also asked for 10 rooms for Lecturers not adequately housed.

The College entered into the discussions faced with two problems. In the light of the tight restrictions then exercised over new building it was feared that any proposal to go ahead with a building on the western site would delay even further the completion of the residential buildings on the eastern site. As regards the longer term the College were reluctant to lose control of the western site for any lengthy period because they could not foresee how the College and its needs would develop. They were therefore reluctant to alienate the land permanently, indeed Henry Clay, then Warden, argued that they were precluded by the Trust Deed from doing that. They were thinking, therefore, of allowing temporary buildings to be placed on the site or, if of permanent construction, with the right for the College to acquire them later. In June 1951 broad agreement was reached with the Social Studies Board which took these views into account. The main features were: the western site would be let to the University on a 99-year lease, the College, however, reserving the right to acquire the building or any part of it for College use after the lapse of 30 years from the signing of the lease or 10 years from the date at which the last section of the building was ready for occupation whichever was the longer period, with a limit of 50 years from the signing of the lease. The Social Studies Board agreed that the building should not be regarded as part of the College for the purpose of applying for building licences or for determination of priorities in the University's building programme.[17] In April 1953 Hebdomadal Council approved in principle the lease of the western site to the University.

The University's resources for financing new building were very limited and Council and the General Board did not regard accommodation for Social Studies as having top priority. Early in 1955 the Oxford City Council offered to lease the western site for a car park provided they could be certain of a lease of not less than five years. The Social Studies Board agreed that the proposed Social Studies Centre was unlikely to be started within five years and that, so far as the Board was concerned, the College could go ahead with the lease. The College did so and the site ceased to be available for University building until at least 1960.

In the meantime, however, as we have seen, there emerged the prospects of a new building for the Institute of Statistics into which it moved in 1964.

The Institute of Colonial (renamed Commonwealth in 1956) Studies also found a permanent home. In 1954 it was decided to establish Queen Elizabeth House under the joint auspices of the University and the Government as a centre for the use of persons of standing from overseas wishing to study in an academic setting problems affecting overseas territories. The Institute, while retaining its identity and University responsibilities, moved its library and personnel into the new premises of Queen Elizabeth House (at 21 St Giles) in 1960. Ernest Oppenheimer, the South African industrialist, made available £100 000 to further all this development.

In 1969 the University began actively to pursue the possibility of a new building to house the Department of Social and Administrative Studies and the Barnett Library and provide general facilities for the Faculty and its growing number of graduate students. The intention was to develop the western side of Wellington Square with the assistance of the Higher Studies Fund. The general idea was approved by Congregation in 1971, it being envisaged at that time that the Institute of Economics and Statistics would ultimately move into the new centre. Financial difficulties led to the abandonment of the latter proposal and in 1973 the plans proved unacceptable to the Oxford City Council. In the summer of 1974 it was learnt that the University Grants Committee had withdrawn the anticipated building grant for the Wellington Square project.

However, a year later the City Council offered the University a 99 year lease of the buildings and site in George Street of the former Oxford Boys' High School. This was nothing like sufficient to provide for all the needs but it was centrally placed and had the merit of having been designed by Jackson. The Centre was completed and came into use towards the end of 1978, the Chancellor, Harold Macmillan, performing the opening ceremony. It provided an adequate home for the Social Studies Lending Library, formerly the Barnett Library; seminar rooms; offices for the Faculty; four rooms for visiting academics; a Students' Common Room, and accommodation for the Computing Unit. The last had been financed and developed by Nuffield College until its transfer.

The Department of Social Administrative Studies, however, still remained in temporary premises, at one time being housed in four separate buildings, until in September 1979 it was provided with adequate accommodation in converted houses, 32–36 Wellington Square. Thus by the end of 1979 the various activities of the Social Studies Faculty were decently housed, but not in one building or in close proximity.

Glossary

Some terms have been used in the narrative which are either peculiar to Oxford University or have meanings there not normally found elsehwere. A short explanation of each term follows.

College In Oxford a college is a self-governing and self-electing body, recognised by the University for certain important purposes. The Colleges admit candidates to the University, i.e. sponsor them for matriculation. They are responsible for discipline within their walls and for the teaching of their undergraduate members. Each College is governed by its Statutes which cannot be amended without the consent of the Privy Council and of the University in so far as the changes affect the University. Colleges are financed by their endowments and by the fees paid by their undergraduate and graduate members. The size of Colleges varies but most are within the range of 300–500 undergraduate and postgraduate members.

Convocation is composed of all MAs of the University who have kept their names on the books of their College. Until 1854 it was the supreme legislative body of the University but in that year a distinction was drawn between the general body of MAs and those who resided within a mile and a half from Carfax. The latter became Congregation and took over much of the authority of the former. In future, Statutes had to be passed by Congregation and were then laid before Convocation which however had power only to pass or reject not to amend them. In 1925 the legislative powers of Convocation were further curtailed, being confined to Statutes and Decrees which had not passed Congregation by at least two-thirds majority. It lost even this power in 1969 and nowadays its main function is to elect a new Chancellor.

Congregation is the sovereign body of the University. It emerged from Convocation and until 1925 was composed of all resident members of that body – residence meant living for at least 20 weeks a year within a mile and a half of Carfax. In 1925 membership was confined to those engaged in teaching and administration in the University. Its decision is essential to all Statutes submitted to it by Council. It elects the majority of members of Hebdomadal Council, receives reports from various University bodies, discusses major issues of policy and passes resolutions, and its approval is required for the appointment of the Vice-Chancellor. It normally meets fortnightly during Term.

Council see Hebdomadal Council

Faculty This is usually taken to mean any branch or aggregate of branches of the studies pursued in the University which is represented by a separate Board. The number of Faculties was increased in the late nineteenth century by the division of the older Faculties. Thus the Faculty of Arts was divided in 1885 into Literae Humaniores, Oriental Languages and Modern History each with its own Board. There are now sixteen such Faculties.

Faculty Boards Each Faculty has a representative Board. At one time the holders of certain Chairs and Readerships in the Faculty were ex-officio members of their appropriate Boards. In addition an equivalent number of other teachers were elected by members of the Faculty other than Professors and Readers. In 1931 the ex-officio element was changed. Boards are now elected from two groups, (1) Official members, i.e. Professors and Readers scheduled in the Statutes, (2) Ordinary members, i.e. all the other members of the Faculty whom are elected by Ordinary members. Each Board may co-opt up to four members.

The many functions and powers of Faculty Boards are to supervise the examinations under their statutory control; to frame lists of lectures; to appoint University lecturers; and to make recommendations to the General Board on matters concerning their area of studies.

General Board of Faculties First established in 1913 to co-ordinate and supervise the work of the several Boards of Faculties. Since 1969 it has been composed of the Vice-Chancellor, the two Proctors and the Assessor, a representative of Hebdomadal Council and sixteen members of Congregation, the Faculties being grouped into two constituencies each electing eight members. It is unusual nowadays for the Vice-Chancellor to attend or to take the chair at meetings of the General Board. This responsibility is undertaken by the Vice-chairman, elected by the Board, who is also ex officio a member of Council.

Under Council the General Board is responsible for the academic administration of the University. It has the duty to consider and supervise all matters connected with the research and teaching activities of the University and to administer the funds made available to it for these activities.

Hebdomadal Council The composition of this body has changed during the past hundred years and the scope of its responsibilities has greatly increased.

At the beginning of the present century Council was composed of four ex-officio members (the Chancellor, Vice-Chancellor, and the two Proctors) and eighteen members elected by Congregation of whom six had to be Heads of Houses, six to be University Professors and six to be members of Convocation of at least five years standing. They were elected generally speaking for six years.

In 1915 the number of College Heads was reduced to three and the number of unofficial members increased to nine. The Vice-Chancellor, on retiring from office, became ex officio a member for one year. The categories of elected members were abolished in 1924, the competition for places being thrown wide open except for the limitation that not more than three could be members of the same College. Since 1969 Council has been composed of the Chancellor, Vice-Chancellor, the Vice-Chancellor elect, the Vice-chairman of the General Board, the two Proctors, the Assessor, and eighteen members elected by Congregation of whom not more than three may be members of the Governing Body of any one College.

Only Council may propose legislation to Congregation. The current Statutes of the University make Council responsible for the administration of the University and for the management of its finances and property. It may now make decrees not inconsistent with the University Statutes without the approval of Congregation being required.

Responsions A kind of qualifying examination set by the University. No candidate could sit the First Public Examination unless he or she had passed Responsions or one of the examinations accepted as an equivalent for it. Until 1920 every candidate was examined in the Greek and Latin languages, also in Arithmetic and in the Elements of Algebra or of Geometry. In 1920 compulsory Greek was abolished. Increasingly the University came to recognise other 'qualifying' examinations, e.g. the General Certificate of Education, and in 1960 the Responsions examination ceased.

School Normally used to describe a course of study culminating in an Examination, e.g. an 'Honour School', leading to a first degree. Sometimes used to describe all persons working in a subject.

Statute The composition, powers and responsibilities of all University bodies, including those which govern the University, are laid down in the Statutes of the University, and all Chairs and Readerships and all Degrees and Examinations are established in this manner. Each Statute has a preamble stating the principle of the measure.

The other legislative form is the Decree which is used for details and not for general principles and for matters judged to be of less significance. Thus Hebdomadal Council and the General Board are established by Statute whereas most of their Committees are established by Degree. Until 1969 all Statutes and Decrees needed to be passed by Congregation before whom they were placed by Hebdomadal Councl. Since that year Hebdomadal Council has the power to make Decrees without their requiring the approval of Congregation.

Vice-Chancellor The titular head of the University is the Chancellor but for a great many years now the administrative work has been undertaken by the Vice-Chancellor. Until 1969 he was appointed by the Chancellor from among the heads of Colleges, the practice being for the office to be held in rotation, according to seniority as head, for three years at a time. Since then there has been an Appointing Committee of twelve members with the Chancellor or Vice-Chancellor in the chair. Its function is to consider possible candidates and propose a name to Congregation not less then two years before the current Vice-Chancellor is due to retire. If that proposal is agreed the Vice-Chancellor-elect becomes ex officio a member of Hebdomadal Council if he is not already a member.

The Vice-Chancellor is ex-officio Chairman of Committees and other bodies of which he is a member. Since 1969 it has been a full time office, the holder being given leave of absence from his College responsibilities.

Notes and References

ABBREVIATIONS

GB Papers and proceedings of the General Board of Faculties.
HCP Papers and proceedings of Hebdomadal Council.
NC Papers and proceedings of the Nuffield College Committee of Hebdomadal Council.
NH The early papers relating to Nuffield College in the University Archives.

1 ESTABLISHMENT OF THE DIPLOMA, 1903

1. *Essays in Science and Philosophy* (London, 1948) p. 33.
2. See A. Kadish, *The Oxford Economists in the Late Nineteenth Century* (Oxford, 1982).
3. *Cambridge University Reporter*, 14 May 1903, p. 774.
4. *Oxford Magazine* (1901–2) XX, 328.
5. *Cambridge University Reporter*, 14 May 1903, p. 766.
6. Ibid, p. 773.
7. Statement of the Needs of the University, 1902, pp. 115–16.
8. Memorials of Alfred Marshall, Edited by A. C. Pigou (London, 1925) pp. 56–7. See also S. Collini, D. Winch and J. Burrow, *That Noble Science of Politics* (Cambridge, 1983) pp. 311–14, 332–4.
9. The paper was divided into International Trade and Currency and Credit, the latter being replaced by Finance in 1906. The main text book recommended was J. S. Mill's *Principles of Political Economy*, and the bulk of the prescribed texts were Parliamentary Papers and Debates of the nineteenth century about economic and financial issues.
10. *Students Handbook to the University and Colleges of Cambridge* (1902).
11. A Plea for the Creation of a Curriculum in Economics and associated branches of Political Science, Cambridge, April 1902, pp. 2–3.
12. *Journal of the Royal Statistical Society*, 1926, LXXXIX, 372. See also *Life of John Maynard Keynes* Roy Harrod (London, 1951) pp. 63–4. Marshall reversed an earlier view that the Tripos should have the title of 'Economics and Social Sciences' or just 'Economics' because it would have opened him to the charge of not keeping good faith with the majority of one on the Historical Board who supported Dickinson's view. But he successfully

opposed a proposal, from Professor Westlake, that a paper in International Law should be compulsory. (Letters to Professor H. S. Foxwell, 18 and 23 February 1902, in the Marshall Papers, Cambridge, 3 (46) and (47).)
13. *Cambridge University Reporter*, 9 February 1904, pp. 454 and 540–541.
14. B. Jowett, then Master of Balliol, wrote to Marshall in August 1881 asking whether he would consider coming to Oxford as Professor of Political Economy (Marshall Papers, Cambridge).
15. *Economic Journal* (1926), XXXVI, 144.
16. Ibid. (1891), I 625–6 and 628.
17. *Memorials of Alfred Marshall*, ed. A. C. Pigou (London, 1925) p. 164.
18. *Journal of the Royal Statistical Society* (1926), LXXXIX, 372.
19. See Collini, Winch and Burrow, *That Noble Science of Politics*, pp. 335–6.
20. A. Marshall, *The New Cambridge Curriculum in Economics* (London, 1903) pp. 27–8.
21. Statement of the Needs of the University (1902), p. 117.
22. Fly sheet to members of the Cambridge Senate of 9 March 1903.
23. Alfred Marshall 1842–1924 J. M. Keynes in *Memorials of Alfred Marshall* (ed.) A. C. Pigou (London, 1925) p. 59.

2 DEVELOPMENTS

1. Master of Peterhouse speaking on 7 May 1903 'a Postgraduate course with a Diploma at the end – like that which, under conditions apparently the reverse of cheerful, they seemed to be talking of instituting at Oxford . . .' (*Cambridge University Reporter*, 14 May 1903, p. 765). In April 1902 Marshall told one of his correspondents that Oxford was making a mistake in planning a postgraduate course in Economics. (Letter from G. Binney Dibble. Marshall Papers.)
2. *Oxford University Gazette* (1906–7), XXXVII, p. 136.
3. Ibid (1907–8), XXXVIII, p. 178.
4. Ibid (1908–9), XXXIX, p. 159. There were, in 1908, five groups of subjects in the Examination for 'Candidates who do not seek Honours'.
5. *Oxford and Working Class Education*, (Oxford 1908) pp. 71–80.
6. *The Story of Ruskin College, Oxford*, 3rd Edition (1968) and W. W. Craik, *Central Labour College*, London, 1964. See also C. Tsuzuki, 'Anglo-Marxism and working-class education' in *The Working Class in Modern British History* ed. J. Winter (Cambridge, 1983).
7. *Principles and Methods of University Reform* (Oxford 1909) p. 118.
8. HCP (1910), 85, pp. 77–82.
9. Ibid, 87, p. i.
10. Ibid, 91, pp. 81–3.
11. *Oxford University Gazette*, XLIII, 739–40.
12. Ibid, p. 779.
13. Ibid, pp. 921–2
14. *Oxford Magazine* (1912–13), XXXI, 380.
15. *Oxford Magazine* XLIV, 132 and 189.

16. 'Oxford and a Business Diploma' by H.E.M., *Oxford Magazine*, 29 January 1914, XXXII, 162–3.
17. 'Sciences' or 'Science' were both used, sometimes in the same document but the singular became more usual.
18. HCP 101, xxxv.
19. Ibid, pp. 217–20.
20. Ibid, p. xcix.
21. Ibid, 102, pp. 171–5 and lxxv.
22. Ibid, 104, p. x.
23. Ibid, 104, pp. 195–8.
24. Ibid, 105, pp. 109–10.
25. Ibid, p. lxvi.
26. *Oxford University Gazette* 1920–21, L1, 192.
27. HCP 101, p. 221.

3 MODERN GREATS 1920–39

1. E. L. Hargreaves, 'Combined Schools at Oxford (1914–23)', *Oxford Magazine*, 1965–6, vol. 6 (NS), pp. 344–50.
2. HCP, 99, p. 279–89.
3. HCP, 113, p. 61.
4. HCP, 114, pp, 169–80.
5. The Preamble to a Statute for an Examination in Philosophy in relation to the principles of Natural Science as an Honour School was rejected in Congregation in February 1923 by 66 to 38 votes. (*Oxford University Gazette*, LIII, p. 328). The proposal had only been approved in the General Board by 11 votes to 6 (G. B. Vol. IX, p. lix). For a brief account of the debate see the *Oxford Magazine* for 15 February 1923 (Vol. XLI, p. 212) which summed up: 'clear that the majority felt that the time was not yet ripe for the scheme'.
6. HCP, 115, p. 85.
7. Ibid, pp. 83–4.
8. The draft was said to be the work of a sub-Committee composed of Professors Adams, Cannan and Edgeworth and Messrs. Barker, Carlyle, Furniss and Price. Adams and Barker were on the Committee for Civil Science.
9. HCP, 116, pp. 144–5.
10. Ibid., pp. 89–92.
11. Ibid., p. 143.
12. GB, vol. IX, pp. 31–2 and xxxiii.
13. HCP 116, pp. lxxi, lxxxiv and xcv.
14. *Oxford University Gazette* 1919–20, vol. L, p. 785.
15. *Autobiography of an Economist* (London 1971) p. 111.
16. *Oxford University Gazette* (1920–1), vol. LI, p. 192.
17. L. L. Price, Obituary of F. Y. Edgeworth, *Journal of the Royal Statistical Society* (1926), vol. LXXXIX, p. 373.
18. See letter by A. J. Jenkinson to the *Oxford Magazine*, 5 November 1920, vol. XXXIX, p. 65.

References 191

19. Ibid, p. 25.
20. Meeting of Oxford University Economics Society in January 1921 when Sir William Beveridge spoke on 'Economics as a Liberal Education'. He defined Economics as 'everything taught at the London School of Economics' (Ibid, p. 155).
21. Ibid, pp. 55–6.
22. Ibid, p. 22.
23. *Oxford University Gazette* 1920–21, vol. LI, p. 76, 153 and 233.
24. *Oxford University Gazette* 1930–31, vol. LXI, p. 579.
25. *Oxford Magazine* 1937–8, Vol. LVI, p. 117. Robert Hall, writing in January 1938, could say 'it is overloaded for all but the best men; and the claims of three subjects prevent any tutor from continuously supervising his pupils' (Ibid, p. 315).

4 CREATION OF A FACULTY OF SOCIAL STUDIES

1. *Oxford Magazine* 1931–32, vol. L, pp. 360–361.
2. R. F. Harrod, *The Life of John Maynard Keynes*, (London 1951) p. 317.
3. *Oxford University Gazette* 1927–8, LVIII, p. 315.
4. Reports of the Board of Studies (1931), p. 145.
5. Reports of Social Studies Board (1932), p. 174.
6. *Oxford University Gazette* 1931–32, LXII, pp. 558–9. It was provided that 'no application shall be brought to the Board of the Faculty of Social Studies the subject of which falls within the province of the Board of the Faculty of Literae Humaniores' (Ibid, p. 621).
7. *Oxford University Gazette* 1937–38, vol. LXVIII, p. 407.

5 DEVELOPMENT OF UNIVERSITY FACULTIES

1. HCP (1928), 141, p. 73.
2. HCP (1929), 142, pp. 59–60.
3. The Library Commission in their report 'Library Provision in Oxford' (1931) had recommended the development of the system of subsidiary special libraries under the control of the Faculties by the provision of accommodation in a new building adjacent to the Examination Schools.
4. HCP (1931), 149, pp. 241–2.
5. GB (1931–2), XIX, p. 292. See also HCP (1931), 149, p. xci and (1932), 152, p. 165.
6. HCP (1932), 153, p. lxxxiii.
7. GB (1931–2), XIX, p. 292.
8. HCP (1934), 158, pp. 163–4.
9. Ibid, p. lxi.
10. HCP (1935), 159, pp. 121–135.
11. Ibid, 160, p. xi.
12. Ibid p. xxiv.

13. Ibid, pp. 145–152.
14. Ibid, pp. 203–212 and xci.
15. Ibid, 161 p. 31.
16. Ibid, pp. 118–9 and p. 1.
17. *Oxford University Gazette* (1934–5), vol LXV, pp. 670–1.
18. Sir Edmund Craster, *History of the Bodleian Library* (Oxford 1952), p. 327.
19. *Oxford University Gazette* (1937–8), vol. LXVIII, pp. 134–5.

6 LORD NUFFIELD'S BENEFACTION

1. The letter is reproduced by Drusilla Scott, *A. D. Lindsay*, (Oxford 1971) p. 231. She added: 'Lord Nuffield had suspicions of Lindsay because of his politics, and so preferred to make this offer through the Chancellor and the Registrar.'
2. See NH/1. for the early discussions
3. HCP (1935), 161, pp. 139–40 and 162, p. 113.
4. P.W.S. Andrews and E. Brunner, *The Life of Lord Nuffield* (Oxford, 1955) pp. 289–90.
5. NH/1. A large part is reproduced in Drusilla Scott's biography, pp. 232–5.
6. HCP 168, pp. 65–72.

NOTE:

The correspondence with W.G.S. Adams, Sir W. H. Beveridge, Miss L. Grier, Professor M. Powicke, and Richard Livingstone is in the Library of Nuffield College.

7 SOCIAL RECONSTRUCTION SURVEY

1. NC VI, pp. vii and 11–12.
2. Ibid. p. 25.
3. NH/4F, p. 2.
4. HCP (1940) 176, p. 156.
5. NH/4F p. 29.
6. HCP (1940) 176, p. lxxxi.
7. NH/4F, p. 35.
8. Ibid, p. 39.
9. Ibid, p. 49.
10. Ibid, p. 72.
11. NC VII, pp. iii–iv.
12. Ibid, pp. 17–19 and vii.
13. NH/4F, pp. 82–3.
14. Ibid, p. 86.
15. Ibid, pp. 115–15A.
16. Ibid VII, p. xvii.
17. Ibid, p. 15 and pp. 25–7.

References

18. Ibid, pp. 23–25.
19. Ibid, pp. 31–3 and xv.
20. Nuffield College Social Reconstruction Survey Report 1941–2.
21. 370 HC Deb. Col. 872.
22. NC IX, p. 119.
23. NH/3/2, p. 48.
24. HCP 180, p. li.
25. Ibid. pp. 143 and lxi.
26. NH/3/2, p. 51.
27. Mimeographed copy in library of Nuffield College.
28. NC VIII, pp. x and xiii.
29. NH2/1
30. NC VIII, pp. 103–4 and 106.
31. NH2/1/1, p. 28A.
32. HCP 182, pp. 169, lxxiv and lxxix.
33. NH2/1/1, p. 31.
34. Ibid, p. 35.
35. NC IX, pp. 151–2.
36. NH3/2, p. 145 and H.C.P. 185, pp. v and vii.
37. NC IX, pp. 87–136.
38. *Life of G. D. H. Cole* Margaret Cole (London, 1971) p. 248.
39. NC IX, pp. 169–72.
40. Ibid, pp. 157–62.
41. Ibid, pp. 165–8.
42. Ibid, pp. 126–8.
43. Ibid, pp. xxvii and xxviii.
44. HCP 185, pp. lxxix–lxxx and xciii.
45. NC X, pp. 3 and iii.
46. NC IX, pp. 99–118.
47. NH2/1/1, p. 33.
48. NH.
49. *Life of G. D. H. Cole*, Magaret Cole (London, 1971) pp. 186–8 and 293–4.
50. NH2/2, p. 154.
51. NH2/1, pp. 31–34.
52. Ibid. p. 33.
53. NC X, pp. 3–7.
54. *Life of G. D. H. Cole* (London, 1971) pp. 245–6.
55. N.C. VII, pp. 61–4 and xxxii.
56. N.C. X, p. 11. The papers, proceedings and reports of the Conferences are in the Library of Nuffield College.
57. *Life of G. D. H. Cole* (London, 1971) p. 243.

8 EMERGENCE OF NUFFIELD COLLEGE

1. NC, I, pp. 29–38.
2. NC, X, pp. 59–62 and 55–6.

3. NC, II, pp. 31–4.
4. Ibid, pp. 57–60.
5. NC, VIII, pp. 49–50.
6. Ibid, pp. ix and x.
7. Ibid, pp. 65–66.
8. NC X, pp. 25–30.
9. Ibid, p. 43 and pp. 55–6.
10. Letter from A. D. Lindsay to A. L. Poole, 28 February 1944.
11. NC, XI, pp. 11–12 and p. xiii.
12. NC XII, pp. 13–15 and 21 and *Oxford University Gazette* 1946–47 LXXVII, p. 156.
13. NC XI, pp. 12–13.
14. NH 2/2, p. 173.
15. *Oxford University Gazette* 1945–6, LXXVI, p. 43.
16. Report of Commission of Inquiry, Oxford 1966, Vol. I, paras 278–9 and para. 79.

9 TRAINING FOR SOCIAL WORK

1. *Oxford University Gazette* 1918–19, Vol. XLIX, pp. 445 and 520.
2. Ibid, 1935–36, p. 396, and see HCP Vol. 161, pp. 141–4.
3. *A Survey of Social Services in the Oxford District* (Oxford University Press I, 1938, II, 1940.)
4. NC vol. II, pp. 29–30 and xix.
5. Ibid, vol. IX, pp. 23–24 and viii.
6. Ibid, p. xvii and NH/BH.
7. *Oxford University Gazette*, 1945–6, vol. LXXVI, pp. 296–8.
8. Ibid, 1928–9, vol. LIX, p. 154.

10 INSTITUTE OF ECONOMICS AND STATISTICS

1. HCP (1934) 159, pp. 133–5. An early draft (early 1932) is to be found at p. 175 of the Social Studies Board Reports. It mentioned that Professor Wesley Mitchell would be spending a year in Oxford as the George Eastman Visiting Professor at Balliol and ought to be consulted. Mitchell, a founder of the National Bureau of Economic Research in New York appears to have been an important influence.
2. *Oxford University Gazette* 1935–36, LXVI, p. 63.
3. Ibid, p. 479.
4. Social Studies Research Committee, Reports, p. 24.
5. Social Studies Board minutes 1937, p. 113.
6. NC I, pp. 20–3.
7. Ibid; p. 19.
8. Ibid, pp. 45–59.
9. Ibid pp. 67–72.

10. Ibid, pp. 79–80.
11. Ibid, p. 89.
12. NC II, pp. 19–22.
13. Ibid, pp. 53–4.
14. NH/2/1.
15. NC III, pp. 3–6.
16. Ibid. pp. 39–42.
17. NC IV, pp. 1–4.
18. Ibid. pp. 13–18.
19. *Oxford Magazine* (1938–9) LVI, p. 316.
20. NC X, pp. 28–9.
21. NC XI, pp. 7–8.
22. HCP (1944) 187, p. 143; 188, p. 23.
23. HCP (1945) 190, pp. 213–8.
24. HCP (1946) 195 pp. 57–60 and 197 pp. 261–2.

11 GENERAL DEVELOPMENTS AFTER 1945

1. Social Studies Board, Minutes, Vol. 2, p. 221.
2. Board of Social Studies, Reports, Vol. 6, pp. 64, 74–5, 97, 99–100, and Minutes, vol. 3, p. 8.
3. Ibid, vol. 6, p. 116.
4. GB (1946), vol. LII, pp. 25–6.
5. Ibid. pp. 137, 205, xxi and xxxix.
6. *Oxford Magazine*, 1945–6, vol. LXIV, p. 359.
7. *Oxford University Gazette*, 1946–47, vol. LXXVII, pp. 88, 114, 155. *Oxford Magazine* vol. LXIV, p. 373 and LXV, pp. 33, 69 and 104.
8. Board of Social Studies, Reports, vol. 6, p. 134.
9. Ibid, p. 161 and G. B. LIII, pp. 323–5.
10. *Oxford University Gazette* (1949–50), vol. LXXXI, p. 845.
11. GB (1955), vol. LXXX, pp. 107–9.
12. Ibid, vol. LXXIX (1955), pp. 119–24, and vol. LXXX, pp. 105–7 and xiv.
13. *Oxford Magazine* 1955–56, LXXIV, p. 328.
14. *Oxford University Gazette* 1968–9, XCIX p. 1411.
15. University Development – Report of the University Grants Committee 1935–47, pp. 72–3; 1947–51 (Cmd 8473), p. 13; and 1952–56 (Cmnd 79), p. 19.
16. NC XIV, p. vii.
17. NC XV, pp. 41–42.

Name Index

Abercrombie, Patrick, 93
Ackroyd, Elizabeth (DBE, 1970), 135
Adams, W. G. S. (Warden of All Souls, 1933–45), 16, 24, 41, 52, 55, 73, 83, 130, 131, 135, 137
Allen, Maurice, 48
Andrews, P. W. S., 125, 146
Ashley, William (Kt, 1917), 4
Aydelotte, F. A., 69, 74

Balfour, A. J., 4
Balfour of Burleigh, 88
Ball, Sidney, 15, 19, 47, 130, 131
Balliol, Master of, see Lindsay, A. D.
Balogh, Thomas (Ld, 1968), 155
Barker, Ernest (Kt, 1944), 24
Barna, T., 125
Barnett, Canon S. A., 130-1
Besse, Antonin, 72, 129
Beveridge, William H. (KCB, 1919; Ld 1946), 73, 83, 92
Bevin, Ernest, 105
Blake, Robert (Ld, 1971), 48
Bourdillon, Miss A. F. C., 135
Bowen, Ian, 155
Bowley, A. L. (Kt 1950), 86, 93, 101-3, 155
Bracken, Brendan (Viscount, 1952), 98
Bretherton, R. F., 42, 48, 59, 135, 146
Broadley, Mrs R., 108
Brown, A. J., 146
Bryce, Lord (1st Viscount), 4, 131
Burchardt, F., 155, 160
Butler, David E., 126

Butler, Harold B. (KCMG, 1946; Warden of Nuffield, 1939–43), 84, 86–91, 98, 106, 118–9, 151-2
Butler, Violet, 16, 27, 49, 130, 134
Cadman, Lord, 85
Cannan, Edwin, 14, 15, 35, 36
Carlyle, A. J., 23, 49, 130
Champernowne, David, 125, 158, 160, 178
Chapman, Sydney (KCB, 1920), 4
Chester, D. Norman (Kt, 1974; Warden of Nuffield, 1954–78), 125, 126
Chrystal, George W. (KCB, 1922), 90-1
Citrine, Walter (Ld, 1946; KBE, 1935), 85
Clark, George N. (Kt, 1953), 55, 93, 101-3
Clay, Henry (Kt, 1946; Warden of Nuffield, 1944–9), 48, 104, 114, 122–4, 125, 158, 182
Clegg, Hugh, 125, 126
Cole, G. D. H., 49, 50, 52, 84, 89–111, 116, 136–7, 154, 161
Cole, Margaret (DBE, 1970), 102, 106–7, 109–10, 113
Costin, W. C., 42, 83
Coupland, Reginald (KCMG, 1944), 41, 85, 116
Courtauld, Samuel, 113
Cunningham, William, 5, 15
Curzon of Kedleston (1st Marquess, 1921; Chancellor of Oxford University, 1907–25), 19, 21-3

Name Index

Dearle, N. B., 15, 27
Dickinson, G. Lowes, 10

Edgeworth, F. Y., 3, 10–12, 136
Emden, A. B., 83
Ensor, R. C. K. (Kt, 1955), 84, 93, 116, 154
Etherton, George (Kt, 1927) 85
Evans-Pritchard, E. E., 59

Fisher, A. G. B., 93
Fisher, Sir Warren (KCB, 1919, etc.), 91
Fogarty, Michael, 125
Franks, Oliver (KCB, 1946; Ld, 1962; OM, 1977), 42, 129
Fraser, L. 42, 48, 50
Fulton, John S. (Kt, 1964; Ld, 1966), 42, 84, 116

Geldart, W. M., 24, 29, 130
Gilbert, E. W., 59
Goldthorpe, John, 126
Goodenough, William (Bt, 1943), 82, 86–91, 96–7, 100–2, 110
Gordon, G. S. (Vice-Chancellor, 1938–41), 83, 88–9
Gordon-Walker, Patrick (Ld, 1974), 48
Green, T. H., 1
Greenwood, Arthur, 93–4
Grier, Lynda, 69, 74, 77, 81, 83, 89, 93, 95, 110, 136
Guillebaud, C. W., 27

Hailey, Lord (KCSI, 1922, etc.; Ld, 1936), 85, 97
Hailsham, Lord (Ld, 1970), 109
Halifax Lord (Earl, 1944; OM, 1946; Chancellor of Oxford University, 1933–59), 63, 69, 88–9
Hall, Robert, see Roberthall
Halsey, A. H. (Chelly), 126, 143
Hardie, F., 42
Hargreaves, Eric, 42, 48
Harris, G. Montagu, 59, 93
Harrison, Austen St B., 83–4

Harrod, Roy F. (Kt, 1959), 48, 55, 57, 84, 116, 154
Hartley, Harold (Kt, 1928), 91
Headlam-Morley, Agnes, 93
Henderson, Hubert D. (Kt, 1942) 27, 58–9, 60, 158, 161
Hewins, W. A. S., 4
Hicks, John R. (Kt, 1964), 125, 167–8
Hird, D., 21
Hobbs, W., 65, 68
Hogg, Quintin, see Hailsham
Hugh-Jones, E. M., 42

Jevons, W. S., 6
Jewkes, J. 178
Joachim, H. H., 31
Jowitt, William A. (Kt, 1929; Earl, 1951), 94

Kalecki, M., 155
Keir, David L. (Kt, 1946), 42
Keith-Lucas, B., 178
Keynes, J. Maynard (Ld, 1942), 6, 11
Keynes, J. Neville, 10
Kittredge, Mr 57, 60

Landon, P. A., 104
Layton, W. (Kt, 1930; Ld, 1947), 27
Lees-Smith, H. B., 15, 19
Leith-Ross, Frederick W. (KCB, 1933, etc.), 85
Lindsay, A. D. (Sandie) (Ld, 1945; Master of Balliol, 1924–49; Vice-Chancellor, 1935–8) x, 30–1, 33, 41, 55, 57, 64–82, 83, 86, 89–91, 93, 95, 104, 110, 114–15, 118–9, 121, 136, 152, 158
Livingstone, Richard (Kt, 1931; Vice-Chancellor, 1944–7; President of Corpus, 1933–50), 58–9, 69, 77, 81, 83, 128
Loveday, A. (Warden of Nuffield, 1950–4), 125, 126

Mabbott, J. D., 174
McCallum, R. B., 42, 48, 116, 161
Macgregor, D. H., 41, 50, 52, 55, 93, 101–3, 116, 137

Mackenzie, W. J. M., 48
MacKinnon, D. M., 161
Macmillan, Harold (Earl Stockton, 1984) (OM, 1976; Chancellor 1959–), 183
MacRae, D. G., 178
McTaggart, J. Ellis, 10, 15
Marriott, J. A. R., 19
Marschak, J., 145, 151, 157
Marshall, Alfred, 3–6, 8, 10–13, 15
Matheson, P. E., 23
Maud, J. P. R. (KCB, 1946; Ld Redcliffe Maud, 1967), 42, 47, 59, 116, 132, 154
Medley, Maria Louise Webb, 47
Mill, John Stuart, 2, 6
Mitchison, G. R., 95
Morley, John, 4
Morris, Charles R. (Kt, 1953; Ld, 1967), 83
Myres, J. L. (Kt, 1943), 31

Norman, Montagu (Ld, 1944), 109
Nuffield, Viscount (1938) (Bt, 1929), 61–2, 63–70, 84, 98–100, 109–10, 127, 129

Oakeshott, Michael, 125
Ogilvie, F. W. (Kt, 1942), 48
Opie, Redvers, 48, 116
Oppenheimer, E., 183
Orwin, C. S., 93

Paton, H. J., 37, 161, 163, 174
Pember, F. W. (Vice-Chancellor, 1926–9), 24
Penson, T. Henry (KB, 1918), 27, 36
Perham, Margery F. (DBE, 1965), 59, 84, 85, 86, 93, 126, 180
Phelps, L. R., 130, 131
Phelps Brown, Henry (Kt, 1976), 42, 48, 60, 146, 147
Poole, Austin L., 121
Portal, Lord (Ld, 1935; Viscount, 1945), 98
Powicke, Maurice (Kt, 1946), 80
Price, H. H., 42, 161

Price, L. L., 3–12, 22, 36
Prichard, H. A., 33

Redcliffe Maud, see Maud, J. P. R.
Robbins, Lionel C. (Ld, 1959), 35, 48
Roberthall, Lord (1969) (KCMG, 1954), 42, 48, 84, 87, 116, 135, 153–4, 161
Robertson, Denis H. (Kt, 1953), 27
Robinson, Kenneth, 125
Rodger, A. B., 42
Ross, David (KBE, 1938); Vice-Chancellor, 1941–4), 99–101
Ryle, G., 42, 174

Salter, Arthur (KCB, 1922; Ld, 1953), 59
Salveson, H. K., 48
Schumacher, E. F., 155
Shackle, G. L. 146
Shackleton, David J. (KCB, 1917), 19
Shove, G. F., 27
Sidgwick, H., 6
Slater, Gilbert, 21
Smith, A. L., 131
Smith, J. A., 23, 35
Streat, Raymond (Kt, 1942), 113
Strong, T. B. (GBE, 1918), 19, 131
Sumner, B. H., 42, 45
Sutherland, Lucy (DBE, 1969), 42, 116

Upjohn, Mr Justice, 128

Veale, Douglas (Kt, 1954; Registrar, 1930–58), 57, 63–7, 69, 73, 78, 86–91, 106–7
Vickers, Geoffrey (Kt, 1946), 85

Walsh, Andrew, 68
Webb, C. C. J., 31
Webb, Medley, see Medley
Webb, Sydney (Lord Passfield) and Beatrice, 20
Weldon, T. D., 41
Wheare, Kenneth C. (Kt, 1966), 48
Whitehead, A. N. (OM, 1945), 1

Williams, H. H., 31
Williams, P. M., 125
Wilson, Charles H. (Kt, 1965), 93, 95
Wilson, Evelyn G., 42, 49
Wilson, Harold (KG, 1976; Ld, 1983), 160
Wilson, Sir Horace, 89–90

Wolfenden, John (Kt, 1956; Ld, 1974), 42
Woodcock, George, 143
Worswick, G. D. N., 155

Young, A. P., 85

Zimmern, Alfred (Kt, 1936), 116

Subject Index

Accountancy, 63—70
African Sociology, 57–9
All Souls College, 52–3, 55, 69, 77
Anthropology, 17, 57
Appeal, 1935–7, 60–2
Applied Social Studies;
    Diploma, 143; M.Sc., 176

Balliol College, 1
B. Litt, see M. Litt.
B. Phil, see M. Phil.
BCL, 25, 29, 162
Barnett House, x, 71, 75, 130–1, 134–9, 179
    Library, 52, 134–5, 136–7, 139, 179, 183
Biochemistry, 54
Birmingham University, 4, 22
Bodleian Library, 52–3, 61, 145–6, 148–9
Business Education, 21–4, 175

Cambridge, viii, 2–8, 22, 65, 67, 169
Catholic Workers College, see Plater College
Certificate in Social Training, 130–2, 140
Civil Science(s), Master of, 24–6, 30, 35
Clapham Committee, 160, 177–9
Clinical Research, 54
Colonial Administration, 57–9
Colonial Economics Chair, 178
Colonial Studies, 86, 179–80, 182
Committee on Economics and Political Science, 14, 33–4, 36, 46–7, 49, 50–1, 132
Committee on Radical Economies, 139

Commonwealth Studies Institute, 183
Congregation, 185
Convocation, 185
Co-ordinating Committee, 59, 69
Council, see Hebdomadal Council

Decrees, 187
Design and Analyses of Scientific Experiments, 157–9
Diploma in Applied Social Studies, 143
Diploma in Commerce and Economics, 23–4
Diploma in Economics (and Political Science), 12–15, 17–18, 20–1, 24, 27–8, 30, 132–3, 140–3
Diploma in Public and Social Administration, 47, 132–4, 140–1
Diplomas, Oxford, 17
D. Phil., 164–7, 176

Economic History, 15–16, 52
Economic Organisation, Chair, 54, 178
Economics and Political Science, see Diploma in
Economics Consultative Committee, 116, 119–20, 122–3, 150, 152–4
Economics Tripos, 5, 12–13, 27, 169
Economists, 42, 56
Economists Research Group, 60, 66, 147, 155
Engineering, 63–7, 69
Engineering Science; and Economics, 175–6; and Management, 175–6

Subject Index

English Language and Literature, 9, 169
Experimental Psychology, 54, 58
Extension Lectures Committee, 2
Extra-Mural Delegacy, 75, 143

Faculty Boards, 15, 186
Finance and Currency, 54
Franks Commission, 129

General Board of Faculties, 186
Geography, 53, 57–9
Government and Public Administration, Chair, 178
Greats, *see* Literae Humaniores

Halifax House, 129
Hebdomadal Council, 186
Higher Studies Fund, 61–2
Historical Tripos, *see* Modern History, Cambridge
Human Sciences, 176

Institute of Economics and Statistics, 144–60
Institute of Statistics, ix–x, 53, 55–7, 60, 75, 92, 112, 117, 119, 144–60, 166, 179, 181, 183
International Committee, 155
International Relations, 168; Chair, 52

Jurisprudence, 169

Library Facilities, 52–3
Literae Humaniores, 1, 6–10, 11, 31, 37, 161, 169
Local Government, 94–5, 178
London School of Economics and Political Science, 3, 20
Lord Nuffield's Benefaction, x, 62, 63–70, 104, 108–10, 115, 117, 128–9, 135, 147, 180–1
see also Nuffield College

Management Studies, 174–5; Centre for, 175
Manchester University, 4, 22
M.Sc., Applied Social Studies, 143, 176

M.Sc., Social Research and Social Policy, 176
Mathematical Tripos, 10
Mathematics and Philosophy, 173
Mediaeval and Modern Languages, 9
Medical Benefaction, 64, 66–8
Metallurgy, Economics and Management, 175–6
Minister for Information, 98
Ministry of Labour, 105
Ministry of Reconstruction, 93–5, 105
Ministry of Works, 95, 98, 105
Modern Greats, *see* PPE
Modern History, Cambridge, 7
Modern History, Oxford, 1–2, 7, 40, 169
Modern History and Economics, 175–6
Modern Humanities, 31–7
Modern Languages, 169
Modern Languages and Philosophy, 173
M. Litt., 162–4, 166, 176
M. Phil., viii, 141, 161–9, 176
Moral Sciences Tripos, 5, 8

Natural Science, Faculty, 26, 31, 33
Nuffield College, 166
  Barnett House, 135–8, 181
  Building, 83–4, 127, 180–3
  Conferences, 110–13
  Fellowships, 75–6, 84–5, 124–7, 177
  Finance, 115–6, 118–9, 123–4
  Independent Status, 127–8
  Institute of Statistics, 147–56, 181
  Lindsay's Views, 70–7, 115
  Scheme of Delegation, 114–22
  Statutes, 84–5
  Students, 127
  Trust Deed, 78, 82, 114, 120–1, 128, 182
  Trustees, 82, 86–9, 91, 100, 110, 120–1
  Warden, 84, 87–92, 97–9, 110, 121, 122
  Women, 75, 81–2
see also Lord Nuffield's Benefaction

Subject Index

Nuffield College Committee, 83, 117, 120, 122

Oxford, vii–ix, 3, 17, 39
Oxford and Working-Class Education, 19, 131

Philosophers, 30–1, 35, 40, 42, 173–4
Philosophy and Natural Science, 31, 33
Philosophy, Politics and Economics, see PPE
Philosophy and Theology, 173
Physical Chemistry Laboratory, 62, 64–6, 69, 72, 78–9
Physics and Philosophy, 173
Plater College, 134, 141–3
Political Economy, Chair, 15
Political Economy Club, 1
Political Philosophy, 54
Political Theory and Institutions, Chair, 16, 178
Politics Consultative Committee, 116, 119–20, 122–3, 151, 154
PPE, viii, 30–45, 161–3, 169–76
 Bipartite Option, 171–3
 Content, 38–45, 170–1
 Origins, 31–7
 Preliminary Examination, 39–40, 170
 Size, 45, 46, 169, 172–3, 176
 Teaching, 47–9, 177–9
Psychology, 53–4, 58–9
Psychology, Philosophy and Physiology, 173
Public Administration, 54, 57–9
Public Finance, 58–9
Public and Social Administration, see Diploma in

Queen Elizabeth House, 183

Responsions, 28, 187
Rhodes Scholars, 18, 28
Rhodes Trustees, 62, 69, 80, 116

Rockefeller Foundation Grant, ix, 55–8, 60, 95, 116, 147, 154–5, 160, 179
Royal Commission on Oxford and Cambridge, 36
Royal Institute of International Affairs, 91–2, 95, 112, 155
Ruskin College, 19–21, 27, 134, 141–3

St Antony's College, 72, 129, 177
Science Greats, 32
Senior Status, 28, 39
Sidney Ball Lecture, 47, 51
Social Administration, Delegacy, 140
Social and Administrative Studies, Department, 140–1, 143, 171, 183–4
Social Anthropology, see African Sociology
Social and Political Studies Association, 130–1
Social and Political Theory, Chair, 178
Social Psychology, 59
Social Reconstruction Survey, 92–104, 136
Social Research and Social Policy, M.Sc., 176
Social Studies; Scope, vii; Board of Studies, 46, 49; Faculty 50, 178–9
Social Studies Centre, 183
Social Studies Research Committee, 58, 64, 71, 115, 145, 157–9
Social Training, Certificate, 130–2, 140
Social Training, Delegacy, 51, 138, 140, 179, 181
Social Work, Training, 130–43
Sociology, 20, 171, 178–9
Special Diploma in Social Studies, 141
Statistics; Readership, 54–5, 157–9; Chair, 160, 178
 see also Institute of

Subject Index

Statutes, 187
Sub-Faculty
  Economics, 50, 179
  Politics, 50, 179

Taylor Institute, 54
Templeton College, 175
Treasury, 101, 103, 113

Vice-Chancellor, 187

Wartime Research Committee, 86, 101, 103, 108
Webb Medley Scholarships, 47, 51
Working-Class Education, 19–21, 131

Younghusband Committee, 140